An Accidental History of Tudor England

*Also by Steven Gunn*

Charles Brandon, Duke of Suffolk
Early Tudor Government, 1485-1558
War, State and Society in England and the Netherlands,
1477-1559 (with David Grummitt and Hans Cools)
Henry VII's New Men and the Making of Tudor England
The English People at War in the Age of Henry VIII


*Also by Tomasz Gromelski*

The Material Culture of English Rural Households
c.1250-1600 (with Ben Jervis, Chris Briggs,
Alice Forward and Matthew Tompkins)

# An Accidental History of Tudor England

*From Daily Life to Sudden Death*

STEVEN GUNN and
TOMASZ GROMELSKI

JOHN MURRAY

First published in Great Britain in 2025 by John Murray (Publishers)

2

Copyright © Steven Gunn and Tomasz Gromelski 2025

The right of Steven Gunn and Tomasz Gromelski to be identified
as the Author of the Work has been asserted by them in accordance
with the Copyright, Designs and Patents Act 1988.

All rights reserved. No part of this publication may be reproduced, stored
in a retrieval system, or transmitted, in any form or by any means without
the prior written permission of the publisher, nor be otherwise circulated
in any form of binding or cover other than that in which it is published and
without a similar condition being imposed on the subsequent purchaser.

A CIP catalogue record for this title is available from the British Library

Hardback ISBN 9781529333749
Trade Paperback ISBN 9781529333756
ebook ISBN 9781529333770

Typeset in Bembo by Hewer Text UK Ltd, Edinburgh
Printed and bound in Great Britain by Clays Ltd, Elcograf S.p.A.

John Murray policy is to use papers that are natural, renewable and recyclable products and
made from wood grown in sustainable forests. The logging and manufacturing processes
are expected to conform to the environmental regulations of the country of origin.

Carmelite House
50 Victoria Embankment
London EC4Y 0DZ

www.johnmurraypress.co.uk

John Murray Press, part of Hodder & Stoughton Limited
An Hachette UK company

The authorised representative in the EEA is Hachette Ireland, 8 Castlecourt
Centre, Dublin 15, D15 XTP3, Ireland (email: info@hbgi.ie)

# Contents

*A Note on Conventions* — ix

1. Another Tudor England — 1
2. All Sorts of People — 11
3. At the Coroner's Court — 27
4. In Sickness and in Health — 47
5. Families and Households — 61
6. Houses and Homes — 81
7. Townscapes — 101
8. Landscapes — 117
9. Seedtime and Harvest — 133
10. Wild and Tame — 151
11. Places of Work — 171
12. Faith and Festivity — 189
13. Crime and Control — 207
14. Trade and Travel — 221
15. Carts and Wagons — 235
16. Boats and Ships — 249
17. Ways of Dying — 261

*Acknowledgements* — 275
*Illustration Sources* — 277
*Bibliography* — 279
*Index* — 295

# A Note on Conventions

When quoting from inquest reports, we have used inverted commas and original spelling for English statements included by the clerks, apparently as the jurors said them, and for Latin phrases. We have expanded common contractions, replaced '&' with 'and', inserted some minimal punctuation, and modernised capitalisation and the use of i, j, u and v. When translating from the Latin sections of the reports, we have used modern English spelling and no inverted commas except when quoting direct speech.

We have tried to use the units that would have made sense to the sixteenth-century jurors who provided our information. Distances are given in miles, yards, feet and inches, and areas in acres, though their miles and their acres varied across the country and their miles were probably longer than those we have calculated when reconstructing journeys. Weights are in stones, pounds (lb) and ounces. Times of day are given to the nearest hour, as the jurors gave them, and periods of time to the nearest hour or fraction of an hour. The smallest fraction our jurors mentioned was one-twelfth of an hour, or five minutes to us, but quarter- and half-hours were common. Dates are Old Style but with the year taken to begin on 1 January.

Money is given in pounds, shillings and pence, where £1 = 20s. = 240d. Modern equivalents are notoriously hard to calculate. One popular conversion tool reckons £1 in 1500 worth £666 at 2017 values, or enough to buy nine stones of wool, and £1 in 1600, after a century of inflation, worth only £138, or enough for two stones. Another converter puts the equivalent figures at £787 and £197 and reminds us that by 2023 the equivalents were £1,005 and £252. As we shall see, such figures must be taken with a pinch of salt when entering a world where jurors might think a house worth 13*s.* 4*d.* and a cow worth 16*s.*, 20*s.* or even 26*s.* 8*d.*

# I

# Another Tudor England

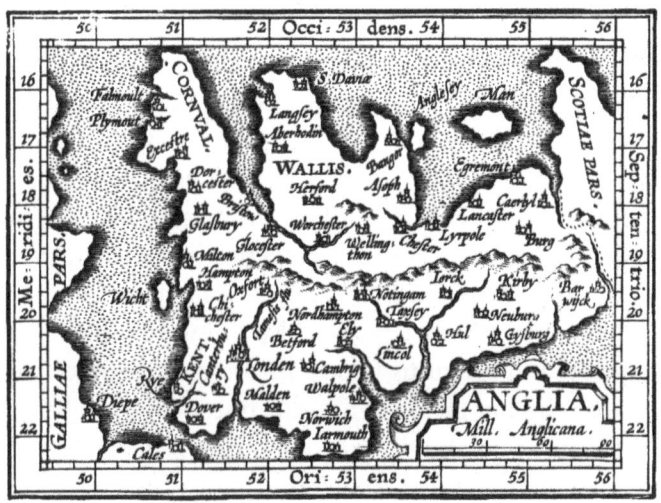

On Monday, 6 July 1579 William Shakespere went for a wash in the River Avon. Suddenly he fell into the deep part of the river, where he drowned. Three months later, on Friday, 16 October, Anne Bulleyn took a pail to a pit on the common at Bramerton in Norfolk to fetch water, slipped on the edge and fell to her death. William was not, of course, William Shakespeare of Stratford-upon-Avon, the aspiring actor, poet and playwright, but William Shakespere of Warwick, the corviser or shoemaker. Anne was not Anne Boleyn, the feisty wife of Henry VIII, but Anne Bulleyn, the nineteen-year-old maidservant of Francis Corye of Bramerton.

When we think of Tudor England, we tend to think of kings and queens, courtiers and adventurers: Henry VIII, Elizabeth I, Sir Thomas More, Sir Francis Drake. Or we reflect on great events that shaped national history: the Dissolution of the Monasteries, the defeat of the Spanish Armada. We conjure up iconic buildings – Hampton Court, Longleat House, Hardwick Hall – or the plays of Shakespeare and Marlowe, the music of Tallis and Byrd. Or perhaps we remember the founders of great local institutions: Archbishop Whitgift at Croydon, Archbishop Holgate at York, Lord Williams at Thame, Lawrence Sheriff at Rugby, William Wyggeston at Leicester.

There is a different history of Tudor England, the history of the several million subjects of those kings and queens and how the great changes of the day affected them. Historians have explored it with dedication, finding evidence in the most ingenious places, from parish registers, churchwardens' accounts and estate maps to shipwrecks, hedges and slagheaps. Rebel demands, government investigations and the records of the law courts have been squeezed to understand the disorder sparked by competition for land and food, taxation and religious turmoil. Ordinary people have been put back into the big picture of Tudor history, and rightly so.

But there is a third kind of Tudor history, the history of what ordinary people did all day. Many conventional sources shed light on everyday life, but they leave gaps. Waged work shows up better than unwaged, and work better than leisure, except when the moral disapproval of the authorities was so great that they tried to control it. Borough records mostly tell us what went on inside the town walls, parish church records what went on in the church and the churchyard. Depositions in court cases were answers to questions that were asked for a reason, to find evidence relevant to the case. Conflict, change and resistance generated more evidence than simply getting on with things. But getting on with things is what most people did most days.

This book aims to present that third kind of history, a history of everyday life. The idea is not new. In different ways historians of different parts of Europe have been writing such history for a generation, and the Germans even have a word for it, *Alltagsgeschichte*. Archaeologists spend much of their time reconstructing the daily lives of ordinary folk, though in England they have more to say about the Romans and the Vikings than the Tudors. For historians, what we can explore is limited by the sources at our disposal. Our key sources here are some 8,888 coroners' inquest reports into accidental deaths filed between 1500 and 1600, like the one produced at Warwick on Wednesday, 15 July 1579, by the Warwickshire county coroner, John Savage, investigating the sad end of William Shakespere, or that put together at Bramerton on 17 October by Ralph Dyxon over the body of Anne Bulleyn.

Such records survive much more systematically for the sixteenth century than earlier periods thanks to two pieces of legislation. First an act of parliament of 1487 commanded the coroners to hand in their inquest reports to the assize judges. They brought them back to the court of King's Bench in Westminster, where they were filed away. Then an act of 1510 ordered coroners to make sure they held inquests on all sudden deaths and not just homicides, and to do so speedily, so that bodies would not lie 'longe above the grounde unburyed to the great noyaunce of the Kynges leage people'.

The reports take us into every corner of Tudor England, with inquests from around half the country's 9,000 or so parishes. They show us where people lived, where they went to work, where they travelled. They give us glimpses of safe and risky things to do. People died reading books as well as practising archery, mending clothes as well as felling trees. Administrative idiosyncrasies led the records to be kept separately for some counties and great towns, so we have none for Durham and Lancashire, only some for Cheshire and only one year's worth for London. In contrast we have them for Monmouthshire, which in some respects was treated as an English county; they survive in large numbers for the Lake Counties, where records are otherwise thin; and we get a flavour of London life from inquests held just outside its cramped boundaries, at St Martin's in the Fields or Charing Cross, at Clerkenwell or Tower Hill.

The victims, all 9,291 of them, form a cross-section of Tudor society. They were wide-ranging in age and social position. Apart from stillborn infants, the youngest whose age we know was eight-day-old James Swyft, who fell out of bed and into the fire while sleeping with his drunken widowed mother. The oldest, said to be about 106, was John Wynde, a thatcher understandably described as old, weak and debilitated, who fell from the roof of a stable when reaching out for his thatcher's needle. At the top of society was seven-year-old George, Lord Dacre, inheritor of a peerage title dating back nearly a century and of lands worth several thousand pounds a year. He died at the Thetford house of his step-father and guardian, Thomas, duke of Norfolk, trying to adjust his wooden vaulting horse, four and a half feet high and more than six feet long. When he pulled an iron pin out of a back leg, the horse collapsed and crushed his head. At the bottom were the homeless and sometimes unidentifiable poor, like the nameless girl who fell off the steps of a windmill at Cockayn Hatley in Bedfordshire after a night sheltering in the beacon house, where those tending the fire beacons to warn of foreign invasion kept themselves out of the weather.

The numbers of victims from different parts of England were roughly proportional to the population of each county at the time. We can show this by working backwards from the numbers reported in the censuses taken from 1801, or by using the musters of the militia, meant to include all able-bodied men for the defence of the realm. Yorkshire had the largest back-projected population, the largest militia and the most recorded accidents, followed by large southern and eastern counties with prosperous agriculture and rural industry, such as Norfolk, Suffolk and Kent. Small or thinly populated counties like Rutland, Worcestershire or Leicestershire had fewer militiamen and fewer accidents. The matches for individual towns are less close, but it is reassuring that while returns from Bristol, Exeter and Norwich are thin, the other very large provincial centres, Newcastle and York, led the way by a large margin. So we can use the inquests to compare the hazards of life in different parts of the country.

On the other hand, the inquests are not robust for fine-grained statistical analysis. The match between accidents and population is less close than we might like, for the ratio between the number of reported accidents in a county and its estimated population varies widely. Bedfordshire and Huntingdonshire look improbably dangerous and Rutland positively lethal, with seven times as many accidents per resident as Hampshire. The main cause was apparently the inclusion or exclusion of reports from the largest towns: Hampshire's score includes almost no records for Southampton, Portsmouth, Winchester, Alton and Basingstoke. Devon, Cornwall and rural Northumberland are also under-represented, apparently because coroners or villagers were just less diligent there than elsewhere before the 1580s and 1590s, when they reached more usual levels. Even within other counties, more remote areas were under-represented, for it has been shown that an improbably high proportion of recorded suicides and fatal accidents occurred in places easily reached by major roads. And deaths at sea, out of sight of land, were not covered by county or borough coroners but came under the jurisdiction of the lord admiral.

There are other limitations on what the reports tell us. Because some activities were more inherently dangerous than others, inquests do not record all aspects of life in equal depth. Accidents that did not prove fatal did not prompt an inquest. Some fatal accidents certainly were recorded but still do not appear in our series, for example when pardons were granted to those who killed others by accident, but no corresponding inquest report can now be found. Some inquests themselves refer to other deaths at the same danger spot for which no report survives. While the number of available inquests increased decade by decade, rapidly until the 1530s as the filing system developed and thereafter in rough proportion to the overall rise in population, it levelled off towards 1600 despite ongoing population increase, probably as more reports began to be retained with the records of county assize courts.

There are smaller issues of accuracy. Some reports, about one in a hundred, make mistakes, most commonly giving an inquest date before the date of the accident, so that one or the other must be wrong. This was an especially easy slip to make when copying Roman numerals, where a missing x or v or i can make all the difference. Greater inattention – or conceivably ignorance – led to rare comic malapropisms. One clerk twice assures us that Thomas Hancoke 'scandalizavit' – offended – an elm tree before he fell off it, rather than 'scandavit', or climbed it. Other reports are too badly damaged to read. A few files are entirely lost, or perhaps await discovery among unsorted records at the National Archives. Very occasionally, when two copies of the same report were filed, they contained different details, one hour out on the time of death for example, one day out on the date, a cow, rather than a mare, being driven down the road by someone who tripped and fell onto a pitchfork.

All this means that we cannot produce watertight statistics for the accident rate per head of population, even for the fatal accident rate per head of population, nor can we be certain that a particular victim died at two rather than three in the afternoon. More fundamentally, we are dependent on what the inquest jurors told the coroner. If they chose to cover up a suicide to spare the family from shame and the forfeiture of the victim's goods, or misclassify a murder to favour the killer, then we may be none the wiser. If they left out details we would like to know, we can usually get no further.

The proportions of different causes of death recorded may also depend on the dynamics of the inquest process. Drownings made up 43 per cent of reported accidental deaths, for reasons we shall explore. But drowning was also a frequent method of suicide, so families were anxious to establish before the law that their kinsfolk had died by misfortune. Carts were involved in more than one in seven fatal accidents because they were widespread and because they were unstable combinations of woodwork, animal power and human miscalculation. But as moving objects with valuable components they were prime targets for coroners, keen to levy lucrative forfeitures on vehicle owners. We shall have to think carefully about coroners, jurors, witnesses, and the stories they told, about how the coroner's court operated and how people thought about accidents.

Yet for all their difficulties, the reports enable us to write a book about Tudor history in which Henry VIII must share his space with Henry Pachet of Stockingford, Warwickshire, who was crushed in a coal-pit collapse at Merevale in June 1587, a book in which Elizabeth I looms no larger than Elizabeth Geffe of Ampthill, Bedfordshire, who was tending a malt kiln at five in the morning in April 1594, set fire to her clothes and was too weak to put out the flames. It is a book in which Wolf Hall was the place where John Colt was kicked in the stomach by a sorrel-bay mare on 5 July 1577 and died at 11 p.m. the following day. Yet it is a book that shows how the everyday life of the people intersected with the doings of the great, and how the headline events of Tudor history could affect anyone and everyone.

The great men and women of Tudor England do appear here, but they are on the margins. Thomas Howard, earl of Surrey and then duke of Norfolk, was lord treasurer to Henry VII and Henry VIII and led the English army to crushing victory over the Scots at Flodden in 1513. For our purposes he was the owner of a young horse that ran wild on a Lambeth street and trampled Agnes Wodehous. Thomas Cranmer was the archbishop of Canterbury who held Henry VIII's hand on his deathbed and wrote the Church of England's first Book of Common Prayer. For us he was the brother-in-law of Henry Byngham esquire, who was killed when Cranmer's palace in Canterbury burnt down on the night of 18–19 December 1543. Sir Thomas Gresham was a pioneer of economic thought, a government adviser on coinage and state debt and a public benefactor, founder of the Royal Exchange and Gresham College at London. But our focus is on Henry Heywarde, the fifty-year-old yeoman who had charge of Gresham's horses at his country house, Intwood Hall in Norfolk. At 11 p.m. on 13 January 1564, Heywarde was in bed in his chamber above the stables when he was woken by the restlessness of the horses below. He hurried to calm them but fell downstairs in his haste and broke his neck.

As for kings, queens and big events, they are here too, but seen from new angles. Henry VIII changed England for ever by dissolving the monasteries, selling many of the monastic lands and enabling the conversion of the buildings. At Stone Priory, Staffordshire, in August 1538, dissolution led to Henry Skatergoode being hit on the head by a stone thrown down by the labourers dismantling the bell tower. By 1542 half a dozen others had been killed by collapsing walls or chimneys as religious houses in Cambridge, Gloucester, Huntingdon, Lichfield, Wigmore and Wymondham turned into demolition sites. Monastic buildings were still being adapted years later. In 1567 a stone column with an iron bar running through it, presumably robbed from the priory, fell on Barnard Benneson in 'the newe worke' at Watton, Yorkshire, and in 1570 John Hedd fell thirty feet when taking down old timbers at Amesbury Priory in Wiltshire. Meanwhile the monks disappeared. The last identified monk to suffer an accident was a canon of Alvingham Priory in Lincolnshire who fell into a mill-pond in 1532; the last friar was an Augustinian drowned at Forebridge, Staffordshire, in 1534.

Elizabeth's reign is famous for the spectacular entertainments mounted to amuse the queen and impress her subjects. May Day 1559 saw one of the first, a firework display on the River Thames outside Whitehall Palace. John Penne was taking part, but drowned when a small barrel of gunpowder caught fire and the crew overturned his boat trying to escape the explosion. She also liked to tour the country on progress, staying with her leading subjects. In August 1561 it was the earl of Oxford who hosted her at Castle Hedingham, but it was William Smythe of Havering-atte-Bower who was knocked from his horse by an elm tree as he drove his father's cart to the castle with supplies for the queen's party.

The Spanish Armada of summer 1588 presented the gravest invasion threat of Elizabeth's reign, and preparations to meet it energised all England. In February and May there were mishaps with a gunpowder mill in Surrey and a cart loaded with 'salte peter water', a vital ingredient for gunpowder, in Suffolk. Already in

February 1586, not long after the war with Spain began, Margaret Wyllys had been hit on the head by a stray branch as she watched men in a Cambridgeshire park felling ash trees requisitioned to make pikes. At musters in April and July there were firearms-training accidents at Leighton Buzzard and Stafford. On 14 July, five days before the Spanish fleet was sighted off The Lizard, Thomas Dickyns of Burton Lazars, Leicestershire, charged astride his gelding towards a 'quyntell', a target on a post, brandishing 'a gavelocke of yron', a javelin. What it would have done to the veterans of the Spanish army is doubtful, but as it glanced off the post and flew off sideways it accounted for Robert Pares, lying on the ground nearby.

The study of a subject such as this raises moral and emotional problems. It is hard not to feel the agony of events like those at Plumstead, Kent, on Thursday, 9 June 1580. Joan Jenninges was a young widow with several daughters. At seven in the evening, she was out of the house where ten-week-old Petronella lay in her cradle. The family's black, white and spotted sow rushed in, overturned the crib, and bit hungrily — avidly and cruelly, said the jurors — into the baby's head. Elizabeth Keye, spinster, perhaps a teenaged family servant, found Petronella dead. We have done our best to avoid condescension or voyeurism in writing about tragedies like this. One of us pulled a pot full of scalding tea over himself as a toddler and the other has been rushed to hospital after a hornet sting on the neck. In other circumstances, in sixteenth-century circumstances, we might very well have been dead. It behoves us to write with respect about the people of the past and their misfortunes. But it is important that we do so. Without a coroner's report Joan and Petronella might be, at best, digits in a reconstitution of the population history of their parish. What the coroners' inquests equip us to do is bring them and their world back to life.

# 2

# All Sorts of People

The victims of our accidents are drawn from the whole range of Tudor society. They illustrate its age structure at a time of rapid population increase, from perhaps two and a half million to four, its social and occupational structure at a time of economic change. They exemplify the health problems that came with age and disability. They show its openness to long-distance migration and cultural change and, conversely, its attachment to local identities and old traditions.

The coroners' reports had to identify the deceased and the cause of death, but levels of detail varied widely. Identification might go beyond a name to an age, a social status or occupation, a place of residence, a family or employment relationship. Inquests gave some indication of the position in society of just over half of our victims, the residence of more than one in three. They noted the age of more than one in five, a proportion that grew from the 1550s, presumably influenced by the introduction of parish registers in 1538.

The very young and very old were certainly at risk of accidental death, but not unusually so. If we count only victims whose age was given, those under fourteen seem to have suffered twice as many fatal accidents as we might expect from their share of the population. The under-fives, even considering how numerous they were as the population grew, look as though they were especially hard hit. But it was naturally easier to give precise ages for the young than for adults. Such precision could be extreme: Barnard Prescott died at the age of two years, four months and seven days. Many adults, in contrast, were given ages only in round numbers, if at all. Our 1560s inquests recorded six men aged thirty, seventeen aged forty, and only seven in between. If we add to our count of children those described as a child, girl, son and so on, and compare them with the total of all victims given any age or description, then the tally of child victims comes to 27 per cent, much closer to the 34 per cent we might expect if childhood were neither unusually dangerous nor unusually safe.

More striking is the small number of victims, only a fifth as many as we might expect, described as aged or over sixty. The exact ages of the old may have been obscure and many no doubt died of sheer old age, or diseases they were too weak to resist. Perhaps as their lives became more constricted, the old were less exposed to accidents, though some died trying to do things they might have managed when younger. Helen Seward could not stop herself falling into the river as she washed a linen cloth, thought the jurors, as she was so old and weak. William Awdeley fell off the top of the haystack in his barn on account of his senility and bodily weakness. Those identified as very ancient were few, but perhaps locally well known. Centenarian John Wynde the thatcher was joined by the ninety-two-year-old Coventry almsman Thomas Prynton, by Catherine Grene of Hertford, fourscore and ten, and by two Gloucestershire veterans, Jane

Blisse of Whaddon at ninety-two and Margery Dymocke of Horfield at ninety-eight.

The most striking imbalance was one of sex. Far more men than women died in reported accidents, just as they had done in earlier centuries. Of the victims identified by gender – and almost all were – 77 per cent were male. This may have been because men were thought worthy of more notice than women, but the sex ratios at different ages suggest that it was more complicated than that. Girls suffered proportionately many more accidents than adult women. For every girl under fourteen whose death was reported there were 1.7 boys, for every woman over fourteen there were 3.4 men. Adult women faced terrible dangers in disease and childbirth, but these did not register as accidents.

For women, social location was far more often a matter of marital status – and the assumptions about work and residence that went with it – than of occupation. One midwife and two seamstresses succumbed to accidents. There were more than a hundred female household servants and more than 400 spinsters, largely interchangeable categories for young unmarried women. More than 250 women were defined as the wife of their husband and thirty-two as singlewomen, a term fading from use over the century. At the other end of the life cycle, ninety-nine women, many of them aged, were noted to be widows. Adult men were on occasion defined as a singleman, a bachelor or the husband of a named woman, but for very few of them was that the main descriptor.

Far more numerous for men were occupational labels. At the top of the social hierarchy these were about rank as much as profession. Knights, esquires and gentlemen constituted around one in forty of the male victims whose status was identified, one in ninety of all males. This was not far out of line with estimates that put them variously at 1 per cent to 4 per cent of the population, increasing over the century. So the lives of the rich were not especially safe, though they faced fewer dangers at work than most. That their rank was effectively hereditary was brought out by the fact that some gentlemen expired at the age of two or three.

The range of occupations identified among those below the gentry was remarkably wide. There were lattice-makers and wafer-sellers alongside the many farmers and the more predictable crafts. The numbers involved are too small to generate more than broad-brush statistics, but they certainly show the difference between rural and urban society. In the countryside at least two-thirds of identifiable male victims worked in agriculture, whereas in towns it was less than a fifth. Towns were centres of commerce and communication: proportionally four times as many townsfolk as countryfolk who suffered accidents worked in dealing and retail positions, and nearly five times as many in transport. Tellingly the differentials were even larger in the three dozen largest towns. Fishing and mining were more common in the country, metal-work, leatherwork and tailoring in towns. Weaving, building and food and drink preparation were present everywhere, but weightier in the urban world.

These findings echo those that historians have made from other sources, such as the remarkable survey of all the adult male inhabitants of Gloucestershire, 88 per cent of them with identified occupations, made in 1608 to register men for the militia. Comparison with that listing enables us to ask whether any occupations occur surprisingly often among our victims and thus which jobs may have been unusually dangerous or unusually safe. Of course, Gloucestershire was not typical of the whole of England – no county was – but it had large agricultural and textile manufacturing sectors, mining in the Forest of Dean, and transport arteries by road and river, so its inhabitants represented most significant areas of the economy.

For most occupational groups, the Gloucestershire figures match ours. Agriculture looks dangerous: 53 per cent of victims worked in farming, but only 46 per cent of militiamen did so. However, if we assume that many men in rural Gloucestershire not assigned to an occupation were agriculturalists, then the numbers come into balance. Fishing, mining and building show roughly the same proportion employed in Gloucestershire as meeting with accidents. Accident figures for metalwork, woodwork and leather-work look a little low, but many victims described merely as urban labourers may have been working in those industries. The same may apply to the dress trades – tailoring, shoemaking, glove-making and so on – and to the commercial and retail sectors, though the disproportions there are larger. They start to look like low-risk jobs. The ultimate safe billet lay in the textile industries. More than one man in seven in Gloucestershire, admittedly a major cloth-making area, wove or processed cloth, fewer than one man in fifty who died in an accident.

Work in transport was dangerous. One victim in thirty-five worked on a boat or a ship, whereas it was one in eighty men in the Gloucestershire militia. And one job sticks out as lethal. Accident rates in food and drink preparation were unusually high. Some of that was down to brewing, for though brewers were comparatively few, three times as many died in accidents as one would expect. The greater culprit was milling. One man in a hundred in Gloucestershire worked in a mill, one accident victim in thirty. Watermills, windmills or horse-mills offered too many ways to die. The risk must have been worth it: there were increasing profits to be made in milling as food demand rose over the century and millers' reputation as crafty profiteers presumably had some foundation.

Occupational titles allow us to examine other kinds of change. The balance among agriculturalists between yeomen, with larger family farms, and husbandmen, with smaller family farms, on the one hand, and labourers, who were employed on the big holdings managed by yeomen or gentlemen, on the other, can be used to chart the spread of large-scale farming for the market, agrarian capitalism as it has been called. By this test, counties where farming was at the capitalist end of the spectrum by the nineteenth century were already full of labourers in Tudor times. Hertfordshire and Bedfordshire topped the table in 1851 for the most farm labourers per family farmer, followed by other southern and eastern counties. Bedfordshire had the most labourers per family farmer among our victims too, with Hertfordshire, Huntingdonshire, Norfolk and Rutland also high at around three labourers per yeoman or husbandman. Conversely northern and western counties harboured many family farms into the Victorian age, and Yorkshire and Cumberland, Staffordshire, Shropshire and Worcestershire, Devon and Somerset were similar in Tudor times, each with one labourer per family farmer or fewer.

Having established the identity of the deceased, the report moved on to the circumstances of the fatality. These nearly always included a date, often a time of day to the nearest hour or space of a few hours – doubtless known from some combination of church clock bells and the position of the sun – and sometimes a precise location. But accounts of events ranged from the briefest mention of drowning in a pond to slow-motion descriptions of complicated cart crashes. The time of death, whether instant or after a period of hours or days, was specified in about half of the reports. The first finder of the body was often named to exclude them from any suspicion of homicide. Such details enable us to sketch wider kinds of social change and social interaction.

Poverty grew over the century under the impact of population growth, social change, famine and inflation. Official responses ranged from relief to repression. At one end of the scale, wandering without work, vagrancy, was a punishable offence. At Gayton, Norfolk, in June 1536, Dorothy Grene felt the full force of the law. A Yorkshirewoman haunting a distant county, aged around thirty and sturdy enough to work, she fitted all the stereotypes of the scrounger. Having asked several people for alms, she was arrested by the two yeomen who served as village constables. They did their duty, as the jurors recognised, under the recently passed act for the punishment of sturdy vagabonds, tying her behind a horse and whipping her. She made so much noise that she spooked the horse. It dragged her up the road, giving her the injuries from which she died three weeks later.

Such treatment makes it easier to empathise with John Carter. As he wandered about at Fittleworth, Sussex, in May 1530, he was warned by a local gentleman that he was to be brought before Sir Henry Owen, the nearest justice of the peace, and punished for vagrancy. He hid up a willow tree to evade arrest but fell into a stream and drowned. Larger towns turned steadily to the systematic incarceration of the apparently idle or refractory poor in workhouses, often named after London's Bridewell hospital. There they were to do productive but tedious work. Mabel Ockford, crushed by the beam of a malt mill as she drove the horse that worked it at the 'Bridwell' in Gloucester in 1589, was presumably an inmate.

The worst crises of poverty came in years of disastrous harvests and soaring food prices. Pauper deaths evoke the agony of years like 1557, when an unidentified beggar died of exposure at night on the bank of the River Nidd on Tockwith Moor, Yorkshire, or 1596, when a wandering pauper fell down the cliff at Church Hougham in Kent. But the indigent were always present. Some were young. Robert and Elizabeth Thorppe, who died collecting alms in the villages of Knaresborough Forest in 1523, were twelve and six. Some were old. Elizabeth Purseglove, who died begging at Chilcote, Derbyshire, in 1531, was eighty. Slowly the poor laws consolidated a system of organised parish relief, and Thomasina Pease sounds like a beneficiary: being exceedingly poor, she lived in 1576 at the charge and cost of the parishioners of her home parish of West Hanningford, Essex.

Beggars could move considerable distances. Some tried their luck a mile or two away, often in the nearest town, others four or five miles. Some begged alms at the houses of their neighbours, others at the gates of the rich. Many victims were known by name to their neighbours, and some had work in better times. Unknown wanderers – nine could not be named by the jurors – must have gone much further. One had been around long enough to acquire the evocative nickname 'Elizabeth at Gode sent us'.

Most vulnerable, as today, were those without shelter in winter. Jane Jackson, needy, weak and feverish from lack of food, died of exposure in a field at Bingham, Nottinghamshire, in March 1541. Some begged respite in barns. The Arnold family, John, Margaret and their children, slept a night in January 1579 in John Parker's barn at Darmsden, Suffolk. There the two children suffocated under forty-nine sheaves of falling wheat. Thomas Gray, an elderly beggar, was wandering the streets of York with nowhere to sleep on the night of 2 March 1568 when he saw an opportunity. At the city walls on Fishergate there was an opening at the top of a door into a room in the postern gate, a building which still survives. He climbed up a piece of wooden board until he could reach the gap and pushed his arms and head, then his chest, over the top of the door. As he struggled to get inside, his feet slipped off the board and he was jammed. Cold and weak, he hung there until he died.

No wonder a place in an almshouse or hospital was attractive. Victims who were inmates typify the admission criteria of age and inability to work. Nicholas Lytster, with his room at the hospice of St John of Jerusalem in Clerkenwell, was seventy, old and debilitated. John Burton, living in a hospital for the poor in the suburbs of York, was old, debilitated and lame. Alice Bonsan of 'Almeshows Strete' in Setchey, outside King's Lynn, was an octogenarian widow, weak and debilitated. Others died around St Leonard's Hospital, Northampton, the Magdalen Hospital of Allington by Bridport, Dorset, and the Westwick Gate at Norwich, presumably annexed to the hospital nearby.

Around one in a hundred of our victims were not English. By far the most numerous and least legally distinct were the Welsh. They were present in the border counties but also scattered further afield. No jurors ever identified a victim as Welsh in the way they did the Scots or the Irish, though they came close with the names Ralph Howell alias Welshman and Lewis Powell alias Welshman. What marked the Welsh out were their patronymic names, often going beyond fathers to grandfathers or great-grandfathers, like Cadwalader ap Huw ap Dafydd, Tomos ap Huw ap Dafydd and Ieuan ap Ieuan ap Hywel ap Siencyn, three Montgomeryshire labourers who died sleeping in a barn at Little Ness in Shropshire in August 1580. These patronymics were already turning into the now familiar Welsh surnames borne by the likes of Lewis Bowen, Edward Evans, John Morgan, Catherine Powell and Margaret Prichard.

The Irish were ruled by the same monarch as the English, but in a separate kingdom. Few appeared in the inquests. Eight passengers drowned in a small boat sailing from Ireland to Minehead, but they were unidentified. In contrast, seventy-year-old Margaret Laurence of Bristol was characterised by the jurors as an 'Irysshe woman', and others' names – Margaret Iryshe, James Irisheman or Anthony Cannon alias Iryshe – may indicate recent migration. Gaelic names occur rarely if at all, even in anglicised forms: Richard Gorman, Richard Kellegh, Silvester Megham and William Neele might be candidates. The other Irish individual to appear in the reports was not a victim, but Patrick the Irishman, the vagrant who found Thomas Witt in a collapsed gravel pit at Radley, Berkshire, in 1551.

Though often at war with the English, Scots appeared both in the North and further afield. William Wilson, 'Scotishman', was found dead in Cumberland in 1532 with an unexplained wound in his neck. Richard Kempe, another Scot, was settled at Boroughbridge in Yorkshire, but two Scots in Cambridgeshire were more transient. Agnes Clerk, alias 'the Scottes woman', was begging for food when she fell into a ditch in Jesus Lane, Cambridge, in 1534. William Hobson had more resourcefulness but equally little luck. He died three weeks after attempting to entertain the inhabitants of Over just before Christmas 1523 with what he described as a game used in his country. It seems to have involved his lying on the ground on his back, bracing himself against a beam or doorpost, while six men tried to pull him along with a rope. As the six men could not move him, he tried bracing himself with one leg rather than two and the leg broke.

Among continental Europeans, the Dutch, who might include varieties of Germans, were commonest. They appeared first as sailors and migrant craftsmen – a smith in Southwark, shoemakers in Cambridge and Sussex, brewers at Thetford and London – and then later in the century as religious refugees. Sometimes they were identified by their place of origin or that of their ship. Sometimes they can be guessed at by their characteristic names: Adrian Gossen, Marcus Vanwestergam and so on.

Two victims neatly fitted English prejudices. One was that the Dutch arrived in floods to mount unfair competition to English workers. Hubert Peecke lived at Sandwich, where a church for Protestant clothworkers exiled from the Low Countries was established in 1561. Inside ten years the community outnumbered the English-born population of the town. Hubert drowned in July 1568 when he went out of Sandwich to the 'newe haven' at Worth nearby to bathe with other aliens called 'Duchemen'. Another view of the Dutch was that they readily drank to excess, so it would have been no surprise that Elizabeth, 'a Duchewoman', perhaps linked to the German copper miners active in the area, was drunk when she fell into the River Greta at Keswick in November 1574.

The French appear in our records only as visiting sailors, the smaller Spanish and Italian communities hardly at all. Those of African origin may be hinted at by the small child killed by the waterwheel at a Sussex iron-forge in 1588, Joan Blackamore, though the surname was also used by those whose ancestors hailed from villages of that name in Essex, Hampshire and Somerset.

Regional identities within England were also strong. The Cornish had the most distinctive surnames and place-names – John Treffrye of Egloshayle, Thomas Trelowyn of St Blazey – but other parts had favoured personal names. Cuthberts, named for the sainted bishop of Lindisfarne, met mishaps in the far North. Randles and Ranulfs died in Shropshire and Derbyshire, bordering Cheshire from which the name of its Norman earls spread. Jurors also used distinctive local words. Household servants were called grooms in the West. Small carts were coops in Yorkshire and putts in the South and south-west. Fords were waths in Yorkshire and the Lake Counties, and streets were gates from Northumberland to Nottinghamshire. A small bridge was a brow in Huntingdonshire and a prey in Surrey. A tree-stump in the south-west was a moot.

Small watercourses showed the most variety. They were becks or sikes in the Lake Counties, Yorkshire and the North Midlands. The southern equivalent was stream, used from Berkshire and Suffolk southwards. Brooks were scattered widely but concentrated in the Midlands. Yet more local terms appeared on occasion: a burn in Northumberland, a greive in Westmorland, a fleam in Staffordshire, and creeks on the coast of Essex and Kent. In East Anglia a small pond was a pulk.

England was also diverse in its response to the most obvious cultural changes of the century, those of the Reformation. One sign of this was the names people gave their children. Protestant enthusiasm for Bible characters, perhaps even a tendency to identify godly England with Old Testament Israel, brought in a kaleidoscope of previously rare names. From the 1560s to the end of the century, starting with children born and christened around the time of the Books of Common Prayer of 1549, 1552 and 1559 and under the influence of the English Bibles of the 1530s, we meet, from the Book of Genesis alone, Abel Metcallf and Seth Holmes, Abraham Gilbert and Sarah Sele, Issac Goryng and Rachel Kinge, Jacob Moore, Dinah Nurton and Joseph Sanders. Exodus and Judges inspired the parents of Moses Foster, Jethro Wilcockes, Aaron Norman, Joshua Withell and Deborah Poulter. The prophets added Jonah Hollande, Zachary Nedham, Ezekiel Harper and Baruch Spencer. Minor characters from the New Testament also appeared, with Nathaniel Danyell, Zacchaeus Spanner and Cornelius Williams, with Theophilus Thacker and Titus Talworth, with Martha Crandall and Tabitha Polhell. Lastly came the names of spiritual virtues, adorning Grace Caype, Mercy Panckeherst and Prudence Carter.

These new names spread fastest in the southern and eastern counties, where religious change took hold more quickly. Seven of these victims came from Kent, five from Suffolk. The eight Abrahams who had accidents between the 1570s and 1590s fit the story, six hailing from East Anglia and the south-east. Meanwhile the Renaissance admiration for the classical world brought in

Greek and Roman names at the top of society – Hercules Raynsford esquire – and at humbler levels, with Arrian Appetharpe, Cassandra Heycoke and Trajan Fawcett.

Earlier in the century, in contrast, unusual names had often come from local saints or other historical figures. Anglo-Saxon abbesses inspired Kenburgh Ryxon, Mildred Harwyn and Frideswide Skarborow; a countess of Normandy, Gunnora Browkes; and a countess of Mercia, Godiva Dawe. The heroes of romance, though never numerous, ran from Roland Warnar, who fell drunk down the stairs of the White Horse Inn at Dunstable in 1524, through the occasional Lancelot, Tristram and Tryamour, to Roland Nicholson, a labourer who came off his horse at East Tanfield, Yorkshire, in 1590.

The commonest names were persistent. Before 1530, more than a quarter of male victims were called John, another quarter either Thomas or William, and a third quarter Richard, Robert or those royal and martial names Henry, Edward and George. Not much had changed by the 1590s. No feminine name was quite as dominant as John, but before 1530 Margaret and Joan or Jane each accounted for nearly a fifth of women, Alice for one in seven, and Agnes and Elizabeth each for one in ten. Joan was still strong in the 1590s, but Margaret and Alice had slipped back. The great gainers were Mary, risen from rarity to more than one in twenty, and Elizabeth, the leading name by a short head at one in six. What parts attention to the Bible and loyalty to the Tudors played in their rise is hard to know.

It is easy to get trapped inside the world of the accident reports, squeezing out intriguing detail and telling patterns. But it is important to remind ourselves that the victims were real people living in communities – the same communities that reported on their deaths – who appear in other records. Some parish registers noted the circumstances in which those buried had died and our victims feature in those. The registers of Grantchester mark the steady toll of Cambridge students drowning in the river. In Southwark the register noted the burial of Katherine Robyns or

Robynson, a butcher's wife slain by a beer cart, on the day following her inquest in 1545.

Pardons for accidental homicide sometimes confirm the details of inquest reports. Thomas Egglesfeld of Sutton on Derwent, Yorkshire, gentleman, for example, shot an arrow at a mark on the wall of a house on 19 May 1511, not knowing that Elizabeth Smyth was inside. The arrow punctured the wall and hit her in the left side, killing her instantly. He was pardoned for her death on 28 February 1512. William Bryswood of Hardwick, Nottinghamshire, shot a crossbow bolt at a robin on a hedge on 28 July 1537, unaware that John Doughty was lying behind it. John died on 3 August and William was pardoned five months later. John Lyes of Little Tey, Essex, shot John Bucke with Richard Pare's fowling gun at Wakes Colne mill on 16 July 1596, not realising it was loaded, and was pardoned in the following February.

Wills can fill in more of the life behind the death. Few accident victims made them. Many had no property to leave, many died too suddenly to make the normal deathbed dispositions. But some came from the propertied classes who had reason to keep a draft will, and others lingered long enough to make their wishes known. Sussex and Yorkshire provide eloquent examples.

Some wills shed bright light on the interval between mishap and death. James Poke of Mountfield was crushed in a marl-pit collapse on 10 June 1578, digging for a mixture of clay and chalk added to light or sandy soils to improve their fertility, and immediately made his will. The vicar and several neighbours and relations were there to witness as he made careful provision for his wife Winifred and their unborn child. Next day he was dead. William Ridges of Forest Row was hit in the left thigh by an exploding gun barrel and died later that day, 20 September 1589. He 'made and declared' a will, presumably hurriedly, dividing his goods and leases of land between his wife and children. One of the witnesses was Adam Adamson, the man who fired the gun.

The affairs of the young esquire William Staveley of Ripon Park, Yorkshire, were more complex. He was kicked in the right leg by the horse of William Vavasour as they rode through York together on 27 March 1598. Carried off, deeply wounded, to the house of John Stephenson in Coney Street, he took two weeks to die. He already had a will, meticulously dividing his lands, goods and money among his family. But the day before he died, five witnesses added to it 'wordes uttered' by him 'as his last will and testament'. He was thinking about land and cash, but most insistently, perhaps feverishly, about horses. He left his bay and white geldings to his nephew William and his little white mare to Robert Harrington. For the man who cared for his mounts, Marmaduke Brian 'alias horseman my servant', there was a bequest small, but gratefully detailed: two cows, pastured in summer in the lime-kilns at Pennacroft, with two loads of hay to feed them in winter for twenty-one years.

Those with less to leave than Staveley also made poignant provision. Robert Elwood of Bowland House, in marshy Watton in the East Riding, fisherman, had made a will two years before he drowned on 1 August 1559 in a sinking boat with his wife Katherine, Ellen Elwood and another couple. He left houses and plots of land in Aike to his sons, including Roland, who, the coroner noted, had custody of the salvaged boat. He left each son a hull net for fishing. He left his lease of land in Leven Carrs to Katherine, who would not survive him to enjoy it. Nor could she act as executor, a task she was to have shared with all his children, including the child in her womb as he made the will, 'when yt shall plaise God to sende yt into the worlde'. Was that child Ellen?

The few victims who had public careers tempt us to reflect on their characters. John Somer was mayor of Sandwich in Kent four times between 1512 and 1525 and the town's MP in 1523. The town records suggest that he was irascible, involved in an unseemly row on the quayside with a former mayor and several knife-fights with other councillors. This rather fits his end, hare coursing in a field at Eastry in April 1526. His hound went after a hare, but the hare escaped. Doubtless infuriated, Somer dashed after the hare on his horse to drive it back towards the hound. He cannot have been looking where he was going, for he smashed his head into the branch of an ash tree so hard that he broke his neck.

Others were more discreet but perhaps too comfortable. John Glanvile, MP for his native Tavistock in 1586, rose smoothly through the legal profession, working for all the right people, West Country powerbrokers like Sir Walter Raleigh and the earl of Bedford. By 1600 he was a justice of the court of Common Pleas at Westminster. Riding on his expensive bay gelding at Tavistock at eight on a summer evening, he was thrown to the ground and hit his head on a stone. A persistent tradition, reinforced by his bulky funeral effigy, held that it was the corpulence born of his prosperity that made him fall so hard.

Glanvile's effigy makes him one of the very few accident victims we can picture. Walter Elmes and Thomas Magnus, clergymen commemorated by brasses, share the distinction. Elmes was rector of Harpsden in Oxfordshire, where his family were lords of the manor. On Friday, 15 July 1511, presumably a hot day, he took off his clothes, went into the Thames and drowned in deep water. Magnus met his end in 1550. He was a veteran diplomat, member of the King's Council in the North and accumulator of church posts across the northern counties, including the rectory of Sessay, Yorkshire. He fell from his horse when it bolted in Sessay High Wood after a sixteen-mile ride. Despite his advanced age, eighty-six, he lingered five days.

Such men are known to history in a way that most of our victims are not. Yet the brute facts of life and death conspired to put them all into the picture of society that the inquests equip us to draw. It is a picture, as we have seen, that ranges widely, from young to old, from rich to poor, from farmers to craftsmen, from Godiva and Kenburgh to Dinah and Martha, from the Welsh to the Dutch. For the details of that picture we depend on the information extracted from local society by the regular machinery of the English state. Let us visit the coroner's court.

# 3

# At the Coroner's Court

How can we trust what the coroners' reports tell us? Historians have debated the question and for the most part their verdict has been cautiously positive. They write of the inquest jurors' 'activity and initiative' and of the reports' 'factual strength', 'superior detail', 'immediacy' and 'ring of reality'. But we should think through the issues for ourselves. How were the reports created and what kind of evidence do they present?

England had had coroners since the twelfth century. Tudor local government handbooks, frequently reprinted, instructed that when someone died in sudden, or violent, or suspicious circumstances, the coroner should be called in by local officials or other honest men. He should come without delay and order a jury to be summoned. Parish constables or town bailiffs drew a jury together and the jurors were sworn in. Coroner and jurors viewed the body and the jurors answered to the best of their knowledge the coroner's questions about the circumstances and cause of the death.

Elizabeth's secretary of state, Sir Thomas Smith, explaining the government of England to her continental neighbours in 1583, claimed that inquests were held 'commonly in the streete in an open place', but that cannot have been practical in all English weathers. Public buildings often served: churches, rectories, castles, guildhalls, inns. Each county had several coroners at any one time, elected in the county court. In little Rutland they often worked in pairs, but in larger shires they concentrated their work in different districts. Variations in jurisdiction gave cities, towns and some great landlords their own coroners, while the lord admiral's officers investigated deaths at sea and the royal household coroner cases near the court. Occasionally there were unseemly disputes. At Oxford rioters overturned the table at which the city coroners were sitting, threw old shoes at the mayor and aldermen, and even broke the mayor's mace, as they insisted that Wolvercote lay in the county's jurisdiction, not that of the city.

County coroners were the sort of administratively competent and legally trained gentlemen who occupied many other local offices, though they rarely made it to the top level of county governance as justices of the peace. Borough coroners were town worthies who worked their way through the gamut of civic posts but generally strayed no further. All in all, coroners seem to have been able enough to do their job though varying in ambition and sophistication, as a glance at the range of their signatures, from the workaday scrawl of a John Wylkynson at Boston to the practised elegance of a Francis Sandys in Somerset, might suggest. Some were very experienced. Kent's William Webbe served for fifty years, and he and Bedfordshire's Richard Sampson heard more than 130 accident inquests each.

Some days were busier than others. Alexander Metham held two inquests on 17 February 1582, one at Sheffield and one at Bradfield, seven miles away. Elizabeth Cooke died at 7 a.m. on 27 March 1588 and Mary, servant of William Spencer, at 5 p.m. that day. Richard Sampson held Elizabeth's inquest at Eaton Bray on the 28th and Mary's at Heath in Leighton Buzzard on the 29th. The press of business encouraged efficiency, though speed was easier in towns than the countryside. Detailed calculations have shown that the average time six different Sussex county coroners allowed to elapse between the finding of a body and the holding of an inquest ranged between three days and twenty-three. It made sense to use one jury to investigate separate incidents in the same place. But some cut corners. On 24 February 1579, Edward Payne of Huntingdonshire used a jury at St Neots to pronounce on three deaths, one from early February and two from the previous June, and on 15 April 1580 he called a jury at St Ives to wrap up one death that had occurred two days earlier and two that were left undated.

Reports were mostly composed in Latin, the usual language for legal records. The jurors spoke their verdict in English, so there was a translation process in which technical terms were often left unchanged, as were particularly descriptive phrases, when a horse 'dyd sturte aside or out of the waye' or a bather was 'duckyng yn of his hed'. Occasionally whole passages came in English, and for us they provide the most vivid sense of the court's findings. At Guildford in April 1545, for example, the jurors reported that one-year-old Peter Baronsbe

> did rise from his bed alone by hymselff and went to make water at a hole, beinge in the wall in the lofte of the sayde house where he lay, and so went to the hole; and in his retorning from the sayde wall he fell from the syde of the steyeres of the chambr; and in his fallynge his face restid upon the vi [sixth] stepp of the sayde steyres; by reason of the which stepp beinge veri sharp-edgid, the sayde Peter was sore wounded in hys face; and so by misfortune he came to hys deth and none otherwise.

The basic details were backed up by enumeration of the injuries on the corpse, handbooks asking for 'the lenthe, bredthe, and depnes of al woundes'. Some reports were cursory, but many were precise. John Estoft was a twenty-six-year-old tailor caught in twilight gunnery practice at Hull between seven and eight in the evening on Monday, 25 September 1598. The wound to the left side of his body was one palm wide and reached through to his intestines, part of which protruded from the hole. His side was charred and his hip bone shattered.

Objects implicated in the death, whether animate – a horse that kicked – or inanimate – an axe that slipped – were known as deodands, things to be given to God, and were confiscated by the royal almoner to be applied to godly uses. Most often they were probably redeemed by the owner for cash. The horse and cart of John Byxe of Bapchild, Kent, for example, were judged to be worth £1 13s. 4d., but John settled with the almoner for £1 6s. 8d. Jurors had to value them, ideally by inspection. Some juries insisted that they could not estimate the value of carts they had not seen. Some items – hot water, a dead dog – were judged to be worth nothing, but those worth a fraction of a penny – two wooden pegs, a string for tying up barley – were solemnly valued. The values assigned resembled those assessed by neighbours listing the goods of the deceased for probate, on the low side of market rates, but not unrealistic. They give us a sense of a material world very different from our own, but finely graded.

Coroners were increasingly followed up by the clerks of King's Bench if they failed to enquire properly into these deodands, just as juries increasingly faced litigation in the court of Star Chamber over the manipulation of verdicts – suicides wrongly found to be accidents, for example. As the latest historian to examine the system, Matthew Lockwood, has concluded: 'from the early sixteenth century the oversight of coroners and their inquests was relatively widespread, rigorous, and effective', leaving 'few opportunities for corruption or incompetence'.

While the coroners asked the questions and framed the report, choosing what details to include, it was the jurors who decided what had happened. It is important to think who they were, what their position was in local society and whether they were likely to understand the circumstances behind accidents. They were supposed to be respectable adult men, honest and law-worthy men as some reports put it, between twelve and twenty-four in number, drawn from the parish where the inquest was held and those closest to it, the outsiders helping both to make up the numbers and to keep some check on village cover-ups.

Jurors were drawn from a broad middle band of village and town society. They were the kind of men widely engaged in local affairs, as churchwardens, constables, manorial court jurors and charity trustees. Husbandmen, yeomen and craftsmen were over-represented compared with their poorer neighbours or with the gentry. Maturity and independence were valued, for fathers were prominent and servants, who were generally not heads of a household, overlooked. As literacy spread, increasing numbers of them could sign their names.

Status mattered. Gentlemen or even esquires were called in for controversial cases, and if a spokesman or foreman was named, it was usually the juryman of highest social rank. But social weight was balanced by expertise. At Newcastle, the keelmen who worked the boats carrying coal down the Tyne from the mines of Northumberland and County Durham and the mariners who manned the port's sea-going ships took many seats on juries, especially for mishaps on the river, although they were poorer and had less stake in town government than the bakers, brewers or shoemakers, let alone the great merchants.

More specific inside knowledge was also sought. Those who found bodies or who were working with the victim were named on juries for their insight rather than excluded for their bias, as were probable relatives of the deceased. Another sign that jurors understood how accidents happened was that they occasionally went on to suffer them. The Servatius Franke who sat at an inquest at Cobham in Kent in 1581 was most likely the same Servatius Franke who fell off a ladder at Cobham fifteen years later. A few, perhaps self-important, nominees declined to serve and were fined or roundly condemned, but a good excuse could work. William Strynger paid no penalty for his absence from a postponed hearing in 1555, since he was so ill that he could not attend without danger of death.

Such postponements, like the debates laid bare in Star Chamber cases, show that juries made serious efforts to enquire effectively and agree a verdict. They could be honest, even apologetic, when they could not work out what had happened. Sometimes we know they discussed the location of a set of footprints or the precise position of a body. We can imagine them at Nuffield, Oxfordshire, on 21 February 1533. They concluded that William Juster must have overturned the cart he was driving from Henley-on-Thames to Latchford by steering its right wheel over the roots of an ash tree growing by the road where it ran by a body of water. The cart carried a chair and, as he spilled out of the cart into the water, the chair fell on his head and the cart landed on top of the chair, pressing him down until he drowned.

This may not have been exactly what happened, but the comfort to us is that it must have been a credible story at the time. Otherwise, the jurors and the coroner, at risk of prosecution, would not have dared tell it. In other words, the report tells us about life in the sixteenth century, even if it does not tell us for certain how poor William ended up underwater with the chair and the cart on his head by the road just beyond the ash tree.

Witnesses were certainly involved. Some accidents were said to have been seen by up to forty neighbours and sometimes individual witnesses, even children as young as seven, were named. Those who had spoken to the victim on their deathbed helped. William Burneham, who had been in a fight but had also got himself jammed between his cart and a gatepost, was said to have told his neighbours 'This bruser of my carte wyll onys be my dethe'. Corpses were examined thoughtfully. As the jurors looked at the right side of George Rydyoke, lying in his windmill, it was evident that 'too of his rybbes was broken and also his right arme', by reason of which 'it dyd well and suffycyently appere to the said jury' that it was these injuries, suffered as he was dragged into the mill's machinery, that killed him.

Occasionally medical advice was called in. In one case, the opinions of four surgeons were sought to decide which of three wounds had proved fatal. In another, two surgeons carried out an autopsy that found long-standing problems with the victim's lungs, liver, spleen and gallbladder. Those who buried the dead without permission were reprimanded. One grieving widow was told that she had laid her husband to rest in manifest contempt of the law and as a wicked example to other lieges of the queen. The parishioners of Mickelham in Surrey exhumed Thomas Cleygate for the coroner to see sixteen days after burying him, but the constables and other inhabitants of Harwich refused to disinter the putrefied body of a young sailor on the grounds that it would spread death and plague among them.

For the most part inquests were punctilious, distinguishing, for example, between the slightly different ways in which different victims died in the same accident. Sometimes, however, those involved told convenient half-truths and jurors chose to believe them. The best examples are a stereotyped series of cart crashes beginning in mid-century. While the rules of deodand were flexible and inconsistent, legal writers stated with increasing clarity that objects or animals that were moving should be held responsible for causing an accident. As Anthony Fitzherbert put it in 1538, coroners should 'inquire what things were then moving'. In more than half of cart accidents early in the century, only the wheel that struck a victim was declared forfeit. After 1540 this proportion fell below half and after 1560 below a quarter, on the understandable basis that the rest of the cart and usually the draught team must have been moving too. It now suited the owner of a cart drawn by several animals for as few of them as possible to have been moving at the time of impact, as in a verdict of 1548 which explained that 'there was none defalte in the seid oxen, bull and mares for they were immedyatlye stoppyd and dyd as moche as in theym laye to hold backward'.

No doubt some drivers really did manage to do as it was claimed Richard Dunckley did, shouting 'Whoo, whoo' at his horses when the cart rode up onto a bank beside the road, so that they were all stationary when the cart fell over. But the advantages of such accounts were clear when each of the draught animals alone was often more valuable than the cart or its load. In the 1540s and 1550s, only one in ninety recorded cart accidents involved this sort of story, perhaps one in forty if we add some vaguer narratives. In the 1560s and 1570s it was one in twenty explicitly and perhaps as many as one in ten overall. By the 1580s almost one in twelve cases explicitly featured teams standing still at the driver's command.

We can find other useful fictions. From the 1580s a suspicious number of those who drowned washing horses were said to have slipped off the back of the horse and tried to swim to safety, lessening the likelihood that the horse would be judged forfeit. Other details helped create a story that made sense. Many children were described as looking into water, often at a reflection of their own face, before they fell in and drowned. Since presumably in most of these cases no one was watching or they would have pulled the child out, this took an observation about what children often did, and used it to account for the drowning. Such fictions may dent our confidence in the inquest reports as blow-by-blow narratives of individual incidents, but they leave them firmly intact as evidence for the kinds of things people did. Before using that evidence, there is one more question to answer. What did the jurors mean by an accident?

The sixteenth century had inherited a series of contradictory ideas from the classical and early Christian worlds. Philosophy viewed accidents as an unanalysable category of unpredictably multi-causal events and literary theory as a key plot device for drama. Mythology provided Fortuna, a goddess who played heartlessly with the fate of her victims, but whose favour might be wooed by the forceful man of action. From astrology came the view that the stars might induce a *dis-aster* for the *ill-starred*.

Christian recognition of God's power over earthly affairs ranged from a rather general foreknowledge of events and disposition of circumstances to a barrage of providences affecting the life of every individual, community and nation.

How many of these notions swirled in the heads of inquest jurors is hard to say. Providentialism and astrology featured in the sensational ballads, murder pamphlets and almanacs of popular reading culture. Chaucer's *Canterbury Tales*, widely circulated in manuscript and then repeatedly printed, included a chilling sketch of the horrible deaths mischance could bring: the carter run over by his cart, the scalded cook, the child in the cradle chewed by a sow. On the positive side, health and safety advice was on offer. Early in the century, the clergy were charged to warn women every Sunday not to lay their children too close to them in bed lest they smother them and not to leave them alone at home near fire or water. Later, the agricultural writer Thomas Tusser dispensed sound counsel in rollicking verse such as

> Take hede how thou layest the bane for the ratts,
> For poysoning servant, thy self and thy bratts.

Traditional religion offered many preservatives against sudden death, feared because it deprived the victim of the chance to make a deathbed confession and receive the last rites to hasten the way through purgatory. There were prayers against sudden death, promises that those attending mass would be spared that day, saints trusted to intercede against a sudden end. The new Books of Common Prayer dismissed purgatory and spurned superstitious remedies. Nonetheless they included requests at morning prayer that we might not 'runne into any kind of daunger', at evening prayer that God might 'defend us from al perilles and daungers of this night', and in the litany that the Good Lord would deliver us 'from lightning and tempests, from plage, pestilence and famine, from battaile and murther, and from sodayne death'.

People must have talked about accidents, because local chroniclers recorded them. Among the lightning strikes and building collapses there was the occasional celebrity victim like Sir Jacques Granado, soldier and courtier, his head smashed on the wall of the privy garden at Whitehall when his horse veered off course as he rode before the king and queen in 1557. Some mentioned accidents that appear in our inquests. Henry Machyn recorded the firework display at which John Penne died, 'the Quen's grace and her lordes and lades lokyng out of wyndows' as 'mony fell in the Temes, butt ... on man drownyd'.

In legal terms it should have been clear what an accident was. A death by misfortune was a sudden death which was neither a suicide, nor a homicide – murder, manslaughter or self-defence – nor a divine visitation, a death with no discernible secondary cause. Telling words and phrases recurred in each category of inquest report. Homicide victims were slain by someone else, usually murdered feloniously with malice aforethought. Suicides slew themselves feloniously at the instigation of the Devil and not having the fear of God before their eyes. Those who died by divine visitation became ill, then languished for a significant period, then died. Accident victims died by 'infortunia', 'mala fortuna' or 'fortuna sinistra'. This was rendered into English in lawyerly terms as misfortune or misadventure but might be given by jurors more plainly as 'unfortune' or 'evyll fortune'. Accident reports often included references to the suddenness or unexpectedness of events and to chance, even 'inffortunat chawnce'. These narratives usually led up to a clear finding of homicide, suicide, misfortune or visitation, and on the filed copies the King's Bench clerks helpfully noted which of the four it was.

Some deaths tested the boundaries. Here the wording might take pains to show which side of the line an incident fell. Jane Stonarde, for example, fell into a pond by misfortune and against her will, not meaning herself any harm. Her drowning was definitely not suicide. When John Thurkyll fell on top of Ralph Otley by misfortune and unhappy chance as they wrestled for recreation and out of familiarity with one another, it was without malice or premeditated harm and neither of them had a weapon. Ralph's death was definitely not homicide.

Sometimes jurors knew they had to make a clear choice between different possible causes of death, for example an injury and an illness in cases of domestic violence. Jane Lee conducted herself badly and negligently in her work, so, on 9 September 1566, her master, a Lincolnshire yeoman, gave her three blows on the shoulders with a small stick. He did so without any malice aforethought and afterwards she remained in good health until 28 September. Only then did she become sick with a fever, dying on 2 November. Thus, concluded the jurors, she died by divine visitation and in no other way. Less clear-cut was the case of Alice Sherwood. She died after a beating from her mistress, wife of a Taunton tanner, on 4 December 1581. The hazel rod used, it was noted, was just over a yard long but only one and a quarter inches round, and while the marks of the blows were still visible on Alice's arms, the information that she was already ill convinced the jurors that she died by visitation.

Another tricky category was death in custody. Juries found verdicts of divine visitation in the cases of Roger Coxsall, injured while being arrested by the watchmen at Clare, Suffolk, and of Thomas Bewley, put in the stocks overnight, drunk and disorderly, by the constable at Bolton upon Dearne, Yorkshire. We should of course remember that the kind of men who sat on juries and agreed these verdicts were the kind of men who had household servants whom they sometimes felt they should beat, who served their turn as watchman or village constable and might have to put troublemakers in their place.

Some juries made careful use of the small but significant distinction between death by misfortune and homicide by misfortune. Domestic violence cases where no other illness could be blamed, for example, or deaths at football that clearly resulted from the actions of another player, like a leg-breaking tackle, could be treated as homicide by misfortune. Then, while the responsible party was in no danger of a murder trial, he might need to buy a pardon. Other jurors may have used death by misfortune as a proxy for self-defence in cases of sexual assault. William Wylson apparently proceeded so violently as he attacked Eleanor Foxe to rape her that the knife she held in her right hand struck him in the thigh. Classifying this as misfortune cleared Eleanor of any responsibility for William's death, even from the need to obtain a pardon, although she was holding the knife that killed him. A suspicious number of other amorous young men stabbed themselves in the thigh or the stomach. At least some of the same middle-aged jurors who thought it reasonable to beat idle servants thought it reasonable to protect young women like their own daughters from rape.

Jurors were not always so sure. Take the death of James Whettell of Lyneham, Wiltshire, on 25 September 1567. About one o'clock that afternoon he met John Woodroff of Whitley and they fell out, Whettell publicly speaking opprobrious and unbecoming words against Woodroff. They went their separate ways. Later, around four o'clock, at the 'longe barrowe' at Lyneham, as Woodroff headed home, Whettell attacked him with sword and dagger and wounded him several times. Woodroff drew his sword and, going backwards while defending himself with a buckler or small shield, fell to the ground, where he lay holding his sword in his right hand. As Whettell continued his furious attack, he ran onto the point of Woodroff's sword. He died instantly from a wound in the left side of his chest, six inches deep and two inches wide.

The jury probably had trouble agreeing that version of events. They did not report until 28 April, seven months after the death. Their findings included phrases often used in reporting murders: Whettell attacked Woodroff with malice aforethought and in his anger. The point that Woodroff was going backwards, indeed lying on the ground, recurred in narratives of self-defence homicide. The language of accidents was there too: they met by chance and Whettell fell on Woodroff's sword by misfortune. The stated verdict was that Whettell had feloniously killed himself, a suicide verdict, by running onto the sword. Yet one clerk wrote a note on the report that it was a self-defence case, another that it was a death by misfortune. In the end the self-defence note was struck out and the misfortune one left to stand. We may well wonder. Might this have been a duel tidied up after the event, two antagonists meeting at a landmark, the long barrow, to settle their earlier dispute with its unbearable public insults, Whettell the gentleman with the fashionable sword and dagger, Woodroff the yeoman with the more old-fashioned sword and buckler?

Those involved in a death were not always confident of the likely inquest verdict. At least a dozen accidental killers fled the scene, village bowmen, for example, being unaware of the distinction drawn by lawyers that mishaps in archery practice approved for the defence of the realm should be counted accidental. Some sought sanctuary. William Fermor, chased by villagers after he stabbed a workmate in the leg, made it over forty miles from Staplehurst in Kent to the sanctuary of St Martin's Le Grand in London.

There were other grey areas. Some reports left things unclear over suicide and in many marginal cases jurors valued the goods of the deceased, which would be forfeit if suicide was confirmed. More than half of them drowned and others poisoned, stabbed or shot themselves, but it seems harsh to suspect those trampled by horses or savaged by bears of contriving their own ends. Epileptic attacks, post-injury infections, deaths by exposure and lightning strikes in their different ways hovered between misfortune and divine visitation.

Two particularly complex and emotionally charged topics were abortion and infanticide. When Eleanor Hipstone died immediately after taking a drink made with branches of yew, intending to destroy the infant in her womb, the jurors did not categorise her death, but the clerks counted it as misfortune. When Martha Fysshoocke drank a mixture of rat poison and the juice of yew leaves with the same intention and died two hours later, the jurors were clear that it was suicide. Her clothes were confiscated and sold back to her mother for 6s. 8d. Stillbirths, especially those not immediately reported or those suffered by unmarried mothers, were readily suspected as cases of infanticide, but they attracted a range of verdicts. Even an unidentified baby discovered with her throat cut and another abandoned naked by her mother overnight and found partly eaten by pigs were classified as having died by misfortune, though the mother of the second was castigated as not having God before her eyes.

It should not surprise us that different juries could look at similar deaths and come to different conclusions, or indeed that some cases were left in question. Some verdicts do seem astonishing. Lucy Careton was found to have walked close to a windmill with the wicked intention of killing herself by a blow to the head from the rapidly turning sails. In a nearby windmill three years later, Francis Richardson was found in a chamber hanged by the neck from a rope thrown over part of the mill. The jurors concluded that he must have been playing with the rope when it suddenly 'did compasse' his neck so that he was hanged by misfortune. Perhaps the jurors knew things about the victims or their circumstances that they did not put in the report. Perhaps they leapt to generous or bigoted conclusions.

Many caught up in accidents were held to have contributed to their own death in some way. A common formula, that a victim had not foreseen the danger of their actions, was often combined with the understanding that children could not be expected to grasp risk as adults did. Three-year-old Elizabeth Turner played by the River Stour and fell in, explained the jurors, since she lacked discretion due to her age and was unaware of the danger of drowning. As children grew up, the jurors' comments gained an increasingly critical edge, poor judgement or even impudence and wantonness replacing lack of discretion. Adolescents could face full-blown scorn.

Victims were blamed more directly in around two hundred reports. Negligence was mentioned most often, as when Peter Harris 'was skoulded thorow hys owne necligens by mysfortune'. It applied mainly to activities requiring concentration, driving carts, handling firearms and so on, but it could stretch as far as climbing ladders or just walking along. It could also be used in the aftermath of an accident to explain its consequences. John Ildesley died because he negligently continued to walk about and go to work every day with an unhealed wound in his foot. Carelessness, imprudence or recklessness were similar, rashness or hastiness a little more specific. Robert Chapman bent down too rashly as Isabel Batson passed him hay and punctured his head on her pitchfork. Equally undesirable was excessive confidence in one's own ability.

Some terms were ambivalent. Ignorance might be excusable or culpable: not knowing the right path to take was different from not knowing how many people could travel safely in a boat. Not paying due attention to one's safety might involve reckless helpfulness, like jumping into a pond to help a drowning bull, or unsafe working practices, like cutting sedges too close to the water's edge. Others were forgetful. Ten-year-old William Hopkyn was sitting, asleep, on the front of a cart. Waking up and forgetting where he was, he fell from his seat and was run over.

Foolishness was more pointed. Cecily Warner played foolishly with a bull. Others ignored warnings. Alexander Godbye sat on a churchyard wall, watching archers shooting at targets alongside. They told him several times to get down, but he would not and got an arrow in the head. Elizabeth Albott sat with Robert Phyppes watching men throwing the sledgehammer. Francis Robynson warned everyone before he threw, but Elizabeth got up, ran off and was hit. The jurors made their view crystal clear by repeating that if she had stayed by the wall with Robert Phyppes she would not have been hurt. Matthew Jones warned James Horne not to touch his master's black horse, but James thought little of the advice and patted the horse on the loins. It kicked him.

Individual fault might be emphasised to clarify what should be forfeit. At Newcastle from 1587, following the appointment of two new town coroners, those who fell into the river were always said to have done so by their own negligence. This form of words made sure that owners in the great port city would not keep losing their boats. Conversely the role of the deodand could be personalised. A waterwheel murdered a fuller, a horse feloniously murdered and killed a boy, a cart murdered and killed its victim.

Nowadays, encouraged by uninvited enquiries about whether we have had an accident at work, we are concerned about third-party negligence. On occasion this was tackled explicitly. Servants who left small children in dangerous places might be called negligent, as might those who did not take precautions with firearms or steered ferries badly. There are also suggestions of collective negligence. John Dobbekyn thought the ford he used to cross a small drain in the Lincolnshire fens was a sufficient passage for the king's subjects, but he drowned because the local inhabitants had put a dangerously unstable foundation underfoot.

The system of forfeiture of course made for a rough and ready punishment of many kinds of negligence, for those who drove or rode badly enough to kill could lose their cart or horse. Negligence was also implied when practical remedies were prescribed to forestall danger. Some house owners were ordered to fence their moats. When John Coffe fell from the cliffs at Swanage as he raided seabirds' nests, it was said that the climb was so dangerous, two other men having been 'byffore thatt tyme ... in lyke maner kyllyd', that such attempts 'ought utterly to be denyed'. We are even closer to modern concerns with the case of Richard Parrett, a labourer killed working at the bottom of a well. The jurors fined the tenant of the property for his negligence in not providing Richard with any protective clothing or other necessary things.

One village saw both individual and collective fault. Snodland in Kent suffered drownings at two different mills four years apart. In the first case it was found that the millpond was so close to the footpath, and so unprotected, that five children had drowned in it within the jurors' memory. The coroner therefore ordered the two farmers of the mill to divide up the length of the path and each shut off his section from the pond at his own costs, giving them a deadline to do the work on pain of a substantial fine. In the second case, it was the inhabitants in general who were charged under penalty to repair the road on the eastern side of the tidal mill to make it safe.

Occasional incidents prompted legislation. The manor-court jurors of Southwark passed several regulations in response to accidents. Larger measures came from a Herefordshire inquest in January 1581. On 1 December 1580, John Swannycke and James Meiricke were at either end of the ferry barge at Wilton, steering it across the River Wye. A sudden gust of wind frightened a horse and its trampling drove Swannycke from his post. The rudderless boat turned in the wind and sank. Swannycke and sixteen passengers drowned.

Seventeen years later an act of parliament providing for local taxation to fund a bridge to replace the ferry made its way through the Commons. At first reading, Sir Thomas Coningsby, a combative Herefordshire MP, opposed it on the grounds that there were too many taxes on his poor county already and that there were so many bridges on its rapid rivers that the cost of maintaining them all would be prohibitive. But a committee was established to work on the bill, led by his colleague Sir John Scudamore. It included experienced legislators, representatives from interested constituencies such as Gloucester and the Brecon Boroughs, and Herbert Croft, one of Coningsby's local rivals.

The final version of the bill, passed into statute in February 1598, pulled out all the stops in justifying its provisions. The ferry carried trade to Ross-on-Wye and beyond from Herefordshire, Monmouthshire, Brecon and most of South Wales, but the river it crossed was 'very furious and dangerous, and with a small rayne doth suddenly swell and ryse uppe'. The ferry boat had often sunk, so that thirty or forty people had 'not longe since' been drowned, while others had had to swim for their lives or been trampled by other passengers or their livestock. A bridge should be built within seven years at the cost of the county's inhabitants, bolstered by voluntary contributions gathered in Wales. Tolls were to pay for the bridge's upkeep and compensate the lord of the manor who currently rented out the ferry. All was to be done under the supervision of the county's justices of the peace, Scudamore, Croft and the cantankerous Coningsby among them. The bridge, built in sandstone, survives to this day.

Accidents evoked emotional as well as practical responses. Chroniclers called them sad and pamphleteers went further: doleful, pitiful, mournful, woeful, lamentable. In a handful of cases the jurors' language suggested their feelings. Bodies were said to be grievously smashed, victims cruelly ill. One tragedy sticks out. On the afternoon of 12 May 1565, Thomas Roydon, esquire, and Edward Fen, gentleman, left the house of Francis Weldon, esquire, at East Peckham in Kent for a swim in the Medway at Branbridges. Thomas stripped off first and went into a deep pool of the river called 'Nokeweare Poole'. He swam for a short time and then felt himself caught by the current. He called out to Edward for help and Edward leapt in. The rescuer, impeded by his partly undone boots, was able neither to help his friend nor to save himself and both drowned, dying, as the jurors said, sadly and distressingly.

Deeper questions were raised by accidents. The hotter kind of Protestants sought zealously to detect the providential hand of the Almighty at work in the everyday. So was random misfortune sufficient explanation for a fatal mishap, or even the kind of pragmatic reasoning so prevalent in the jurors' verdicts, that an accident occurred because a riverbank was too slippery or a horse too restive? References to the will or providence of God were scattered thinly through inquest reports from the 1560s on. In most cases we can guess why they seemed appropriate. A great tempest or the escape of one person when others perished might fairly be seen as an act of God.

One coroner specialised in providence. This was Martin Cotes, who operated in North Kent from 1573. In December 1581 he presided at Gravesend over a case in which six passengers survived the sinking of their boat and three did not. Perhaps this prompted reflection on God's inscrutable will. The survivors, said the report, had been restored to life by divine providence. Cotes's inquests returned to normal for the next three years, but from 1584 he adopted the formula he would use from then on, that victims died by misfortune, which is divine providence.

If any coroner was going to use such language, then Cotes was the man. His other job was as clerk to the chapter of Rochester Cathedral, where the atmosphere was one of advanced Protestantism. The dean had gone into exile when Mary restored Catholicism and three of the canons got into trouble under Elizabeth for not wearing the proper vestments. Cotes complicates any easy contrast between blind faith in providence and practical reasoning about accident prevention, for he was the coroner at the Snodland mill inquests with their solid safety recommendations. He also retains an air of mystery because he found many more drownings to be accidents, rather than suicides, than most coroners did. Was he the model Christian, merciful to the grieving, or the canting puritan hypocrite, on the take from those who wanted to keep their family's goods and reputation?

One accident set out especially starkly the conflict between providence and pragmatism. On Sunday, 13 January 1583, the scaffolding on which the spectators stood collapsed at a bear-baiting show in Paris Garden, Southwark. Five men and two women from all over the metropolis were killed and many others injured. The coroner's jury recounted how the larger than usual crowd had been warned by those minding the scaffolding to stand still when the old, weak timbers began to creak, but they took no notice and ran from one side to the other until all fell flat.

John Field, the militant puritan preacher who had once been curate of St Giles Cripplegate, home parish of one of the victims, had no time for such worldly reasoning. Inside five days he rushed out a forty-four-page pamphlet, arguing that the city magistrates had neglected their duties in allowing a thousand or so Londoners to prophane the Lord's Sabbath day by crossing the river to attend 'that cruell and lothsome exercise of bayting beares'. He admitted that the spectators' gallery was 'very old and rotten' and unusually crowded. But he maintained that the comprehensive nature of the collapse was a sure sign that the event was a 'fearefull example of

God's judgement'. Masters should, he suggested, keep their servants from such vanities, and townsfolk should recognise such 'vaine pleasures' as 'sweete poysons', and rather seek after 'the comfortable worde of salvation', especially on a Sunday afternoon. The lord mayor was convinced, resolving that the collapse gave 'great occasion to acknowledge the hande of God for such abuse of the sabboth daie' and 'contempt of Gods service'. But the showmen and their customers were not so easily persuaded. The bear-baiting was soon going strong again.

Neither coroners nor jurors were perfect in their diligence or understanding. But they tried hard to work out what had caused their neighbours' deaths. They made thoughtful use of the distinctions set out in law, of the evidence of witnesses, corpses and accident sites, of ideas about chance and providence. Sometimes they apportioned blame or suggested safety measures. In so doing they opened a precious window on everyday life. The need to consider disease as a cause of death by divine visitation kept it in their minds as they reached their verdict. But their reports also give us much other detail about health good and bad, about disability and the search for medical help. As we begin to watch the people of Tudor England through the window of the coroners' reports, we can start with sickness and health.

# 4

## In Sickness and in Health

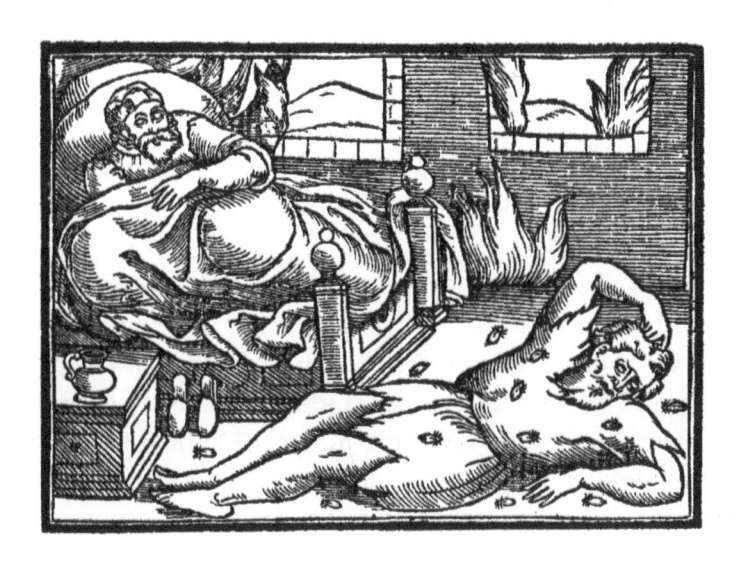

The coroners' inquests reveal much about the dangers posed to health by sixteenth-century life, though not always in the terms we would choose. Contemporaries made little distinction between infectious diseases, other medical conditions, and symptoms. Anything from whooping cough through gout to a headache could be called an illness. They often used generic terms such as sick, infirm, debilitated or lame. Even when they were specific, we might be not much the wiser. The 'fymbroke' afflicting John Jeffe's stomach, for example, was probably some kind of hernia, but it is hard to be sure.

More importantly, because the inquests recorded only fatalities that might be hard to explain, they ignored straightforward deaths from epidemic disease. The plague outbreaks that cut regular swathes through city-dwellers or the childhood fevers and gastric infections that killed so many in their early years scarcely feature. None the less, the inquests tell us a great deal. The famous epidemics do appear. Roger Hogge was already fatally ill with the 'pescilence' or plague when he accidentally cut himself with a knife in 1526. Burning ague, probably typhus, made Agnes Rusholme too weak to escape the current of the Ouse as she walked along its shore in 1555. The 'great lax', or dysentery, made James Nycols soil his shirt and breeches in 1552 and drown in the attempt to wash them. The lax also made for disastrous nighttime trips to the privy, like that of John Birde, who fell down the eight stone steps that led to his chamber in 1580 and smashed the back of his head.

Agues or fevers were common. They were often so intense, thought the jurors, that they clouded victims' judgement, like the 'hot fevers which were so fierce that they took away people's memory and senses' that the Welsh soldier Elis Gruffudd remembered coursing through the army in 1544. Dorothy Cawthorn, a household servant, ran such a high fever that she lost her reason. She got out of bed between four and five in the morning and bludgeoned a hole in the kitchen wall, only to drown outside. John Morley, a Yorkshire husbandman, was 'bysett with a sekenesse called a woyd ague and . . . owt of his mynde and wyt'. Driven by this wode – furious or wild – illness, he went out of his house at 7 a.m. and down to his death in the River Aire, chased in vain by two of his servants.

Fevers peaked at certain times and places. The bad harvests of 1555–6 were followed by waves of fever, probably typhus in 1556–7 and influenza (dubbed the new ague or 'newe dysease') in 1557–9. Together they produced the worst mortality crisis of the century, killing perhaps a tenth of the population. Nearly one in five of all our accidents involving these conditions happened in 1556–9, nearly one in ten in 1559 alone. Other fevers, sometimes called quotidian fevers, rising to a peak on a daily cycle, were probably malarial and spread by marshland mosquitoes. Nearly a quarter of the fever cases in the inquests occurred in marshy Lincolnshire or on the banks of the Yorkshire Humber. There were fevers in the villages of the Holland fen, in the Lindsey coastal marsh and in the Isle of Axholme, where Dorothy Cawthorn battered down her wall.

Other infections were less deadly but still debilitating. Elizabeth Pristone was suffering from 'knigcough', kinkcough or whooping cough, when she died in a Yorkshire 'snaw dryfte' in 1570. Margery Chesshyre had the 'tysycke', perhaps tuberculosis or bronchitis, when she fell into the fire with a pain around her heart. Stephen Frenche's leprosy made him wash his legs in a pond where he drowned.

The contemporary idea that much illness was related to diet fitted some conditions better than others. Kidney stones caused Thomas Page such maddening pain that he ran off and fell into a ditch. An attack of 'the splen and colicke' so convulsed Thomas Michell that he fell off his horse. Edward Baker, a Gloucester minstrel, had such severe 'gowte' that when he cut his leg on a piece of timber, he bled to death.

Cancers were recognised by contemporaries, though their terminology did not always match ours. Robert Langwith was ill with a 'canker' and William Baker with 'the cankers' when they suffered fatal falls, William after visiting a surgeon. Two victims said to have lost their judgement through intense pain were Elizabeth Richardson and Isabel Thornton. The first was suffering from a 'rotten brest' and the second was ill in one of her breasts for two months before she gave birth, developed fever and felt her breast swell greatly.

Sometimes symptoms leading to accidents were vividly described, but their cause is hard to know. Falls might be ascribed to 'a swymmyng in hys hed', 'a decines [dizziness] in the bran', or a 'quothe', a fainting-fit. Several victims had headaches severe enough to be called 'a megreme'. The 'palsey', sudden paralysis or shaking, that made people fall off carts and roofs might have resulted from a stroke or a degenerative disease. John Chyttenden often suffered from an affliction in his sides called 'stight', a stitch, which caused such unbearable writhing that he fell off a bridge.

But what lay behind it? More commonplace was the fate of half a dozen swimmers seized by 'the crampe'.

For some jurors, the set of the stars influenced health, as we might expect from the wide publication of almanacs depicting the astrological 'zodiac man' showing how each constellation governed a different part of the body. At Beccles, Suffolk, in December 1544, Simon Reve cut his foot trying to stop his white mastiff fighting with a greyhound. Though the dog-bite scratched him only one-eighth of an inch deep, he died nine days later because, the jurors explained, the sign of the foot was then reigning in that place. At Bow Brickhill, Buckinghamshire, in November 1580, when Bridget Chyvell fell and cut her thigh with a knife, she died instantly because, said the jurors, in that leg and place the sign will rule at that time. Thomas Moulton's best-selling popular medical treatise, *The Glasse of Helth*, did indeed suggest that in November 'this sygne', Sagittarius, 'reigneth in the thyes', so that one should 'beware of cuttyng of thoo places', though it allotted the knees, rather than the feet, to Capricorn and December.

Cosmic influence was also held by some to induce temporary derangement in the form of lunacy. Those called lunatic manifested very unsettling behaviour. Thomas Aston of Wadworth, tanner, went onto the Don bridge at Rotherham, climbed its wall and suspended himself over the water by his hands until he fell and drowned. John Sheffield of Gokewell, Lincolnshire, gentleman, rose from his bed at one in the morning and grabbed a sword. John and Margaret Smale restrained him, Margaret was fatally stabbed and Sheffield himself died later that night.

Others were called, more neutrally, 'insane', but they could still shock. The jurors characterised Henry Clerk as an insane vagabond, wearing no clothes and of such wicked manner of life that no one would offer him hospitality, hence his death from exposure. William Wale, husbandman, insane for a year, won more sympathy, but must have unnerved his friends in September 1530, in the uncertain early years of Henry VIII's Reformation. He set fire to a cartload of hay and stood in the middle of it, perhaps imitating a heretic burnt at the stake. With the help of his neighbours, his servant Jane Moreton pulled him away from the fire and took him home, seriously burnt. There he told them that Blessed Mary had protected him and asked them to take him back so they could see her. At the site, he suddenly fell into the ashes. The neighbours dragged him home again, but he died the following day.

Epilepsy, the falling sickness, loomed large for those explaining accidents, as it did for those offering healthcare. Lady Grace Mildmay, one of the formidable gentlewomen who counted it their charitable duty to offer medical help to their neighbours, placed it first in her list of conditions to be addressed 'because it is frequent . . . lamentable to behold and difficult to cure'. Nearly one in a hundred of our victims suffered from it and some at least of them had fallen many times before their fatal seizure. Yet it did not prevent them from pursuing the normal activities of life. Risk was unavoidable if they wished to earn a living. Alexander Hudson, the jurors recalled, had worked while having the falling sickness and thus often fell over in streets and dangerous places. John Androwes was up a tree, picking apples, when he had his fall, Margaret ferch David walking through a puddle of water and mud, unappetisingly called a 'donghill lake', to drive oxen to pasture. Dorothy Gardiner and Agnes Fourde were doing the laundry, John Gibson and George Lace angling. Richard Catwood was a mason who fell off scaffolding while repairing a church.

Visual impairment played an understandable role in accidents. Around half of victims' sight problems were attributable to old age, while others had always been blind. They were mobile, sometimes in familiar surroundings close to home – gardens, closes, pastures – but sometimes further afield. Nicholas Lewys, blind from birth, was walking down Finkle Street in Donington, Lincolnshire, when he met his mishap. John Mershe was coming home from mass. Juliana Myntyng, seventy years old, blind and lame, was walking the mile from Brasted to Sundridge in Kent.

Mostly they fell over unexpected obstacles, but there were other hazards. John Venn, 'myssynge his waye', went into a cart-house, where he was attacked by a bull. William Coxe met Nicholas Forwoodd leading some geldings out to pasture. Forwoodd could see that Coxe was blind and shouted to warn him about the horses. Coxe stepped backwards and fell into a ditch. Fire was the other great risk. Agnes Manfelde died when she tried to light a kiln and the house burnt down. Margaret Pottenwode, aged seventy, was alone with a toddler who cried when a spark from the fire set light to some straw. She reached out to comfort and protect him, but both were burnt. He died at once and she lingered for three days.

Others had mobility problems. Robert Tappyn, a lame tailor, used a wooden 'crutche' to support himself, but it slipped as he crossed a bridge. Nicholas Ellerkar of Tholthorpe, Yorkshire, gentleman, was up before dawn to walk on his 'crouches of wodd' to a place called 'Ravensike Bank', but he fell into the River Swale. The elderly Suffolk esquire George Henyngham fell into a ditch when his walking stick, graphically called a 'lenyng tree', snapped. John Hounsell, an eighty-year-old husbandman, rose at dawn every day to rouse his servants. Coming downstairs from his chamber in the dark, his staff slipped from his hands, and he fell.

Disability might also be mental. The law made a clear distinction between temporary lunacy and idiocy, a lifelong mental impairment that might be tested by rough and ready criteria such as an ability to count money or to know the days of the week. Those described as idiots or natural fools were sometimes capable of work, but their lack of judgement made them vulnerable. John Marler stayed too long in a flooding meadow and Alice Pyttarde got too close to an ox. Benedict Hutche, though counted an idiot and natural fool lacking reason, worked for an Amersham tanner and, as the inquest recorded, owned a pair of shoes worth 6*d*., a canvas shirt worth 4*d*. and a purse with 2½*d*. in cash. He liked playing around with empty carts, but miscalculated when he pulled a cart full of wood over on top of himself.

Some victims should have known better, valuing their entertainment above their health. Football was a particular draw.

Robert Fowcher, playing at Hemingford Grey, Huntingdonshire, ran very violently, struck the ball and fell as an 'impostume', a purulent swelling in his body, released its unpleasant contents in the presence of dependable witnesses. He died later that evening. Timothy Purcas too was, as the jurors put it, not thinking of the danger to follow when he played in a meadow called 'Churchmeade' at Cressing, Essex. In a rough encounter he broke a vein inside an old ulcer on his left leg, went off to the next field and bled to death.

Only John Cheeseman of Leeds, Kent, disappointed the jurors more. He had long had a hernia in his stomach when, on the evening of Whit Sunday 1588, he was at Anthony Davy's inn with assorted adolescents and young men. They were playing together, jumping or dancing, and John was drunk. Caring little for his hernia – the scorn of the jurors drips off the page – he conducted himself wantonly and in a disorderly manner. Shaking and crushing his body as he fell many times, he made his injury much worse. A great part of his entrails was thrust up out of his belly under his skin and could not be put back in again. He was gravely ill for the next two days, then died of the rupture. So – the jurors hardly needed to add – in their judgement he died not only by misfortune, but also on account of his own bad conduct.

Treatment for medical problems was available, usually at a price and at various levels of expertise. The medical professionals most prominent in the inquest reports are surgeons, who specialised in external injuries and sometimes doubled up as barbers. They were widespread in society, featuring as accident victims, but were also mentioned in inquests on their patients. They mainly worked in towns rather than villages, so the injured came in from their homes or the sites of their accidents: from Stansted Mountfitchet three miles to Bishop's Stortford, from Hursley six miles to Romsey, from Peasenhall fifteen miles to Bungay.

Failed treatments were described to clear the surgeon from blame. Christopher Deacon had fallen in front of a cart when drunk and crushed the bones in his right leg. John Skald, assistant to William Purviche, barber and surgeon, treated him, and his prospects of recovery were good. But three weeks after the fall he accidentally tore the dressing off his wound and bled to death. Two-year-old James Horseley suffered from scall, a nasty but widespread skin disease of the head. At his father's request, a local surgeon treated him with a poultice. He died, but the jurors decided that the surgeon had acted according to his learning and not out of malice.

Things were more awkward when rival surgeons disagreed. John Trabbe, aged twelve, was hit in the forehead by a small arrow, a bird bolt. He was taken to the house of William Breteyn, surgeon, and remained there nine weeks until, apparently out of danger, he went back to his mother. Five days later another surgeon, Richard ap Pryce, persuaded her to try his treatment. John immediately had a fatal 'axes', an attack of illness. Richard Turgood broke his left leg driving a cart and various surgeons tried to cure the wound. Eventually, two weeks after the break, one got Richard's consent to amputate. The patient died an hour later. Of course, success was not guaranteed even when the experts agreed. Henry Siesly showed his head wound to surgeons and physicians, educated scholars of internal medicine. Both pronounced that it was not life-threatening. They were wrong.

Much medicine was practised at home, where remedies could malfunction disastrously. Anne Wyffyn, aged fourteen, had intestinal worms. She ground up some ratsbane – arsenic rat poison – into a very fine powder, mixed it into a pot of ale and drank it to kill the worms, not suspecting that it would kill her instead. Margaret Morlande used ratsbane to make a 'water to kill lyce'. She got up from bed at night to help her husband, a lame clergyman. Feeling thirsty, she reached in the dark for a pot of beer she had left out, forgetting that next to it stood the lice water, which she drank instead. The electuary, a medicinal conserve, that Katherine Aynley, seamstress, shared with her old friend, Alice Johnson, may have been homemade or bought from an apothecary. Either way, Katherine had no idea that it had become harmful. She survived eating it, but Alice's body swelled up and she died ten hours after the fatal dose.

Other home treatments rested on the learned medical principle that good health depended on the balance of the humours in the body. Excess or impure substances might be removed to restore the proper balance by bleeding, purging or sweating. John Persey had a range of internal afflictions for which his close friend, Richard Ciche, a butcher, took blood from the left side of his head the day before he died, using a little cleft stick of hazel wood. As both the wound and the quantity of blood were very small, the jurors were sure that this did not contribute to his death.

There was more doubt about events at the house of John Curtisse, gentleman, at Bishop Burton, Yorkshire, on the night of 23 March 1588. His children, eight-year-old Bridget and five-year-old William, were unwell. His servant Isabel Pecket rubbed their heads with ointment, gave them a 'warme posset drinke', probably of spiced milk and ale, and put them to bed, to sleep and to sweat. Bridget was in a bed, William tied into a cradle, and both were wrapped up, indeed 'overcharged', with many covers. About midnight Bridget cried out for help, begging for some air. Agnes Jackson, another servant, wanted to lighten the burden on her, but Isabel would not let her. Bridget suffered on, dying at about five in the morning. William had already suffocated.

Without means to counter infection, some treatments were a losing battle. Anthony Blanden, aged eighteen, was apprentice to a Suffolk butcher, Thomas Paccebrigge. In late July 1575, he was in his master's cart when it overturned and fell on him. His leg was broken, he ached from head to foot, and within a month 'a swellinge' appeared on his head and jaw. He must have continued to work, because in late September his master's wife struck him twice with a 'stander', maybe a candlestick, as a punishment. His illness worsened, so Thomas sent him home for treatment by his mother. Her cures were useless, so he then stayed three weeks with a surgeon at his master's expense. The surgeon cured his head but not the putrefaction of the flesh below his chin and he returned to his mother's house.

There, in December, the malady attacked his buttocks, another infection appeared above his knee and his uninjured leg became greatly swollen along its whole length. He died on the last day of December, five months after the cart crash. As the jurors concluded with eminent practicality, this could not have been the effect of Anne Paccebrigge's chastisement. She had hit him when he was sitting down, so could not have hit his buttocks, site of the fatal illness. In any case her blows did not even leave a mark. The same logic implicitly discounted the original accident in July. Hence it was his illness, brought on by divine visitation, that killed him.

Given the perils of treatment, some took the advice of medical authors that fresh air and moderate exercise promoted health. Anne Oxpring felt ill and weak, so she went out of her house to revive her feeble spirit with some fresh air. It was midnight and she fell into a well. Several others, ill or recently recovered, drowned while walking in open spaces for recreation.

Hygiene was also a good thing, within reason. Andrew Boorde's regularly reprinted *Breviarie of Health* advised that it was good to wash the hands often, especially in the morning and after meals, but that the face was better wiped daily with a cloth. Some people went outside regularly to wash their hands and others stopped to wash in pools or streams while out and about, their fingers dirty with mud or straw or in need of a clean before milking cows. About one in ten washed their face or mouth as well and a similar number washed their feet and legs. All ran the risk of drowning. Such accidents happened all year, at all times of day and irrespective of age, sex or social rank.

Very different and far deadlier was bathing the whole body in deeper water. Bathing killed five times as many as less ambitious forms of washing, about four hundred victims in all. Medical writers thought it was best avoided because it let disease into the body's open pores – far better, they thought, to put on a clean linen shirt – but their recommendations were clearly ignored and indeed some victims were said to bathe for refreshment or health. Bathing was often hard to distinguish from swimming for exercise, though dozens of the drowned were clearly walking about in the water unable to swim when they lost their footing. Any open water would do, ponds, streams or big rivers. Boys and men of all types did it, clergymen and gentlemen, goldsmiths and locksmiths, tailors and shoemakers, millers and bakers, mariners and watermen, husbandmen and shepherds, labourers and servants, a vagrant in the Wreake at Rearsby and a soldier in the Eden at Carlisle.

Bathing was commonly, as jurors explained, brought on by hot weather or hot work. Accidents clustered in the second half of the working day, nine out of ten between 1 p.m. and midnight, and in the summer months, nine out of ten between May and August and seven out of ten in June and July alone. May to August were indeed the months recommended in the first English treatise on swimming, Everard Digby's *A Short Introduction for to Learne to Swimme*. Bathing could be pleasurably combined with leading animals to water or fishing, but swimming was also a practical skill. Some of those who drowned were trying to cross rivers or streams to pick fruit or fetch wandering livestock, some trying to retrieve items from the water.

Those who bathed took off their clothes, the reports noted – one fastidious cleric even piled 'a lytle hand towell' with his garments – and were naked. This presumably accounts for the rarity and secretiveness of female bathing. Of the four female victims of washing that may have gone beyond the hands, face and feet, all unmarried, one took off her shoes and stockings and waded into a pond at ten at night, two were probably trying to wash from the bank, again in the evening, and only one, ten-year-old Margaret Collyar, went in so deep at five in the morning that when she fell her inability to swim doomed her.

Many bathed in sociable groups of workmates, neighbours and brothers. Sometimes they drowned together. Thirty-four incidents took the lives of two victims and five tragedies accounted for three. Some rescue attempts were striking. William Turner, a yeoman of Hadleigh, Suffolk, rushed from one part of the River

Brett to another to save Thomas Reade, described as his chosen and faithful friend; Turner drowned but Reade survived. The toll was especially grievous among Cambridge undergraduates, many of them, as we have seen, swimming at Grantchester. At least a dozen drowned between 1531 and 1583. No wonder the university authorities tried to ban swimming in 1571 despite the many intellectuals who stressed the classical precedents for its utility and healthfulness, Digby, a fellow of St John's, among them.

Some took risks. Jurors criticised them as too confident in their own strength or insufficiently learned in the art of swimming. Some dived to the bottom of a pond and got tangled up, swam beyond the reach of help from their companions or went beyond the point of exhaustion. But most seem to have chosen accessible places to swim, sites for watering or washing animals, quaysides, fords or washing stairs, moats, sluices or ponds. French Weir on the River Tone in Taunton, where John Clastocke drowned in 1567, was still being used for swimming in the 1920s. Admittedly the Cambridge bather who went in near 'the Ded Mens Pytte' in the Cam with its clutching weeds may have been less wise and many did meet environmental hazards. There were plants, mud, fast currents, collapsing banks and unexpected pits. Worst were pits with fast currents, whirlpools or whirlpits or twirlpools as the jurors called them. These were precisely the dangers warned about by Digby.

Non-swimmers knew they needed to learn to swim. James Astrell went to a pond to teach himself but drowned in deep water. Those unsure of their abilities might use swimming aids. It is not clear whether Hugh Welshman tied his shirt round his neck before entering the water out of modesty or for extra buoyancy, but it did him no good as the sleeve got tangled round his arm. Others were better prepared. Robert Romesey in the Severn at Gloucester and Martin Robinson in the Thames at Southwark buckled on bladders, but they drifted away. Sixteen-year-old Thomas Seyland, servant of a tailor of Chiche in Essex, not only tied two bladders around himself but also kept his friends nearby. When the ropes holding the bladders broke, he cried out to them 'I'm drowning, I'm drowning, for the love of God help me'. Two friends grabbed him by the hands, but they lost their footing and all three drowned.

Any open water might be good for bathing, but some places were especially healthful. All over England were wells, springs or pools reputed to have healing properties. Robert Browne of Penrith walked to a well called 'Bladren Skarre' in May 1583 to seek his health after a long illness, but, as the jurors commented, by the good will of God he was drowned there. Oliver Broughton may have had similar notions when he washed in 'Alum Well' at Kendal. Thomas Paddy had a different idea of the kind of place that might help him. He went to a spot called 'Willow Holme' at Lilford, Northamptonshire, with the intention of healing his body from illness and rested with his back against a willow tree before sliding into the river. Perhaps he had in mind the recommendations of medical books that the leaves and bark of willow – containing the same active ingredient as aspirin – were good to treat ailments from earache and gut pain to sores on the skin and the spitting of blood.

Sixteenth-century life presented many challenges to health. Epidemics spread readily and diet, housing and social constraints could make things worse. Yet people were resourceful in adapting to their situation, in seeking treatment from experts or devising it for themselves, and in trying to maintain their wellbeing. Some of the ways they did that certainly make sense to us – a walk in the open air, a refreshing swim – but circumstances made them riskier than they are today. Others, like bleeding, sweating and home remedies based on rat poison no longer appeal, though we should remember the role of modern drugs in the poisonings that now loom large in accidental-death statistics. While we characterise mental-health difficulties differently from them, we still find them challenging. We have better means to alleviate conditions such as epilepsy, but disabilities of many sorts can still make life limited and dangerous. Their health, like ours, was preserved or tested in the context of their domestic life, where Margaret Morlande cared for her husband and John Curtisse's servants put his children to bed. We should next explore families and households.

# 5

# Families and Households

Households were the fundamental units of Tudor society and the framework for the course of life. Parents, children and servants lived together and often worked together too, for the household was a powerful economic unit. It is no wonder that around one in ten accident victims over the age of fourteen was found by another member of their household.

Some accidents give us a glimpse of a household at work. In March 1598, at West Coker, Somerset, Jane More, wife of Thomas More, was with her servants Mary Hayward and Christiana Osmond, malting grain in a kiln next to the kitchen. Mary, standing on the wall of the kiln, passed her mistress a sieve full of malted oats, but as she carried it to the granary, Jane slipped under its weight and broke her neck. In April 1594 at Bathealton in the same county, Richard Pearce, husbandman, was working with his sons John and Thomas in an outhouse, taking down a large beam from a cider-press or 'appell wringe'. Richard and John used two levers to turn the screws or 'vizees' of the press, while twelve-year-old Thomas stood seven feet off the ground, presumably steadying the beam. The beam fell off the top of the screws unexpectedly and shattered Thomas's skull.

Households also worked together outside. In July 1539 at Buttermere, Cumberland, William Dicson left his wife, children and servants cutting hay while he went to check on his cattle and fell into a beck. In July 1578 at Towcester, Northamptonshire, John Heyford was scything grass in the fields, working with his wife Alice and his two sons. Alice and the boys realised that John's rival, Thomas Cowper, was taking away the cut grass, and she was run over when she tried to stop his cart. In December 1559 at Dallow, Bedfordshire, Thomas Dermar, yeoman, his wife Alice and his servants Agnes Evered, Thomas Ivery and Robert Semar were busy loading wood from a newly felled beech tree onto a cart when the trunk rolled downhill and hit young Mary Owney.

Complex families could be produced by bereavement, remarriage and wet-nursing. Jane Wood died washing a muddy spade in her stepfather's pond, Isabel Gybson was found dead by her stepmother, and John Craforthe fell into a river because, the jurors said, of the inattention of his mother, now married to John Jenyns. John Brigges was the son of Jane Brigges of Teynham, Kent, spinster, but was living with Nicholas and Elizabeth Tobye when, at the age of two, he drowned in a ditch under the negligent care of their daughter Isabel.

Marriage was preceded by courtship, freer among the less wealthy than the propertied but still risky. The unfortunate Jerome Snouke ran fast towards Grace Wyseman to give her a kiss, feeling, as the jurors recorded, an ardent desire of marriage towards her. She was holding a willow rod in her right hand and it poked him in the left eye so hard that he died four days later. Other young folk had similar mishaps. John Beeley and Alice Higgot fell from a first-floor gallery where they were joking together. John Gill ran over to Felicia Clerk, undressed down to her shift as she harvested peas in a hot field, but fell over and stabbed himself in the leg with his knife. George Busche met a similar fate with Juliana Cock in the hay harvest.

We can sometimes picture the scene in more detail. William Prydmore was making a haystack with three women when he resolved to kiss Margaret Goodladd on top of the stack. She resisted, they both fell off, and she broke her neck. William Hykeman, a waterman, was cheekier still. In the marshes at Minster in the Isle of Thanet in May 1588 he saw in the distance two servants from Queenborough, Rose Wylye and Anne Palmer, cutting reeds. He joined them and jested first with Anne, then with Rose. He helped Anne a little with her work, then went back to larking with Rose. Rose joked with him that she had a knife at her belt – maybe warning him to watch his step – and he answered, perhaps quoting a ballad, though not it seems one that survives, 'Hange sorowe, lett wyeffe and chylderen go begge'. He put Rose on the ground and tumbled her about in the reeds until her knife went into his thigh. If these unfortunately placed knives were about self-defence rather than accident, it went tragically wrong in the case of Elizabeth Adam and Jane Haukes, killed in a clinch by the knives in men's belts.

Married life was intended to be, as the marriage service put it, a partnership of 'mutuall societie, helpe and comfort . . . both in prosperitie and adversitie'. Some met this standard better than others. The home of John and Barbara Reder, a Norfolk couple in their thirties, seems a place of fondness. As they sat by the warm fire on a November evening, she reached out to take his arm, only to cut herself on the knife that lay on her apron. Agnes Mayson and her husband William may have had a more teasing relationship. One August afternoon at home she playfully snatched a sickle away from him but cut her right arm. Sometimes the reactions of spouses to accidents suggest their concern. Richard Denway was pulled from the water and taken home by his wife and her neighbours when caught in a storm while fishing. John Webster went looking diligently for his wife, Joan, until he found her, three days after she fell into a stream.

Thomas and Joan Gelder fared very differently. Walking the five miles from Worksop to Carburton on a February evening, he abandoned her at the foot of Sparken Hill, where she died of the cold and, the jurors were not shy of saying, lack of care from her husband. Thomas Henor's wife took a more direct approach, laying about her husband with a staff in a full-blown fight that killed the visitor who interrupted them.

Other couples doubtless failed on the criterion that wedlock was 'ordeyned for a remedy against sin, and to avoyde fornicacion'. We might have our suspicions about Nicholas Sawman and Agnes Raynoldes, wife of James Raynoldes. He got drunk in James Baylie's alehouse at Hollington, Sussex, and they set out to walk to Crowhurst where he lived. They lay down on the ground together near the road, Agnes left him asleep there later in the night and he never woke. Equally inappropriate was the conduct of William Wotton and Sybil Corvesor, wife of John Corvesor. They were treading down a stack of oats in a barn when William, 'in sporte and play', grabbed Sybil, threw her over and lay on top of her, both covered in oats. Only when it was dark did he get up to go, falling from the stack and breaking his neck.

The first purpose of marriage, said the Prayer Book, was 'the procreacion of children, to be brought up in the feare and nurtour of the Lord'. Continual work amid frequent pregnancies could bring traumatic stillbirths. Anne Blacke and Jane Browne bore dead children after falls. Unmarried mothers, often domestic servants desperate to conceal shameful and potentially ruinous pregnancies, had even less chance to pause and less hope of assistance. Elizabeth Bromham gave birth to her son dead in the hall of her master's house for lack of womanly help. Alice Nytynghale fell on her stomach while carrying a basket full of malt. Her daughter died in her womb and when she gave birth a few days later, moved, as the jurors recognised, by anxiety and shame, she threw the child's body into the moat.

Babies were vulnerable both to disease and to the hazards of the home. Infants left by the fire while mothers, servants or nursemaids worked were burnt when their cradle fell, or sparks reached their sheet or bedding straw. Siblings rushing about were a hazard to babies, but babies distracted parents from toddlers. Richard Jeanes, seven months, was hit in the head by a bench knocked over by his four-year-old brother, while two-year-old Jane Foster fell into a kettle when her mother switched attention to the baby. Servants entrusted with babies might be too reckless to foresee risk. Edith Hurley, eleven months old, was left in the charge of twelve-year-old John Deyman. He took her to a dye-house and sat her on the edge of a furnace filled with sixty pints of scalding water. She fell in. The most alarming nursing establishment was that of Hugh Smythe, a labourer of Plumstead, Kent, and his wife Elizabeth. Walter Grete placed his son Barnaby with them, but at the age of fourteen weeks he was left sleeping on a bed while Elizabeth went out to buy food. A poisonous creature – perhaps a snake – which Hugh kept in a chest escaped, climbed up to Barnaby and bit him.

Mobile children faced new perils. One solution was to strap them into fireside chairs, but wriggly toddlers tipped themselves into the flames. Another was to keep them occupied, as Katherine Yett left her master's daughter Agnes Hardyng playing with a metal basin while she went to the neighbours' house for a bag; but Agnes pottered out to a pond. Perhaps it was safer to take them to work, but perhaps not. William Gregorys let his son watch as he mended a cart, but one wheel fell on the boy. Margaret Davy put her daughter Bridget at the side of the road while she helped with the harvest, but Bridget's head was trampled by a cart-horse. Helen Pette took little Edmund to a watermill, but he fell into the millstream as she was shutting the floodgate.

Small children followed parents and siblings into danger. Nicholas Browne wandered upstairs after his mother, Sybil, as she worked around the house, and Mary Fowle went out to find her father at his fulling-mill next door. William Russhe trailed behind his sister and other children as they drove cattle to water. At Terrington St Clement in Norfolk, at nine in the morning on 9 May 1567, twenty-five-year-old Margaret Lyngehoke, wife of Thomas, went out into the garden with a bucket of linens to dry on the hedge. Her children followed behind her, playing, eighteen-month-old Thomas picking the flowers that grew round a pond. Suddenly she saw him in the water and stretched to grab him, but the stake she held on to snapped. She was found drowned, her right arm clutching her lifeless son.

Drowning became a major threat as soon as children could move, claiming three-quarters of victims aged two and three. Most fell into open water, usually near the home, but dozens fell into containers in the house or yard, most often wooden tubs. They could hold as much as five or six gallons and be up to two feet deep. They went by many different names depending on size and shape: keelers, kivers or trendles, cowls, kilderkins or kimnels, hogsheads or vats, soes or stands. Water everywhere was ripe for play. Small children fell into ponds reaching for a goose feather or a barrel hoop, hitting the water with a stick or throwing in stones, trying to fetch a drink in a cup, a dish, or even a snail shell. Houses were also full of scalding liquids. Laurence Thinge pulled out the tap on a 'mesheinge toubbe' in his father's kitchen and unleashed a torrent of boiling ale mash. John Newman was playing and jumping in an unrestrained manner, as any three-year-old might, next to some 'brewyng vesselles' full of 'whott scaldyng wurtt'. He fell into one and died from his burns four days later.

Toddlers at home faced other dangers. Stacked firewood and hay fell readily onto them. They played with animals and came off worst. Most often it was horses, but Dorothy Laken was knocked into a kettle by a greyhound puppy, and George Tynckler and John Choppinge fell into ponds with a young crow and some goslings. Others were indulging in imaginative play. Elizabeth Coosyn rode on a bench until it fell on her. Christiana Jelyan sat by the town ditch making cakes out of mud, Margaret Wymarke washed her straw hat in a well and Isabella Lelonne tried washing some linen in a large water tub.

Small children were not ignored. Nearly half of all victims under seven were found by another member of their household, mostly by a parent or if not by a sibling or servant, often quite soon after they were missed. But they wandered off easily, rich as well as poor. Raphael Champneys, two-year-old son of Justinian Champneys, gentleman owner of Hall Place, Bexley, Kent, fell from a broken bridge in the grounds of the house. Richard Weston, three-year-old son of Richard Weston, justice of the Common Pleas, fell into a trough of boiling liquid playing with his brother in the manor-house brewery.

The very young also went out and about in groups. Bartholomew Ayshebye, said the jurors, went out of his father's house without his mother's knowledge to play with others, as is the habit among boys. Thomas Joye wandered round a tanner's yard looking for the other very small children with whom he usually played there. It was a sign of their mobility that cart accidents were the next most frequent cause of accidental death for two and three year olds after drowning. Carts and horses hit those who sat or lay or played in the street.

As children grew, some risks, such as domestic drownings or open fires, diminished, but open water, carts and animals remained lethal. The more adventurous they became, the more unsuitable the places they played. Many climbed onto carts or field rollers or ran beside them. Recklessness afflicted girls almost as much as boys. Agnes Tinge, playing with other children on the village green, wrapped a halter tied to the wheel-spokes of a loaded cart around her arm and pulled the wheel over her back. Agnes Larwood ran past the turning wheel of a horse-mill to reach a wooden post, playing dangerously as the jurors put it, and was crushed between post and wheel. Susan Bradshawe, aged five, tried to row a boat on the River Trent.

Boys larked about on bridges or in gravel pits, while Edmund Lawton and his friends played with the ropes on a timber crane until the machinery hit him in the head. Thomas, James and Richard Sparke drowned playing together in Cowan Head Water in Westmorland, and Michael Hampton, a shepherd boy from Nuneham Courtenay, Oxfordshire, fell out of the boat he was punting when it became slippery because he and his friends were splashing each other. Others were more inventive. Ralph Holden climbed up the sail of a windmill and fell off when the wind blew it round. Robert Alcocke played with other children in his father's blacksmith's shop, where a scythe and a great hammer fell on his head.

Play was exhilarating, but work beckoned. Few children under the age of seven worked, though some did simple tasks from four onwards, fetching water, carrying food, picking plants, minding animals. For those in the next stage of life, work was significant. While those under seven met their death far more often playing than working, the proportions were roughly equal for those between seven and thirteen. Such older children ventured further from home. Only one in six of them was found by a parent following an accident and few by other household members. Their mobility also took them to places where they found accident victims of all ages, whereas younger children reported only their contemporaries.

These older children did more varied work than the very young. They might be entrusted with errands, as Elizabeth Fairechild, aged seven, was sent from her father's house at Ingthorpe, Rutland, to do business in Great Casterton some half a mile away. They might be left in charge of animals, in groups, or alone, herding cows, oxen, sheep and ducks. Horses were riskiest, as children began to ride and were sent out to catch or watch over them in the fields, to take them to carts or stables, to water them or to lead them as packhorses.

Large numbers of children were servants in households other than their parental home. Among our victims, nearly one in three servants whose age was given was under fourteen, while one in twelve children between seven and thirteen was found after their accident by a master, mistress or fellow-servant. The youngest clearly identified servant to fall victim was aged six, and servants of eight or nine were not uncommon. Anne Symon, Jane Naysse and Thomas Howard each died at the age of ten. The girls were washing pots in a pond and fetching a pole from a watermill, and the boy was unloading straw from a cart. John Springolde, another ten-year-old servant, was not a victim, but the first finder of his master, struck down as he felled an alder tree. Boys working in agriculture might be called labourers rather than servants. Again, some started young, at seven, eight or nine years old.

Many types of work were done by boys and girls alike. They gathered fruit, nuts, herbs and firewood. They dug for turves or sand. They worked with dangerous machinery. Helen Est merely went to a horse-mill to collect her master's malt but stopped to watch the horse and was hit. Twelve-year-old Nicholas Olyver let his eight-year-old brother, Thomas, work the iron winch that raised the bucket of a well, but Thomas could not manage it. The winch spun out of his hands and knocked him into the well as the bucket fell to the bottom. Both boys and girls fetched water, though it was more commonly work for girls, as was childcare. Ellen Adam fell into a well while carrying six-month-old George Ramme, Elizabeth Bromehedd into a stream holding her one-year-old brother, William.

Driving carts was work for boys, some as young as seven. At first these were small carts drawn by a single horse, but by eleven and twelve boys oversaw large and complex teams: five horses, four oxen and a horse, four oxen and two horses. Ploughing probably demanded more skill than driving a cart, but we find twelve- and thirteen-year-old ploughmen. Some children were given tasks that proved beyond them. Michael Nottyngham, aged eight, and Elena Grynnell, aged ten, lost control of their pitchforks and impaled their young workmates. Eleven-year-old Beatrice Davis was sent on business by her master from Chigwell to Romford, six miles away. When she had finished, she took the horse she was riding to John Tyler's house to water it. She sat on the edge of the well while the horse drank, but was so exhausted that she fell asleep and rolled in. Others' determination got the better of them. Nine-year-old Anne Wattes dropped the wooden bowl with which she was scooping water from a pond but took off her shoes and hose, waded after it, got stuck in the mud and drowned.

Children worked with adults to see how things were done. Boys went with their fathers as they drove carts, fished or felled trees. Others accompanied adolescents, herding pigs, milling grain or carrying sacks of malt. Some teaching was planned. On 14 June 1558, at five in the afternoon, at a gravel pit in the fields of Reymerston, Norfolk, presumably a quiet spot, Thomas Cokerell, aged nine, was having a driving lesson. Under the rule and guidance of his father, as the jurors put it, he was driving a cart drawn by two horses and two oxen. Then he got overexcited. Rashly and without consulting his father, the jurors were keen to stress, he ran and jumped into the moving cart, which the startled horses overturned.

Some boys were eager to learn. In April 1552, ten-year-old Thomas Hubbard was sent to the fields at Brundish, Suffolk, with food and drink for the ploughmen. Once there he asked to try ploughing, but as he followed the plough he tripped on a clod and fell, accidentally hit a colt with his whip and got kicked in the head. Others decided to teach themselves. Eleven-year-old Thomas Stone was left alone with John Nele's cart and three horses by Nele's thirteen-year-old servant, Thomas Brittilbank. He climbed onto the shafts and drove around so fast that the cart overturned.

Work could be mixed with play. John Phipp and Richard Banger were meant to be minding sheep and cattle, but one played by a stream and fell in and the other lay on the ground so still that archers practising nearby did not notice him. Thomas Flyntt and four other boys, drawing water from a well in Pontefract Castle, turned the winder so fast that the bucket shot down the well, great fun until the spinning winder hit Flyntt in the neck. At Bromham, Bedfordshire, Robert Audryan was watching over cows with other boys in a meadow near the River Great Ouse. His watching cannot have been very effective, because they were playing a game called 'blyndfeld'. His eyes were so well covered by a 'byret', presumably a cap, that he fell into the river and drowned.

Formal education was available and the century saw many school foundations, but the proportion of children involved declined as they grew older and more able to work. The most dangerous part of school was getting there and back. Five-year-old Edward Benson drowned ladling water out of a pit with his hat on the way to school with Robert Tucker. They were only going half a mile, but at the same age Joan Cheeseman had to walk three miles from the vicarage at Horley, Surrey, where she was learning letters, to her widowed mother's home in Charlwood. She slipped crossing a millstream at four in the afternoon.

Older boys played or swam together, encouraged by boarding arrangements like those in 'the Brethren Hall' at Maidstone Grammar School. The inquests speak of their friendships, of Lewis ap John at Leominster Grammar School and his true friend and schoolfellow John Griffith, of the way Adam Martyne at Crewkerne School went to help John Olford and Robert Hodges when they got into trouble in the water. Yet they also went off on their own. Sampson Butler, scholar of Eton, failed to swim the Thames to reach some tempting nuts on the far bank.

As literacy spread, unevenly by rank, location and gender but also by generation, so reading itself might become a danger. It may have been because his son could read better than he could that Thomas Wulley asked thirteen-year-old Richard to cut open a newly arrived letter and read it to him, only for Richard to hit his head on a stool as he looked for his knife. John Carpynter junior must have been seriously absorbed in his book not to notice someone cutting branches off a nearby elm tree. Eight-year-old Susan Wigmore must have found whatever she was reading even more distracting as she wandered out of the house with a book in her hand and tumbled into a pond.

Fatal accidents inevitably present a parade of negligent or distracted parents, but some cared deeply. Roland Maddocke was asleep in his house in Fletcher Gate, Nottingham, when his daughter Alice cried out, waking him suddenly. Although his wife and servants were in the house, he jumped out of bed to calm her but fell down a flight of steps. The distress of Alice and Richard Crundall when their daughter fell into a well was so loud that their neighbours came running and helped retrieve her body.

Similar concern was evident when parents searched for missing children, couples going together or one parent taking a servant or neighbour. Some looked long and hard. John Turnar found his only son William the day after he fell into a covered pit in a nearby garden. One father looked for his son for three weeks, another for five. Children returned the favour. Anthony Snote and George Aeylerd each hunted with neighbours until they found their fathers buried in pit collapses. Jane Milner's daughter called out her neighbours when her widowed mother disappeared from their home at Greysouthen, Cumberland, undressed, at two on a January morning, having told the girl to go to her room and make her bed. They searched for two and a half days until her mother was found in a drain.

Families were not just about parents and children. Siblings of both sexes played together across a range of ages, and as adolescents and even adults they worked together, but sometimes they fell out. John Hill lashed out at his brother Thomas with a staff and hit their father, Henry, on the head. Ellen Wryghte, a married lady of fifty but described by the jurors as a sturdy woman, was aiming to hit her brother Robert Barker when she grabbed her husband's 'wodehooke' and cut herself. Grandparents rarely lived with younger generations, but they stayed in touch. Ten-year-old Thomas Hunte and two-year-old Robert Haven died alone on their way to their grandfathers' houses. Six-year-old Hester Skinner went with her mother to visit her bedridden grandmother but fell into a scalding kettle.

Children and servants interacted in complex ways. Some accidents suggest an idyll where servants were big brothers and sisters. The servants of two Kent yeomen lifted their master's small sons into the dung-cart for a ride back from the fields. All went well until the carts overturned. Servants carried children in their arms or put them up on horses to ride behind them. Other incidents were more ambiguous. When Joan Large, servant of Margaret Denyll's father, held Margaret over a river by her belt until the belt broke, was she entertaining her or threatening her?

As children grew, relations could be tense. William Riddye, aged seventeen, was sitting by the fire in William Graye's kitchen mending his shoes with a knife when Graye's twelve-year-old son Simon came in and tried to pull Riddye's chair away so he could sit on it. Riddye kicked him so hard that he fell off the chair and cut his arm. Alice Bennett, aged fifteen, was sitting on a stool in Thomas Onley's kitchen sewing when Onley's thirteen-year-old son John came in. John took the small spit used for roasting birds, heated the sharp end in the fire and burnt a hole in a post by the chimney. Alice 'bade hym rest and leffe worcke or ells she wolde tell his father therof'. 'What, folle,' replied John, 'what hast thou to doo therwith?' He put the spit back in the fire intending to bore the hole deeper and she jumped up to take it away from him. He spun around, the spit stuck into her left thigh half an inch deep 'and when she saw her owne blod she fell downe ded'.

Sometimes we can see the emotional impact of a child's death on a whole household. Agnes Cotton was the three-year-old daughter of George Cotton, esquire, master of Panfield Hall in Essex. Between one and two in the afternoon of 20 February 1578, she was with her mistress, presumably head of the nursery, and some other servants, but she wandered, unnoticed, out of the room. She went to the drawbridge over the moat – a moat that still survives in part around the house – and fell from it into the water. Elizabeth Forgen, crossing the drawbridge, spotted Agnes below and was so terrified that she could not speak, but shouted and howled, bringing George and his wife and servants running out. They could not understand what Elizabeth was trying to tell them, but George followed her down to the moat. When he saw his daughter there, he leapt in, pulled her out by her gown and took her into the house. He tried to revive her by whatever means he could, but to no avail. It must have been harrowing to recount events for the inquest.

Households of every sort had servants. One in five victims who were servants worked for gentry or clergy, one in five for yeomen. Nearly one in three served craftsmen or traders and one in six husbandmen. Artisans had servants who were working assistants as well as some who were domestic staff. Yeomen needed help to work their large farms, care for their children, and keep their households running. Husbandmen's servants provided additional farm labour or worked as young women around the house, like the few servants who worked for labourers. Those who served widows – one in twelve – are a reminder not only of the number of households headed by women, but also of the urgent need for labour of those who inherited a farm or business at the death of a husband. Widows' servants included not only men who drove carts, cared for horses, harvested crops or maintained watermills, but also women who milked cows.

More than half of all the servants whose age was given were between fourteen and twenty-one. This was the classic time for service as a phase of the life-cycle, for training in housekeeping or farming, or apprenticeship in a craft, between childhood and marriage. But one in ten was in their twenties, no surprise in the later sixteenth century when worsening economic conditions were pushing upwards both the average age at first marriage and the proportion unable or unwilling to marry at all. Some were older still. Servants of the gentry might be responsible middle-aged men, while widows, sometimes elderly, found refuge in domestic service.

The difficulty of establishing an independent household may also explain the handful of victims who were described as both relatives and servants of the master of the house. Katherine Dekes was sister and servant to William Dekes, Joan Hill sister and servant to Lewis Hill, Eleanor Spyllett sister to Agnes Wastell and servant to Agnes's husband, Henry. There were also sons and daughters described as servants to their parents. These were not the rambling lineages of the gentry, where younger kin might well serve the landed eldest son. Henry Wastell, for example, was a labourer. Other servants or labourers who shared the master's surname may have been brothers or cousins.

Masters and servants often worked closely together. William Cokerell, carpenter, and his servant William Moryce demolished a house, and Roger Miller, mason, and his servant John Sherecroft built a well. Thomas Wullett, waterman, and his servant William Tompson loaded their boat with timber, and John Wenden, carter, and his servant Robert Becham drove their cart full of cloth. John Spacie ploughed with his master William Skelton, and Francis Hancock carted wheat with his master John Myles. Nicholas Swynforde dug chalk from a pit with his servants, and William Watkys and his servant dragged timber out of a wood. Some masters did prefer to supervise. Thomas Meriall directed his servants as they dug marl, while Thomas Westwoode, admittedly aged fifty, watched his as they sawed up a tree.

Male servants usually worked with masters and female with mistresses, just as masters issued orders to male servants but mistresses to female, sending them to a well for water, to a stream to wash linens, to a creek to catch a goose. The role of wives as mistresses of the house is also evident in the regularity with which they found their female servants dead. But sometimes it was all hands on deck. George Barstable's maidservant Edith helped mend his cart and Thomas Reve took his servant Benetta Leede down to the river at six in the morning to collect the fish in the fish-weir.

Some employers clearly cared for their servants. Thomas Hurleston was throwing barley to George Catelyn to thresh when George, who had a fever, collapsed. Thomas picked him up to carry him out of the barn and revive him but tripped at the barn door, breaking George's neck. Roger Adye was in a field with Jane Smyth and Anne Heneker. One of his heifers ran away, and as they chased it Anne fell and swooned as though dead. Roger and Jane picked her up, comforted and revived her and took her to a nearby house. Other servants were taken to their masters' homes for care, and the trip might be substantial. John Smythe, a joiner who fell off a roof at Southill, Bedfordshire, was carried three and a half miles to the house of his master, Thomas Taylor, at Ickwell in Northill. One master and mistress and their servants and neighbours were even commended by the jurors for their diligent attention to a wounded teenage servant.

On the other hand, the ideal household was seen by contemporaries not only as a reproductive, nurturing and economic institution, but also as a source of order and discipline, secured, if necessary, by the violence of its adult male head. Beatings for children and servants are mentioned regularly in the inquest reports and their purpose was clear. As the jurors put it when William Johnson, a Devon tailor, accidentally hit a bystander while laying into his servant John Deyman, it was a means of instructing and correcting him.

Beaters used whatever weapon came to hand. William Salwey and his servant Richard Walle were ploughing when they fell out, so William beat him with a cattle goad. Robert Wilson, a joiner, used the handle of a saw. It was not only men who wielded the rod. Margaret Wrag was about to chastise her ten-year-old son when he dashed off into his father's smithy. As she chased him, Margaret ran into a metal bar two feet long heated red-hot to make horseshoe nails. Beatings should also remind us that in some accident narratives parental violence might well be covered up by plausible stories of spilled cauldrons and falling objects.

Punishment could be controversial. William Stokeley's wife stepped between him and his stepdaughter Mary Borowe as he was about to beat her, holding their baby son George. The head of William's wimble, a brace-and-bit or similar tool, flew off and hit the baby. Thomas Nycholles, presumably a neighbour, intervened when Robert Wilson was punishing his son. As Robert raised his right hand for a blow and the boy dodged it, the peacemaker was struck on the forehead. Occasionally servants fought back. John Wylde went to his barn to tell John Thorogoode, in a reasonable manner, thought the jurors, what work he wanted him to do.

Thorogoode responded with abuse and then grabbed his master. In the tussle Thorogoode fell onto Wylde's knife. At times servants also argued with one another, drawing knives, throwing flails and tussling over stools by the kitchen fire. They could be hard pressed, running to get things done, and at times their tempers cracked.

Younger servants who could not stand their treatment ran away. William Wallis was only eight when he left his master without permission and froze to death hiding under a pear tree. Peter Eade and Catherine Cok were each nine when they walked out. She died hiding for the night in a wet hedgerow, and he wandered long and hungry in the January snow before expiring. At times the jurors protested too much. They mentioned that in their view twelve-year-old Hugh Thornall had no reasonable cause to leave his master's house and roam his lands and woods for four days and nights in December before dying of cold. They emphasised that while fourteen-year-old John Byby's master, William Smyth, and his wife, Jane, had beaten him before he ran away and slept the night in a field, they had used only a twig and had done it because he frequently carried out his duties in a neglectful and perverse manner.

Households were not isolated units and neighbours and relatives visited one another. Widows seem often to have come to grief on their way to or from their neighbours' homes. Such visits demanded hospitality. Margery Reder dropped a log of firewood on her head while cooking a meal for her husband and their neighbours. When John Saffold and Jane Myllett arrived to see Catherine Scoote, she had no drink at home. John gave her 6*d.* to fetch some and she went off into the village with a pot. By the time she got back, an hour later, her son had fallen into a pond. Neighbourly chit-chat sometimes diverted attention enough to cause a mishap.

Neighbours also worked together, building barns, mending carts or catching fish, and lent household necessities. Joan Hill lost her balance on the way to return a stool her brother had borrowed, carrying it on her head where the wind caught it. Little Cecily Symondes drowned following her mother to a neighbour's house to lend him a shovel. Children went back and forth on errands.

Godiva Woldweryche and Thomas Atkyns were sent by their mothers to the homes of James Wood and Humphrey Frebodye, gentlemen. Such trips may have been to ask for charity. Elizabeth Wyllys presumably had the obligations of the rich in mind when she walked to Sir Thomas Mildmay's house at Moulsham, Essex, in January 1588, in search of food for herself and her family, only to slip and fall.

Neighbours gave support at times of crisis. Elizabeth Burden called her neighbours when she found her husband struck to the ground by an elm tree and Helen Pope's neighbours helped her retrieve a body from a pond. Many neighbours went looking for eight-year-old Agnes Stern when she did not come home from driving the cows to pasture, and two couples from their village helped Alice Rayner's parents search for her. The husbands then served as jurors at Alice's inquest, formal structures interacting with informal, just as it was a neighbour acting as village constable who found the body of Richard Badcock.

Tudor families and households – terms more interchangeable then than now – look both familiar and unfamiliar. Parents and children generally lived together without grandparents or uncles, aunts and cousins, but a wide range of households had servants. Families clearly tried to care for small children but left them freer to wander than we would find comfortable. Our toddlers are still at risk, as theirs were, from ponds and streams and scalding liquids, though our houses are not so full of open fires and uncovered vats of wort and whey. Older children, whether in the parental home or working as servants, were entrusted with considerable responsibilities. Often they coped, sometimes they did not, and sometimes play took precedence. Parents less usually faced the joys and strains of cohabitation with their own adolescent offspring, but more often found themselves training, caring for and at times brutalising household servants of the same age.

It was in the relationships of masters, mistresses and servants that the multiple roles of the household, not only domestic hub but also site of work and bulwark of social order, came most sharply into focus. In these relations and in those between husbands and wives, parents and children, and servants and children, families were places both of comfort and of strife. Individual households were in turn interconnected by ties of kinship and neighbourhood. All these social interactions shaped the lives of households, but so did the practicalities of accommodation. Households lived in houses and houses served as homes.

# 6

## Houses and Homes

Houses and their surrounding yards and outbuildings were the sites of at least one accidental death in five. Building was a dangerous industry, as it is now, and the need for maintenance was constant. But just living in Tudor houses posed a whole range of risks.

Houses and outbuildings shared the same, mostly timber-framed, construction. Fires were frequent and could sweep through whole neighbourhoods. They started readily. Barns and mills were full of flammable material, light and heat came from naked flames, and houses had straw in mattresses and on the floor. Eliza Willson demonstrated the dangers as she looked under her bed for a lost plough-staff at 4 a.m. with a candle in her hand. Yet fires were only fatal under certain conditions and killed, for example, about the same number as attacks by cattle. Escape from a slowly burning building of one or two storeys was usually possible and victims were often those less able to get away. One in three was a child – sometimes left shut in a house by busy parents – and others were elderly or blind.

Some tried to escape but failed. Jane Pulton jumped out of a window and William Robertson was felled by a burning beam. Occasional fires spread too fast to get away. On 2 May 1530, fifty-eight houses burnt down in Long Preston, Yorkshire, but in only two were the residents killed, parents, children and servants together, five in one house and seven in another. The flames spread so rapidly, explained the jurors, because they were fanned by a very strong wind. Fire-fighting could prove deadly amid suffocating smoke and falling timbers. Lancelot Gyttyns was burnt rescuing children and goods, Dorothy Sale and Andrew Penywhite drowned fetching water.

Building collapses were harder to evade than fires and killed nearly twice as many. They happened in flimsy outbuildings – barns, byres, henhouses, a loft propped up with an old axle – but also in substantial homes. In November 1590 Robert Paycock's three-storey merchant's house at York fell in. Sometimes high winds were blamed, sometimes floods or snow-drifts, sometimes the dilapidation or the poor construction of the building. Sometimes too much was stored too high up, grain and firewood in Paycock's case. One collapse in three involved walls, stone where it was plentiful, clay, earth or cob elsewhere. More were failures in the timber of frames and roofs. Jurors knew their woodwork, explaining how couple-spars, rafters, balks, crossbeams, wind-beams, summers, liernes, joists, sills, sidepieces, manteltrees, bay windows and durns or door-frames came crashing down.

The hall was the principal room of the house. Accidents happened in the halls of the gentry, centres of hospitality and social pre-eminence, and in the halls of simpler homes, where children and dogs scampered about amid much of the life of the household. Separate, indeed detached or semi-detached, kitchens were desirable to limit fire risk, but many cooked in the hall. Open cooking fires might be replaced with a brick chimney, but chimneys were dangerous. They collapsed on cooks and were risky to mend or sweep. Whole kitchens could fall, as an old kitchen did on one Staffordshire gentlewoman.

Kitchens were close to wells and sewers, and were littered with water-filled vessels. But their prime feature was fire, making them sociable but perilous. Almost as many met their end falling into household fires as died in burning houses. The fate of Elizabeth Bowne, a frail servant, was more bizarre. Sitting by her master's kitchen fire she was hit by four flitches of bacon falling from the chimney where they were hanging to smoke. Similarly unfortunate was baby Katherine Bradnocke, crushed by a falling side of salted beef while sitting by the fire on a servant's lap.

Larger homes had more rooms. Parlours crop up in the occasional inn or gentleman's house. Cellars with their steep steps and propensity to flood were mostly an urban risk. Chambers, solars or lofts were far more frequent and were above all places to sleep. They were naturally a feature of inns and around one in three of those mentioned were in the houses of the gentry and clergy. But yeomen, husbandmen, craftsmen, even labourers had them too, as open halls were increasingly given ceilings and upper rooms. They saw more accidents than kitchens for a simple reason. Two in three deaths linked with chambers involved falls on the stairs or ladders used to reach them. Flights might be six or eight feet high or more, made of stone or more often of wood, straight or sometimes winding. Others fell through trapdoors or holes in chamber floors.

Some who fell and hit their heads or broke their necks were ageing – sixty, eighty and more – but many were in the prime of life. They crossed the social scale from servants and labourers to the gentry: Roger Westcote of Walsall, gentleman, or Sir Robert Broughton of Denston, Suffolk. Among them was the most controversial accident victim of the century, Amy Dudley, née Amy Robsart, wife of Robert Dudley, Queen Elizabeth's master of the horse and alleged lover. Left alone in the house of Anthony

Forster, esquire, at Cumnor, Oxfordshire, in September 1560, as her husband dallied with the queen, she came down the stairs from her chamber. Falling steeply, she broke her neck and sustained two dents in her head, one of them two inches deep. Debate has raged ever since over whether she slipped, threw herself in despair or was pushed. Even the jurors, led by three gentlemen, may not have been sure, as their verdict took eleven months to settle.

Doors lent themselves to various mishaps. They caused falls as they swung or jammed. Those rushing through them tripped and fell, one hitting his head on a door-latch. Windows were tricky too. Thomas Wardell, a clergyman, rose from his sickbed in York's Bedern Hall and fell out of the window. A servant sat little Margery Skelton next to a loose window and she fell into the courtyard below. Humphrey Polle, a fidgety eleven-year-old, pulled out the wooden pin securing a window cord in his father's house in Leominster. When the window snapped shut the cord throttled him.

Building, demolition and maintenance between them led to one accidental death in fifty. The roof was the most pressing site for repairs, and five dozen men died roofing, with thatching accidents well ahead of tiling. All manner of buildings were thatched: houses, barns, stables, hovels. Tiles were largely reserved for the gentry or prosperous townsfolk. Slates appeared where they could be sourced locally.

There were professionals for each material, thatchers, tilers and slaters, but householders mended their own roofs and labourers helped. November, with harvest done and plenty of straw to hand, was the thatching season, with twice as many accidents as any other month. Tiling seems to have been spring and summer work. New tiles were carried onto the roof on a hod and old or broken tiles thrown down, sometimes carelessly. Thatching straw was carried in yelms, or straightened bundles. It was sewn together with a thatcher's needle and held down by springles, bendy sticks. They could spring back and hit one in the face, but the biggest problems came with ladders. One roofer in five fell off a roof beam, but three in five fell from a ladder. Rungs broke, ladders slipped, feet slid. Some climbed ladders thirty feet high, while others had to tie two or even three together to reach an awkward spot. No wonder John Saunders, a thatcher's assistant, thought it safer to climb off the ladder onto a wooden roof beam. It proved rotten.

A second perilous task, accounting for three dozen deaths, was digging and maintaining wells. Wells, often lined with stone or timber, could be deep, seventy feet or more, sometimes more like a domestic reservoir, eight feet wide by nine feet deep. For deep excavation or repairs, for clearing detritus or retrieving lost buckets, or even, in the case of the intrepid Jane Miller of Brimington, Derbyshire, to check if the water at the bottom 'dyd spryng', workers were lowered into the depths on a rope or by standing on the bucket.

About half the fatalities were caused by falling material, earth, stones or parts of the well mechanism, or by a slip from a rope or a broken ladder. The other big killer was suffocation. Jurors usually attributed asphyxiation at the bottom of wells to the same 'yearth damppe' or 'colpytte dampe' that they described in mines, though once they noted that straw taken down a well, perhaps for cleaning or patching purposes, caught fire to generate choking smoke. Working in teams was common and one or even two helpers might follow someone in trouble down a well, only to share their fate.

Construction and demolition took more lives than roofs and wells combined. Work stretched across the year, though busiest in spring and early summer. One accident in three was a fall, from ladders, from beams, from scaffolds. Most other victims were hit by falling material, collapsing walls and toppling beams. Manoeuvring heavy stone was dangerous, throwing it down from disused buildings equally so. Loose bricks or timbers were dislodged by wind. Sharp axes, pointy nails, snapping ropes or flying mortar boards accounted for occasional builders. The last stages of work, daubing the outside of walls, plastering ceilings, hanging doors, fitting window lattices, brought a few falls. One plasterer in Clapham nailed a board to a house beam and stood on an old stool on top of the board. It proved as shaky as it sounds.

The moment of greatest peril was the raising and dismantling of timber frames. Pairs of curved crucks – jurors mentioned 'towe payre of crokies', 'towe payer of small forkes' or 'a forcklegge' – formed the mainframe of one design, commoner in the West and North. Elsewhere box-frames were built of trusses, tie-beams and rafters. Jurors spoke of posts, rafters and 'coples', of the 'breast beame', 'wyndebalke', 'walplatt', 'raisinge pece' and 'sparrowepece'. Some house beams might be thirty feet long and nine inches wide, and any could fall before the structure was securely carpentered together. Even the wooden pegs that pinned the joints could wound, one catching Robert Waller in the forehead, as could the studs, horizontal strips of wood that formed the wall between the beams, one coming out of a mortice hole and hitting Richard Smyth as he chatted to the carpenters putting up 'a newe frame of a howse'. The stage before erection did for Richard Pretty, as half a dozen men moved part of a pre-assembled timber kitchen on rollers towards the rest of the building, only for a spar to fall on his head.

Professionals and the labourers who assisted them took the majority of casualties, most often carpenters, then masons and bricklayers. But husbandmen and yeomen worked on their own buildings, and even the gentry joined in. George Davell of Coxwold, Yorkshire, gentleman, was hit by a roof he was helping his servants to erect. Thomas Babyngton of Dethick, Derbyshire, esquire, fell off a scaffold as he inspected a wall. Neighbours assembled to raise barns and families lent a hand. Mary Turnor was using a pitchfork to hold up one end of a beam as her husband, William, effected repairs, when the timber slipped and landed on her head.

Any kind of project posed risks. Men died building barns, cart-houses and sheds as well as homes urban and rural. The building ventures of the great cost lives: the stone fireplace of Sir

Thomas Wharton at Wharton Hall in Westmorland, the timber gable of the earl of Pembroke's new house at Ramsbury in Wiltshire, the stone vault of the Queen's Manor at York. Cardinal Wolsey's college at Oxford, taken over by Henry VIII as Christ Church, took so long to build that it killed four decades apart. In 1527 Griffith Dey had his back broken by the timbers he was carting into Oxford. In 1566 three workmates were buried under collapsing stones. Dey's end is a reminder of the deaths that took place on the way to building sites, crashes of carts loaded with stones, bricks, tiles and lime, or the sinking on the Severn near Tewkesbury of two boats carrying a local mason and husbandman with a cargo of bricks.

Furniture was hazardous. Children fell from benches and stools, adults tripped on them or overbalanced when standing on them to reach up high. Tables were places to eat and work. They fell over or came apart, the 'greatt borde' sliding off the trestles beneath. Full-scale chairs were reserved for those who could afford them. Frideswide Sandes, aged seventy-six, who fell asleep in her chair and slid into her bedchamber fireplace, was in the house of Michael Sandes, esquire and MP. Candlesticks wounded those who fell while carrying them, and others came unstuck reaching for a bedside shelf, knocking over an unstable cupboard or finding an unexpected pair of sheep shears on a bedroom chest. Most dramatic was the fate of five-year-old William Bret. At Ringland, Norfolk, on 5 April 1513, he was in the house of Thomas Mere, lord of Brockdish Manor. John Towneshend was in the upper storey, holding a 'hole gemetry of iron concernyng a clok', the complex workings of a medieval timepiece. He dropped it and it hit young William on the forehead, two inches deep.

The yards around houses were full of risks from animals, carts and firewood. The walls, fences and gates around them could be hard to cross. But the most dangerous thing they contained was a well or pond. Three-quarters of water sources where drownings occurred were next to a house, in yards, gardens, closes or orchards. Occasionally they had their own enclosure, a 'well close' or 'ponde close'. A few more were associated with outbuildings such as brewhouses, bakehouses, malthouses or barns. They were understandably lethal to wandering children and those who staggered around in a state of extreme illness. The more shocking figure is the number of women who drowned in them drawing water.

Water collection led to nearly one in twenty of all accidental deaths, one in eight for women and girls over the age of five, killing four times as many women as men. Water was indispensable and was fetched continually. Trips to the well ran all day, apart from a pause around noon for dinner, from six in the morning till seven at night. In summer they started earlier, four or five, and went on till eight or nine in the evening. Accidents peaked in summer, perhaps as more active work in warmer temperatures increased fluid intakes.

Women died at all stages of life, from young girls helping their parents to housewives and widows, with servants to the fore. It was no surprise that when Agnes Trowell, servant of a Coventry weaver, was sent to draw from the Bishop Street well, it was Grace Waters, servant of another household, who found her dead in the water. Risks declined with age, perhaps as strength grew or as tasks diversified. One accidental death in four came at the well for girls aged five to fourteen, one in six for spinsters, one in seven for housewives. Almost any woman could be in peril. The wives of yeomen drowned like the wives of labourers. Jane Daft was a pauper and Mary Goodman an esquire's daughter. Isabella Starre was five when she did not come back from the well at Walton-on-Thames, Helen Warner eighty when she fell into the river with her bowl at Burton upon Trent.

When adult men fetched water, it was generally for specific work purposes – brewing, barrel-making, watering plants – or personal use, for a drink or a wash. Wells were not taboo. Several yeomen and even Thomas Crewkerne, rector of Seaborough, Somerset, died in search of a bucket of water. But if women were not bringing household supplies, men generally looked to boys. At least one in three of the males who died was aged fourteen or under.

Jurors did not distinguish systematically between wells, ponds, moats and ditches. They mixed terms freely to speak of a 'pitt of water or well', a 'ponde or moate', or other variations. But standing or gently flowing water near home evidently provided the great majority of domestic supply. It generated five times as many drownings fetching water as public wells on the street or common, and four times as many as rivers and streams. Some did venture to great rivers for their supplies, the Avon at Malmesbury, the Soar at Leicester, the Derwent at Darley Abbey. There were customary collection spots: in Essex, for example, the 'wateryng place' on the Roding at High Ongar or the 'comon dipping place' on the Blackwater at Kelvedon. But for most the nearest water served best. One wonders how the health of those taking part in the Tudor living history events that have flourished since 1979 at Kentwell Hall in Suffolk would be if they got their drinking water, like Mary Smyth who drowned there in 1574, from a bucket dipped in the moat.

Wooden pails or buckets, occasionally called skeels or kits in the North, were the usual means of collection. Two-thirds of fetchers carried them, some using a pair to cut down the number of trips. Next most frequent were earthenware or stoneware pots or jugs. Then came tankards or cans of leather or wood, flatter bowls or dishes, and metal cookware that could be taken straight to the fire, kettles, cauldrons and posnets. An assortment of small or specialist utensils brought up the rear.

Nearly all of the victims fell into the water, either when stretching to fill a container or picking it up when full and heavy. An insecure footing or means of support was often to blame. Stone steps were slippery, wobbly or icy, wooden boards and beams broke or slid away, tree stumps crumbled underfoot, shrubbery snagged the feet. Wooden stakes or tree branches snapped.

Different techniques led to different problems. Several fetchers used hooked staffs to hold the bucket over the water but lost their balance anyway. Agnes Mannynge and Agnes Wygg each lay flat on their chest to lift out their pail but slid down the bank. At seven and nine Matilda Bustell and Jane Hanley were overcome by the weight of their buckets when they lifted them onto their heads to carry. Wisely filling pails one at a time, as Agnes Daykes did, was to no avail when she slipped topping up the second. Ladling river water into the pail with a scoop, like Cecily Chapman, failed when the scoop was washed away and she stretched to snatch it back.

Those constructing wells aimed to provide remedies. One set of standards was laid out by the jurors when John Cave fell into a newly dug well in the dark. It was dangerous because level with the surrounding ground, lacking an encircling curb and only partially covered with wattle hurdles and boards. Curbs and wooden covers were mentioned regularly, though they posed problems of their own. Curbs tripped people or broke and those who climbed onto them slipped off. Covers slid aside or needed dragging open or pushing back into place.

The jurors called about one well in thirteen a draw-well and many more clearly matched their definition. These were yards rather than feet deep. Their bucket went up and down on a rope or rope and chain. The rope was generally attached to a winding mechanism, a wheel, barrel or windlass. A rarer alternative was a tumbrel or sweep, a long beam pivoting on a post to drive the bucket up and down. The control and distance from the water that such wells provided must have been welcome to those used to stretching uneasily over a pond. Yet things could go wrong. Half a dozen victims lost their balance when the winches or barrels they were holding or leaning on spun out of control. Others reached out too far to grab the well-rope or were dragged into the well by the weight of a full bucket on a runaway rope. Flying wood from broken wheels or tumbrel posts hit a few.

Even the most sophisticated engineering could fail. At Honington, Warwickshire, Thomas Wheler, yeoman, had his well fitted with a 'plumpe' or pump. As he used it on 20 September

1578 it broke apart and one piece hit him in the neck. At Stockbury, Kent, a 'great treadewheele', of the sort used in advanced mines, was installed to raise water from 'a depe drawe well'. On 12 June 1590 Ralph Evans was walking in the wheel and William Gray stood watching him. Ignoring Ralph's warnings, William stepped between the wheel and the axle post to get a closer view. He was caught in the head by a spoke of the wheel, pulled in and thrown out again with a broken skull.

The main uses for all this water were brewing and cooking. Ale was better than water to drink, healthier with antiseptic alcohol and more nutritious with substantial calories, but its production took dozens of lives. Malt kilns killed housewives, maidservants, widows and the occasional male labourer, who collapsed under heavy baskets, lost control of the kiln fire of straw and wood or fell climbing the kiln to stir the malt. Next came mashing, when the ground malt was mixed with hot water in a vat. Women and children fell into the lead and copper boiling vessels and women pouring water or adding malt fell into the vats, one containing forty gallons. At the final stage, when hot wort was drawn off from the mash and left to ferment, a few more adults fell into vats or dropped pans of wort. But in this phase three-quarters of the victims were children. In halls, kitchens and courtyards, oblivious or inquisitive youngsters were scalded or drowned in wort left to stand in wooden keelers or pails, in brass pans or kettles.

Cooking, usually for midday dinner, caused a scatter of other accidents. Food had to be fetched and readied for the pot. Jane Stanter fell off a ladder taking onions down from their hanging place. Jane Moye and Agnes Howe drowned washing tripe, William Browne hanging salted fish in a moat to soften it, while several children fell into tubs of soaking food. William Weston cut himself as he rushed from the kitchen to the hall to return a borrowed knife. The fire had to be maintained. Elizabeth Abrye was carrying an armful of wood to top it up when she stumbled and grabbed a cauldron. Elizabeth Smyth drowned emptying a basket of ashes into the river. Hot whey for cheese-making was another danger, scalding half a dozen children. The perils of baking were more incidental. Juliana Clatter tripped carrying a bowl of dough on her head through the streets of Taunton, presumably to a common bakehouse. Elizabeth Bennet fell into the moat at Birtsmorton Court, Worcestershire, picking leaves to put under the bread she was baking.

It was preferable to head home for meals. John Preist was walking back from the woods for breakfast when he fell into a charcoal pit. But some had them delivered to their workplace, like William Hunte, servant to a bladesmith, whose master's sons brought him his dinner at the grinding mill. Some working outdoors just paused to eat dinner where they were, even in winter, taking shelter under wobbly trees or haystacks. Others took their food to work within the household. Thomas Norman was the horse keeper for Robert Wyseman of East Greenwich, esquire. He took his 'messe of brewes', a thickened broth, to the stable to eat, only to get caught in a fight between a horse and a mastiff. Roger Vanwright balanced a plate on his knees as he sat on a brewing vessel but fell in as he cut his food. Some children snacked in a way that distracted them, eating apples and pears when they should have been concentrating on washing a spade, walking along a ditch or just sitting in an apple tree.

The main danger of eating lay in knives. Altogether one victim in sixty died from a knife cut. Most cuts were incurred in falls. Robert Wymple was eating breakfast and strolling through an orchard, Edmund Feld leaving the table to get some bread, Matthew Henrye walking out of his master's house after dinner, when each took a tumble. Elizabeth Michell was going upstairs with money in her left hand and a knife, bread and cheese in her right. Even those seated at table had their problems. David Lettredge was eating his dinner when he dropped his knife. He tried to catch it between his knees but pushed it deep into his leg. It was clearly a common reflex, as three others had similar accidents. Some just used their knives with insufficient care. William Thomas stabbed himself in the hand opening an oyster and Anthony Baker jabbed himself in the chest straining to cut a loaf.

Everyone needed a knife and not just for eating. John Marchaunt cut himself whittling a stick and Mary Coker cutting a candle. They were cheap, generally valued at between a halfpenny and 2*d*. The large majority of those who had knife accidents were men, but women carried them too, indeed the jurors called Helen Rawson's knife a 'huswiffe knyfe'. Small children picked them up as they lay around the house, but by six both boys and girls were carrying them in jerkin or apron pockets. Older men and women more usually hanged them at their belts, sheathed, unsheathed, or with a broken sheath, but sometimes used pockets or purses or tucked them into sleeves, hose or garters. Carrying on the belt accounts for the high proportion of fatal knife blows that hit the thighs or belly, at least one in three.

Washing-up was riskier than cooking, taking a score of lives, almost all of them female servants. All kinds of vessels needed washing. There were tubs, pails and herring barrels. There were leather bottles, drinking glasses, tankards and cups. There were wooden bowls and treen dishes, earthenware pots and crocks and brass skillets. They were washed in ponds, wells and streams and in rivers as big as the Wye and the Kennet, the Great Ouse and the Tyne. The victims all drowned except for young Beatrice Wylcockes, scalded by the spillage from her grandmother's dish-washing kettle.

Textiles also needed washing, drowning four times as many as crockery and cookware. This too was overwhelmingly women's work. At least half those who died were servants or spinsters and a quarter housewives or widows. The few men who laundered were washing their own shirts, breeches, stockings or shoes, sometimes when unusually dirty: George Tong got muddy going fishing. Women washed household linen – sheets and towels, cheese-cloths, milk-cloths and ash-cloths – and occasionally other textiles such as canvas. They washed their own linen, petticoats, aprons, neckerchiefs and breast-cloths. They washed their masters' and husbands' linen, mainly shirts. They washed all year, though less in the depths of winter.

Most laundry was done in ponds, moats and ditches, and, more often than when fetching water, in rivers and streams with a current to take the dirt away. There were accustomed sites like the washing pools at Much Cowarne, Herefordshire, and Staple, Kent, or the washing places on the stream at Thurlbear, Somerset, the Nene by Fotheringhay Castle and the Severn at Powick. Popular urban spots saw multiple fatalities: Alice Tomkyns and Elizabeth Bennett on the quayside slipway at Gloucester, Jane Stampe and Alice Richardson at the Windows Quay in Newcastle. Some washing was clearly also done at home, where children fell into tubs of water or brine for soaking linen.

Washers used equipment like the 'wasshe betyll' Alice Reyner reached out for when it slipped from her hand as she was beating clothes. For soap they boiled ashes for lye, another dangerous liquid for unwary youngsters. Cloth could be unwieldy in the water, floating away, and out of the water. Alice Andrewes carried her laundry in a pail on her head but lost her balance on the steps to the pond. Alice Malyne found the best way to carry a sheet some ten feet long was to pin it round her shoulders, but the wind caught it and wrapped it over her. She stumbled, 'blyndfelde', into the water.

Clothing could be a trial at other times. Hats and caps of straw or woollen cloth, blown off by the wind, tempted a dozen wearers into the water. Boots filled up and dragged down those who were drowning. Shoes could be harder to walk in than boots. The jurors blamed the soles of Anthony Dyxson's shoes, the slipperiness of Alice Baxter's shoes and the newness of William Bushe's shoes when they slid off riverbanks and footbridges. Spurs too could make walking difficult. Leonard Thorneborgh, an Oxfordshire yeoman, and Edward Holgate, a Yorkshire clothier, were tripped on the stairs by theirs.

Tudor fashion made some garments uncomfortably tight and others unfeasibly large. Henry Daunce, a Bury St Edmunds draper, wore his doublet and hose so figure-hugging in 1526 that he fell into a ford bending down to wash his face. Henry Davies, a weaver of Holme Lacy, Herefordshire, in contrast, was weighed down by his 'great breches' in the River Wye in 1571. Similarly wide breeches may have been the problem at Reading in 1561, when John Yonge's legwear somehow caused his gun to go off unexpectedly. Voluminous cloaks, fastened at the throat, were warm but cumbersome. Several travellers were hampered by theirs when they fell into wintery waters, while Agnes Myles was stifled by her muffler.

Making and mending clothes was both a professional and a domestic activity. The tools were sharp. George Broke stabbed himself in the thigh four inches deep while cutting openings in the front of a doublet with his tailor's chisel. George Wallys's tailor's shears cut Elizabeth Porter as they fooled around. Two men cut themselves on their knives as they mended their shoes. William Hammon sat at the feet of his mother, Joan, as she sewed linen. She threw a pair of shears forcefully – recklessly, said the jurors with some hindsight – onto the table and they fell off. William knocked his knees together in the attempt to catch them and drove one point into his thigh.

Emptying the bowels and bladder was as necessary as eating and drinking and rather more dangerous. One in four victims was weakened by illness or old age and a few were drunk. Toilet facilities were no respecters of persons. Three clergymen met their ends in search of relief, three boys of five or under, two men of eighty or more, a girl of seven and a widow of sixty. Night-time toilet trips were especially hazardous. In the dark one could fall finding indoor facilities or merely standing upstairs urinating out of a hole in the wall. One could fall outdoors on the way to the privy or on the way back. Strange surroundings increased the risk, as Richard Fyer found when he fell from the stairs on a trip to the latrine on his first night at the Maiden's Head Inn at Gravesend.

Facilities varied in sophistication. Mary Vynten and Thomas Parker used manor-house moats. William Fryshe headed for an old well and others to the nearest ditch or pond, often in a yard behind the house. John Wright stood on the water-gate of the mill where he worked and aimed for the millstream. Those working on boats took their chances over the side. Others seem to have headed for rivers because there were latrines there, on the Sherbourne at Coventry for example, or the Avon at Charlecote. Boards to stand or sit on or more elaborate wooden frames must have been a help, but they broke beneath the unlucky.

Sometimes the best arrangements were to no avail. Geoffrey Lyteljohn had a 'jaques' set over a pond in the north-west part of his garden at West Meare in West Hatch, Somerset. When the seat broke at 3 a.m. he fell to his death. John Dunkyn, a Cambridge baker, had a 'sege pytte' in the corner of the garden behind his house just outside the Trumpington Gate. It too had a seat, but he fell drunkenly backwards into the pit where he was, as the jurors evocatively put it, 'qweasomed' by the stench. Cess pits were best dug deep, but that made them perilous: Robert Morfote fell nine feet down a latrine, Alice Whytehede into six feet of fetid water. Chamber pots should have been a safer alternative, but Juliana Sheile drowned washing one out, and Alice Foxhall fell downstairs heading for the window to empty the 'waterboll' of her bedridden husband.

Sleep, lastly, was no refuge from danger. More than one accident in forty involved sleep or bedrest. Some were on their way to or from bed, usually falling downstairs or stumbling outside into water. The range of disasters befalling those who stayed in bed was for the most part predictable – fires, floods, house collapses – but there were variations. Beds were high enough that adults could fall from them and break their necks but low enough that animals could attack babies left alone. Some shared their sleep with discarded knives or even a loaded gun.

Accidents do not throw much light on the practicalities of sleep. Some seem to have slept alone, but there are instances of husbands and wives, parents and children, siblings and servants sharing. There are occasional mentions of sheets, pillows and other bedclothes. Except in the case of a few invalids spending the day in bed, mishaps were spread evenly across the hours of darkness, from going to bed at six, seven or eight to rising at five or six. Signs of the early modern pattern of segmented sleep, whereby two periods of rest were broken for part of the night, are ambiguous at best. Those active at night were often engaged in specialised work, were travelling or had criminal intentions. Our best candidate for a segmented sleeper may be Thomas Asleugh, who rose from his bed at 2 a.m. and went into a close by his house to do some work, yet the jurors seem to have found his behaviour unusual.

There were less conventional but very practical places to take one's rest. Some met with accidents sleeping on carts, pausing their journey or lulled by gentle motion. Kilns offered winter warmth and may have needed watching overnight. Kitchens or halls with fireplaces were also cosy and half a dozen victims, usually servants, set themselves alight sleeping too close. Barns and stables hosted not only the vagrant poor and itinerant labourers but also farmers keeping an eye on their crops. In addition to the hazards of any building they were full of restless animals, rolling carts and stacked produce, comfortable to sleep on but subsidence-prone. William Baten thought the barn a sensible alternative to his master's house when he got home late, realised the whole family were asleep and did not wish to wake them. It was a good plan until he got stuck climbing in above the locked barn door.

Those who dozed off outdoors, rather more than those who met their end in bed, took some strange risks. A few died of exposure, caught out by exhaustion, drink or social exclusion. But far more settled down for a daytime nap in an ill-chosen place, as often around noon as later. They slept under trees, logs or woodpiles, next to carts, behind field gates and by archery targets. They slept on the sides of wells and bridges and the banks of rivers. They slept in saltmarshes where they were caught by the rising tide, or under a bridge where they were swamped by the rush of water from a lock.

Some were children, others ill or drunk, but many just seem to have been taking their chance of a rest. Several were described as tired from their labours and some must have been exhausted, falling suddenly into wells or ponds as they finished work. Their behaviour made sense to their contemporaries. Elizabethan labour legislation allowed for half an hour's sleep during the working day between May and August, the months when two-thirds of these fatal naps fell.

Materials and construction techniques determined both what it was like to make and mend Tudor houses and what it was like to live in them, but so did habits of building work and domestic life. Building and repair were constant tasks because housing materials were more perishable than they are now, the population was growing and its distribution was changing, as some towns expanded and the growth of rural industry pulled people to particular areas of the countryside. Building, roofing and demolition are still dangerous jobs now and DIY has its perils, but well-digging is less pressing and we can be profoundly grateful for that Tudor invention the water closet. Our houses are less prone to collapse, but vulnerable to fire as theirs were, though largely for different reasons, as we cook and heat with electricity and gas and live among flammable furnishings. Stairs are still a major hazard, especially for the elderly.

Home brewing has become both rarer and safer, but the most drastic change for the better is the advent of tap water, eliminating the terrible toll that fetching water and washing laundry took on women. Clothes are still problematic but in different ways. We are less likely to chase dropped hats or drown in waterlogged cloaks, but wry press stories regularly remind us of the proportion of falls directly attributable to trousers, socks and underwear. Napping at work may be less accepted now and, in any case, the more sedentary work that many of us do makes it safer. Knives still kill, but now in violent confrontations rather than as accessories to everyday life.

It takes an effort of the imagination, perhaps aided by a trip to a preserved or reconstructed house, to imagine a Tudor home. But is that any less true of the towns and cities in which some of those homes sat? Their names, streets and landmarks are familiar. They have often kept their roles as regional hubs or district centres. How different were they from the towns we know now?

# 7

# Townscapes

In Tudor England about a quarter of the population lived in towns, but those towns were of very different sorts. London was in a class of its own as both the capital city and the leading port. It grew rapidly over the century, tripling or even quadrupling in size, to a population of 200,000 or more. Behind it came half a dozen regional centres with around 10,000 people each, then two dozen or more cathedral cities, county towns or major ports housing a few thousand. Seven hundred or more market towns had populations that could be as small as a few hundred, but served as local economic hubs and in some cases industrial centres.

Nearly a quarter of our accidents happened in towns. Coverage is wide but not comprehensive, with accidents recorded from about two towns in three and strange disproportions. It is a rough measure of their relative size at the time that we have seventy-seven accidents from York and seven each from Leeds and Wakefield, but not that we have two each from Shrewsbury and Church Stretton. As a result, Newcastle, York and Coventry must represent the other big regional centres, and places like Hereford, Cambridge, Leicester and Maidstone the cathedral cities and county towns. And we cannot put too much weight on statistics. Although every recorded accidental fatality at Witney involved a firearm, we should not conclude that the blanket-making borough was the gun capital of Tudor England. Nonetheless, accidents can tell us a great deal about urban life. We might begin with contrasting examples from South and North.

Southwark in Tudor times had a bad reputation as an under-regulated place to which city folk crossed the river in search of decadent fun. Like most of London's suburbs, it was booming. By 1603 it had more inhabitants than Norwich, the largest provincial city. For respectable Londoners, Southwark might be summed up in one accident. At 8 p.m. on 21 August 1565, in St Saviour's parish, James Johnson, alias Harvie, was in an alley called Deadman's Lane. The alley led towards the Clink prison. He was very drunk and lying on the ground asleep. When he had woken up and was, as the jurors put it, barely possessed of a healthy and calm mind from his great drunkenness, he went on along the alley. Proposing to empty his bowels into a ditch, he let down his breeches. He bent over, still light-headed, and fell in face-first. Hobbled by the breeches, he suffocated in the water, mud and filth.

Drink was prominent in Southwark life, in famous inns like the Green Dragon in Foul Lane, where the iron winch of the well fell on Helen Holland in 1518, and beyond, where brewers' drays ran over wandering toddlers. Its many breweries were associated with the large immigrant presence south of the river. One brewer died in a collapse at the ill-repaired 'bere hows' of the Florentine Guido Portinari, while one of the fighting dray-horses or 'beer horses' that killed Katherine Robyns or Robynson was owned by a brewer called Henry Duram alias Pykelheryng. His family nickname probably alluded to the role of pickled herrings in provoking drinkers to quaff deeply of their Flemish beer. Some Southwark immigrants were accident victims or the parents of victims: Margery Petirson, wife of Dierick Petirson, Jan Tylman, stranger, father of Samuel Tylman. Others were first finders of victims – Matthew Romerkyrk, Dutchman – or jurors.

Other industries flourished in Southwark, less regulated than the city of London. The borough's accidents featured not only brewers and the coopers who made the beer barrels, but weavers and leather-workers, cappers and cap-thickeners, goldsmiths, wire-drawers, pinners and a tipsy tinker, who fell backwards off his stool while holding a cauldron up to the light. Imprisonment contributed to the local economy and prison staff and prisoners died. William Johnson, bagman at the Marshalsea prison, was hit in traffic. Robert Alec succumbed in prison to a head wound incurred while resisting arrest. Robert Saxton, a London haberdasher, tripped getting out of bed in the Marshalsea.

Southwark was a crowded place. Carts came in and out with all kinds of cargo. Small boys ran excitedly along Bankside and fell into the river. People stumbled home through dark streets after a hard day, Joan Symons falling into the Thames on a November evening between work in St Olave's parish and Rose Alley, a new development of close-packed housing near the river. Neighbourly relations could be tense. Henry Thomas, leather seller, kept two mastiffs at the back of his house in St Olave's. They used to get through the dilapidated fence between his property and that of William Fletcher and bite Fletcher and his servants. Fletcher had warned him before witnesses to mend the fence and keep the dogs in. Between four and five in the morning on 4 June 1571, one of the dogs spotted William Wakering, who worked for Fletcher as a leather dresser. It broke the metal staple to which it was chained, squeezed through the fence and attacked, soon joined by its partner. They bit poor William in the throat, head, neck and legs, and he died two days later in his master's house.

Southwark life was strongly shaped by the Thames. People died bathing in the river and drawing water for drinking and washing. Watermen plied their dangerous trade, falling overboard as they manoeuvred with oars and boat-staffs or fended one boat off from another. The river carried supplies of all sorts into London. At ten one August night, William Lye and John Swylam were out in the boat of their master John Napton, looking for food for the dogs at Napton's 'puddinghouse' in the city parish of St Magnus. The dangerous waters running under London Bridge dragged the boat onto one of the arches and it overturned. When craft needed mending, Southwark was the place. Two boat-repairers fell off campsheds, piled edgings to wharves. Thomas Fermery, a shipwright of Paris Garden at the borough's western end, was crushed under one of the big barges that brought grain downriver as his team first washed it and then slid it back towards the water on a roller.

Newcastle too was growing. It also owed a lot to its river, four-fifths of its victims drowning in the Tyne. But in other ways it was very different. Whereas Southwark had little direct contact with international trade because big ships could not pass London Bridge, Newcastle was a cosmopolitan port. Accidents involved ships and sailors from Amsterdam, Dordrecht, Haarlem and Roosendaal, from Rouen and Saint-Valéry. The eastern coasting trade added vessels from London, Southwold, Lowestoft, Wells-next-the-Sea, King's Lynn and North Somercotes, and sailors from Dover, Burnham, Hull and Scarborough. There were local ships too, the *Anthony of Newcastle*, *Martin of Newcastle*, and *Michael of Newcastle* and the *John of Brandlings*, named for the merchant family who provided mayors in successive generations.

The inbound cargoes are rarely described, though the Haarlem ship was bringing in Baltic rye in the hungry 1590s. The outbound loads must often have been coal. The keel-boats that brought it down the Tyne and transferred it to ships for onward trade were involved in a dozen accidents. The docks employed porters and shipwrights who died at their work. The Tyne also found victims among those who overindulged. James Richeson had drunk too much when he fell between his keel-boat and the bank, and so had Robert Burrell when he ended up in the river on 1 January 1541, finding his way home in the dark to his room in the chapel of St Thomas on the Tyne Bridge.

The growth of the town bred building. Timber was insecurely stored, an oak beam falling on Margaret Gibson, a merchant's wife, as she walked along the street. It was sawn up on sawing-horses, one of which collapsed on Elizabeth Lawson, a miner's daughter. Lime for mortar and lime-wash came from lime-kilns on the Ouse Burn, a warm but suffocating place for thirteen-year-old George Nycolson to spend an October night. The buildings on the Quayside demanded high scaffolding, like that from which Nicholas Stabbes fell forty feet.

Accident sites clustered along the river, from Elswick, past the Quayside, New Quay and Windows Quay to Sandgate and Ouse Burn, and on to the Ballast Shore, St Lawrence, Hawk's Nest, Hebburn Staithes and Wallsend Burn. Other mishaps came at landmarks now lost: the Close Gate on the city walls, the Magdalene Cross just outside them, the Carmelite friary by the Castle. But today's central streets also featured. Richard Tomson fell in the Bigg Market. Agnes Burrell tried to shelter in an oven when she woke to find her home in Sidgate burning down. Elizabeth Newton fell into a tub of water in her house in Pilgrim Street at eleven at night and could not get out.

We can trace accidents in many other towns and cities to streets still familiar today. It was in Biggin Street in Loughborough that Margaret Cowper was kicked in the head by a gelding tethered outside a blacksmith's shop. Baldwin Ward fell off a horse in Pool Street, Bodmin, and William Twickten off a cart in Gold Street, Northampton. St Margaret's Road still leads up to the bridge in Bradford-on-Avon, as it did in 1549 when John Lyne got jammed between the roadside bank and the axle of his master's cart. Runaway bulls attacked Richard Arnolde on Middlegate in Newark-on-Trent and Laurence Macham in Gowthorpe, the street leading west from Selby Abbey.

At Nottingham, we still have Fletcher Gate, where Margaret Wyld fell down a well, Long Row, where little Grace Huthwaite tripped into a pan of hot wort, Hollowstone, where half a cartload of hay flattened Richard Draper, and High Pavement, where falling wood hit Richard Hall. Etnam Street, Leominster, where young Edward Hacklutt fell into a pan of scalding whey, still has many old houses, but Borehamgate in Sudbury, where little Nicholas Bowser was run over by a cart, is now home to a 1970s shopping centre.

Sixteenth-century Coventry was obliterated by the bombs of 1940, but the names survive. There is Spon Street, where a young woman drowned in a cloth-dyer's well. There are Bishop Street, Smithford Street and Little Park Street, where a girl slipped off a ladder she climbed after a walk with her mother in Cheylesmore Park. And York has the most impressive roster of all, with accidents all around the city, in or near Stonegate, Davygate, Goodramgate, Petergate, Newgate, Pavement, Hungate, Fossgate, Walmgate, Coney Street, Castlegate, Cargate, Fishergate, Skeldergate, Bishophill, Micklegate, North Street, All Hallows Lane, Common Hall Lane, Lendal, Marygate and Bootham.

Urban streets were much more likely to be paved or cobbled than those in the countryside. At Boston and Taunton, Worcester and York, walkers and riders skidded on paving or hit their heads on stones as they fell. Street repairs were disruptive. At Coventry in 1557, a municipal cart, full of pebbles, drew up on a road in West Orchard ward to unload. Margaret Scales refused to move out of the way, and as the cart slid down the street it crushed her against a wall. Though street furniture, like paving, was meant to make towns safer, it could do the opposite. John Peke hurt himself jumping over roadside rails in Portsmouth, and John Smith's horses pulled his cart over a toddler as he left them to close the chain at the end of Blackman Street on the way out of Southwark down to St George's Fields.

Some town streets could be as treacherous as country lanes. Though the High Street at Worcester was paved, running water cut a 'hollow rote' which made Peter Chaundeler's cart fall over. There were drownings in potholes in Baldock High Street and near the marketplace at Kilham. In an age before street lighting, towns were dark. On a winter's night at Northampton, Elizabeth Harteshorne became disorientated coming back from her neighbour's house, fell and broke her neck. On a November evening in Lyme Regis, Elizabeth Palmer was walking on the harbour wall, the famous Cobb, outside the 'Cob Gate', but fell off onto the 'Chessell' or gravel beach below. On a January evening in Maidstone, Elizabeth Dollynge carried a full 'can pot' of drink to her fellow-servants working on Matthew Wood's boat. The wind blew out her candle and she stumbled into the Medway.

Marketplaces were central to the life of towns, busy with traffic, animals and traders selling goods from stalls to the townsfolk and their rural neighbours. There were accidents with carts and horses around the markets at Kettering, Leighton Buzzard and Malton. A Gloucester butcher inadvertently stabbed himself as he chased two runaway heifers down Grace Lane, leading off the market in Westgate Street. At Leicester, on Saturday, 16 January 1563, William Insley was sitting in a 'shomakers stalle or standyng' in the Saturday Market when a tempest blew it down. Tired shoppers sought refreshment in nearby inns, like John Ray's at one end of the Market Square in Cambridge, where Jane Molle fell down the stairs. Marketplaces served for celebration, like a 'May game' at Cambridge in 1527, and martial display, soldiers training on 'the Cowe Market Place' at Leighton Buzzard in 1588.

Urban houses were more likely than rural to have multiple storeys and storage cellars, both of which could prove dangerous, as could touches of sophistication like the newly installed bay window that fell off a house in Narrow Marsh, Nottingham. Some were solid enough to survive to the present day. Garnett House in Kendal, for example, where Edward Redhed fell off the roof in May 1561, is now the Castle Dairy. Others could be flimsy. John Wrangham was sitting on a stool in his house in Grimsby when the entire roof with its six pairs of beams fell in. Yards around town houses posed the same risks as those in villages, with their wells and cesspits, stacks of firewood, dilapidated sheds, and occasional fruit trees. Larger town houses – that of Richard Tredway, esquire, at Beaconsfield, for example – or urban inns – the Crown at Coventry, the Spread Eagle at Witham – had stables or yards where horses might misbehave.

Most towns were growing, and building was constant. The sites were dangerous and not just to children who played on them. Timber fell on builders at Worksop and Tring. Falls from ladders or scaffolds killed a carpenter at Carlisle, a mason at Godalming and a tiler at Waltham Abbey. At York, Miles Tomson was still assembling his scaffold, ready to tile Alderman Thomas Harryson's house in Micklegate, when a rotten spar broke beneath him. Working on congested streets invited trouble. William Waterden was thirteen feet up a ladder at Stowmarket when a cart came past and knocked the ladder down. Sourcing and transporting materials were dangerous too. There were fatalities in lime, sand, gravel or clay pits in a dozen towns.

Churches were usually the largest buildings in towns, and their roofs and towers were high. At Northampton, a piece of the ironwork of the great bell of All Saints' church, weighing 33¾ lb, broke off as the bell rang for evening prayer at Halloween 1569, fell through an opening in the bell tower, bounced off the wall of the church, and broke open the head of John Dambroke, son of a local haberdasher. The buildings or sites of religious houses long outlived the Dissolution. St Martin's Priory, Richmond, was a landmark for those crossing the Swale in 1548, as it is today on the Coast to Coast Path. There were accidents near what had been the Prior's house at Taunton in 1560, at the Coventry Charterhouse Mill in 1582, and in the Abbey Pond at West Malling in 1599. Friaries were particularly concentrated in towns, giving their name to Frere Street in Sawbridgeworth and Friars Row in Nottingham, accident sites in 1565 and 1572. There were two drownings in the yard of the Cambridge Franciscan Friary, in 1528 and in 1537, one of them a scholar who dropped a book in the pond while studying with William White, the Friary's warden.

Other landmarks used by the jurors included urban or suburban chapels like St Aldhelm's, Malmesbury, and St Margaret's on Gosford Green, Coventry, or medieval hospitals, like those at Andover, Leominster and Northampton. Street crosses were important markers. A horse dragged Robert Parsonys along the streets of Nottingham as far as the Hen Cross. At Northampton, Becket's Well survives today, named for the archbishop who met his nemesis, King Henry II, at the town in 1164. Near it, outside the town's Dern Gate, octogenarian William Freeman fell into a ditch after walking the two and half miles from Great Houghton in January 1557.

Castles also stood out. At Worcester, the castle was dilapidated by 1570 and the monastic buildings were mostly converted to house the college, now the King's School, but jurors could pin down an accident on the Severn by explaining that 'the Colledge barge' was crossing the river from 'the Colledge gate' when the victim fell out near 'the Castell Hyll'. Accidents took place in Castle Street in Reading and by the riverside castle mills in Hereford, Thetford and York. In other towns, the castles were still in residential or administrative use and saw everyday mishaps – with firewood at Eccleshall, gunpowder at Taunton, washing at Fotheringhay, swimming at Newark – while in others their primary use was as a prison.

Town walls were an important badge of urban identity but not always well maintained. On a windy November day in 1553, four-year-old Richard Sone and three-year-old Joan Middelton sat playing in the shelter of the northern city wall at Chichester. A sixty-foot section collapsed on them. At Coventry, Thomas Alsopp was standing in what had been the cemetery of the Greyfriars when a maypole fell over. It missed him but hit the city wall behind and dislodged a stone, which struck him on the head. Carlisle's walls, in contrast, were well defended, especially at times of tension. On 6 April 1543, as Henry VIII fought to dominate Scotland,

Thomas Newlandes was keeping a night watch from the walls and fell to his death. On 7 February 1561, as Mary, Queen of Scots, planned her return to her kingdom, Thomas Atkinson fell from his watch on the castle walls. On the city's Newgate, on 22 February 1570, as English exiles gathered in Scotland after the failed revolt of 1569, a practice gunshot hit Richard Highmore.

Gates were congested spots. Horses kicked Thomas Bate by the Austin Gate at Newark and Anthony Coke by the Bailey at Lincoln. Along the walls ran multipurpose ditches. The London town ditch served as a watering-place for frisky horses, and the Cambridge town ditch and the King's Dyke, the inner ditch at York, as high-risk latrines. Thomas Prynton left the Bablake almshouse at Coventry to reinvigorate himself in the healthy air by the city wall, said the jurors, but being aged, weak and of poor eyesight, he slipped into the flooded ditch. Smaller walls sealed off urban plots. There were falls from walls and crushes against them at Carlisle, Coventry and Nottingham, and a collapsing churchyard wall at Orton. Lastly there were walled pounds for stray animals like the 'olde pynfold' at Woburn, near which William Androwe fell from his horse.

Water supply was a constant problem. Water was collected at risk of drowning even from substantial rivers, and ponds caused similar problems. Some towns made more use of public wells, but they too could be hazardous. Stephen Gantan was drunk when he tripped on a stone and fell into a well near the Exchequer Gate in the Cathedral Close at Lincoln, but others drowned sober. There were deaths in the Coventry Broad Well in 1566, 1570 and 1576, and such incidents encouraged the replacement of open wells by pumps with lead piping. In January 1589, Richard Sandes was mending one of them, soldering the pipes, when he died of suffocation. The Coventry jurors blamed a 'dampe' arising from the earth, but solder fumes in a confined space doubtless added to the risk. London too was bringing in parish pumps by the 1570s, but it had led the way centuries earlier with fresh water brought along conduits to the heart of the city. It was in the conduit field in

Holborn that Lucy ap Thomas stood to watch men practising archery in 1569, only to be hit by an arrow in the forehead.

Town rivers saw accidents of many other sorts. They were such a part of local life that they were known interchangeably by the name of the whole river or the name of the town. At Maidstone there were deaths in the 'Medeway Water' or 'Maydstone Ryver'. The Nene was the 'Northamptone Ryver' at Northampton and 'Oundell River' at Oundle. Rivers did duty for laundry, fishing and bathing, particularly dangerous on tidal reaches, as William Chapman, William Lucas and William Robinson found when the tide overwhelmed them on the Ouse at York in September 1540. They also served to wash and water animals. In February 1541, Elizabeth Tempyll, servant to a shoemaker, took the household's black cow with a white face to St Leonard's Landing on the Ouse in York to drink water. The river was frozen and the cow fell through the ice. Elizabeth and three other young women tried to pull her out with a rope tied to her horns, but the ice broke under them. Perhaps they should have gone to the recognised 'watteringe place', though that did not help Francis Mawson when he rode a grey mare into the river and she stumbled on a log in the water.

River traffic brought trouble on wharves. At York there was the King's or Queen's Staithe on the Ouse, where Matilda Almonde slipped on the wet bank, unloading peat turves from a ketch, and George Dodd overbalanced, trying to cross the river after an evening in John Jackson's inn. At Gloucester, Nicholas Capper had to clamber across another boat to reach his own at the congested main quay. The lowered mast on which he stepped slipped away from him as he carried his son Francis and they both drowned. On the other bank of the Severn sat Llanthony Quay, where a brasier and a capper were swept away while bathing. At Hull, the wooden staithe behind her mistress's house on the River Hull had a hole in it through which Agnes Wynship fell. At seaports like Dartmouth or Weymouth, harbour drownings might make up half or more of all recorded deaths.

Many towns had grown up as river crossings and bridges were central to their lives. Some had special names used by the jurors: the Long Bridge at Tewkesbury, the Great Bridge at Bedford, the Stonebow Bridge and the Wye Bridge at Hereford. Bridges were dangerous for those crossing them, those mending them and those beneath them in boats. Thomas Bradshawe was repairing the Over Bridge at Gloucester when he lost his balance trying to prise away a piece of rotten wood with a mattock and fell into the Severn. A timber beam twenty feet long fell off one of Reading's bridges over the Kennet and hit Richard Bett on a barge beneath, smashing his head, only to be claimed back for repair of the bridge.

Towns were centres of manufacture as well as trade. Mishaps occurred in workshops and smithies, breweries and malthouses, tanneries, dye-houses and fulling-mills. Grain was ground in watermills, horse-mills and occasionally windmills. But as important as industry for most towns was agriculture. Townsfolk ploughed and harrowed the fields at Biggleswade, Hereford, Ledbury and Southwell. They drove horses out of standing corn at Amersham, harvested grain in the west field at Newbury and in 'Footes Meade' at Ilchester, and dug for marl to improve the soil at Goudhurst. They had accidents in urban barns at Bampton, Cranbrook and Elham. Hay was cut in the meadows outside Stafford and Stone, Sudbury and Tonbridge. On the Widemarsh at Hereford, Piers ap Robert was trampled by a black gelding, and on the marsh at Cricklade there was no one to help John Carter when the horse he had been sent to fetch at six on a June morning turned recalcitrant.

Horses for travel and livestock for market were not the only animals. Guard dogs were dangerous, pigs roamed freely, and cows were common. Just beyond the city walls at Carlisle, at the site of the Blackfriars, lurked the moody black cow of Christopher Wilkinson, musician. She had already injured Christobella Bowlie, whose family warned Wilkinson to take better care of her, before she killed Anne Sewell in 1595. Urban dung was piled up in muckhills – young Agnes Wryxton hid behind one while Richard Wallyssh tried out a handgun in the lane behind her father's house at Woburn in 1548, only to be hit by a misfired shot – then spread on the surrounding fields. There were accidents with dung-carts at Coventry, Nuneaton and Tutbury, at Ware, East Harling and Worstead, heading out of Westgate Street in Canterbury to St Thomas Hill, heading into Leominster to collect a load for carriage to the fields. Back into town came wood to feed the insatiable need for fuel, as townsfolk went out anywhere from North Molton to Wymondham, from Ambleside to Romsey, felling, collecting and carting firewood.

Recreation as well as work filled the green spaces around towns. Gloucester's children played on Gaudy Green, and Bath had the Abbey Green, where John Richardson was hit by a falling maypole. At Coventry, there was Gosford Green, where a stray arrow killed Henry Jones at archery practice. Edward Bugge's meadow outside Harlow and the 'comen mede' to the west of the parish church at Bromley hosted football games.

Between the towns and the fields, lastly, lay the suburbs. Some towns were surrounded. Oxford saw accidents in Grandpont to the south, at Broken Hayes, Osney Bridge and Walton outside the Westgate, in the parishes of St Giles, St Mary Magdalen and Holywell outside the Northgate and by Magdalen College outside the Eastgate. London had the most elaborate constellation. We have already visited Southwark, but there were many more.

Between Westminster and the city proper lay the legal quarter and the parishes of St Clement Danes and St Martin in the Fields. Here were grand courtier houses, preferably with a Thames frontage like Arundel House, where one of the earl's watermen fell from his row-barge on a windy day in 1560, but also the homes of many tradesmen. There were butchers to cater for London's huge demand for meat. William Randall, servant of a St Clement Danes butcher, was carrying a calf through St Martin's slung across the saddle of a horse at eight on a February night, when the horse stumbled into a pit and fell on him. There were blacksmiths and brewers who got into fatal fights. Brickmakers used clay from the Ossulstone pits where Henry Williams died in a collapse. The busy river tempted four-year-old Robert Tompson to jump from St Clement's Wharf onto a boatload of hay, but the water ebbed and pulled the boat away.

All round London the traffic was awful. At Holborn Bridge Thomas Hyknam was squeezed between the wheels of two carts and at Stamford Hill in Hackney Anthony Kynges fell out of his coal cart. At St Giles in the Fields, Anne Gryffyn, riding a gelding from Knightsbridge to London carrying a sack of peas, met a cart pulled by six oxen coming away from the city. She rode into a ditch to avoid it and the horse fell on her. On the river, at Erith in November 1531, two gentlemen and three yeomen of London were on their way to Gravesend in a wherry rowed by two London watermen. They steered the boat too close to a ship sailing at full speed and one gentleman drowned when it sank. Two Lambeth watermen drowned in September 1579 alone. One fell backwards out of a boat, drunk, as he crossed from Westminster Bridge to Stangate. The other, more excusably, found he could not climb across three boats to reach a fourth that he was meant to row away.

Yet the London suburbs also offered relaxation, not just the beer-drinking and bear-baiting of Southwark, but also more rural pursuits. On Sunday, 1 June 1578, William Robertes, an ironmonger of St Mary Magdalen parish, Milk Street, fancied a swim by the osier beds in Lambeth Marsh, but went too far out of his depth. Other city folk died bathing at Stratford, Stepney, Putney, Kew and Walthamstow. On Saturday, 22 May 1568, John Willyamson went a mile out of London with four other men to Shoreditch to look for birds' nests. It must have been hot work, for he drowned bathing in a pond in Bishopsfields.

Tudor towns were in some ways as we would expect them to be. They could be crowded and tense, troubled by the very trade and traffic, industry and entertainment that made them special. We recognise the compulsion to go into town to do business or have fun and the desperation to get out into the fresh air. They ranged from cosmopolitan economic and cultural hubs to modest market towns. The patterns of their streets, bridges and quaysides, sometimes reaching back beyond the Tudors to the Anglo-Saxons or the Romans, have often survived to our own day. As we walk those streets and imagine some of our accidents, sometimes standing by the very buildings where they happened, the Tudor past can feel close. Then we think of the open wells, the laundry in the river, the runaway bulls and the dark winter nights.

Perhaps our biggest problem is to get towns in proportion. In England today urban areas occupy only about a tenth of the landscape and yet more than four in five of us live in them. Tudor towns were not only physically smaller, as the names of the villages around Tudor London remind us, but housed far fewer of the population. They were also more closely tied into the countryside, not just as markets but as farming centres, as haycarts came in, muck-carts went out and harvesters went back and forth. Even the types of food and firewood coming into each town depended on the landscape in which it sat. We should set out on a tour of rural England.

# 8

# Landscapes

The face of Tudor England was varied. Thousands of years of human occupation, of felling, planting, hunting, herding and digging, had amplified the natural differences between regions founded on geology, glaciation and climate. The result was a landscape of many particularities and some striking contrasts. Different landscapes suited different kinds of farming, and those variations in turn generated different social interactions and different daily risks. And those differences were all the more consequential at a time when some three-quarters of the population lived in the countryside.

The Lake District, for example, was a land of fells, where storms struck suddenly. They caught walkers on Mossdale Fell, Knock Fell, Langdale Fell and Middle Fell in Stainmore Forest; Isabel Burnyate as she came over the Lorton Fells from Keswick after selling a red woollen cloth in the market, and nine-year-old Thomas Grenehow as he looked for his master's sheep on Penrith Fell. Others fell from the rocky hillsides, in Patterdale coming home from Keswick or from the cliffs at Dillicar near Lowgill.

The lakes too were treacherous. Boats went down on Windermere and Grasmere and a fisherman fell into Ullswater. The fast-flowing rivers claimed many victims. Ten drowned over the century in the Eamont, thirteen each in the Kent and Derwent, fifteen in the Lune, thirty-two in the Eden. Rivers and becks were generally crossed not by bridges but by slippery stepping stones, hipping-stones or coggling-stones as the local jurors called them. The cattle roamed widely and could be aggressive. A cow gored Janet Dogsoun at Scalthwaiterigg, and a bull tossed Juliana Jacson at Bampton Grange. The mines of coal, lead and copper were deep.

Life in the low-lying fenlands of Lincolnshire, Cambridgeshire and Huntingdonshire was very different. Here the cows that attacked Agnes Symmes at Frampton and John Gausby at Weston were pastured on the marshes. Hay was cut on the fens, at Calf Fen in Soham and Ouse Fen in Over, and carted back for fodder. Horses were bred too, causing accidents in Ewerby Fen and the Common Fen at Milton. There were wildfowl, like those Richard Preise of Gedney was hunting when he fell into a pool at Holbeach. There was peat, like that loaded in the cart from which Oliver Hutchonson fell in the West Fen at Isleham. There were thatching materials, like the sedges Alice Arche was clutching when she fell through the ice at Holme Fen.

Drainage ditches were frequent and treacherous, especially for the vulnerable, a feverish Alice Harpeley at Gedney, an aged Catherine Pynchebeck at Whaplode as her walking staff slid away. Their depth created special hazards. William Holdsworth of Boston was carrying cloth to a fulling-mill on two packhorses when one horse slipped down a bank into a channel at Skirbeck. He scrambled round between horse and water to push it out, but he and the horse both drowned. The bigger channels were navigable, but that brought other dangers. John Marshall sent his servants Thomas Doncaster, Eleanor Rowethe and Katherine Fracy by boat across the River Welland to milk his cows in Deeping Fen, but the boat overturned. Whittlesey Mere claimed more victims than Windermere. And at the far edge of the fens, beyond the salt-marsh, stood the sea. Thomas Wood was coming home to Whaplode with his fishing nets when a 'thyk mystye ayer' descended and he lost his way. He stayed afloat as the tide came in, grasping a rope tied to two stakes, but eventually he drowned.

Between the fells and the fens were many different landscapes. There were dangerous hills in the Pennines, where Thomas, Jane and Otwell Crabtre perished when their house below Kinder Scout was demolished by drifting snow. There were stretches of moorland, bleak to cross, like that between Grasby and Holton le Moor at the northern end of the Lincolnshire Wolds, where young, sick Richard Lambert died sheltering under a gorse bush.

Along the southern and eastern coasts and in the Norfolk Broads and Somerset Levels lay marshes with resources to match those of the fens. Locals died cutting sedge, shooting wildfowl, fishing in the 'commen fysshing ryver' at Sutton in the Broads, dredging for oysters in the creeks around Gillingham. They fell from the marsh walls of Essex and into the drainage rhines of Sedgemoor. At Tunstall in the Broads, Walter Ferrier was working in 'a windmyll to cast water out of the marshes' when he caught one finger in the machinery and got dragged in. Rising tides or rain-gorged channels caught those herding sheep or hurrying home from church.

Though these landscapes were distinctive, there was open water everywhere. The great rivers of lowland England claimed many victims, more than a hundred in the Thames, between fifty and a hundred in the Trent, Severn and Avon. Large lakes such as Aqualate Mere in Staffordshire lured people in for fishing or fowling. Lesser rivers, streams and ditches emptied into greater watercourses and between them sat innumerable ponds, wells and pits. Some were merely holes in the ground filled up by the rain, but most were made on purpose, for drainage, defence, fish-keeping or water supply. Some fishponds were large, up to 120 feet long and ninety feet wide, and even simple garden ponds might be substantial. The 'little ponde' into which Bridget Wyllie fell was sixteen feet square and eight feet deep. Moats accounted for one drowning in sixty, concentrated in and around East Anglia. The moats of imposing houses – Buckenham Castle, Caister Castle, Wressle Castle – were significant obstacles, though some moated sites were much humbler. On a really dark night it might be impossible to tell if a drawbridge was up or down, as Elizabeth Grove found at the house of William Try, esquire, at Frampton on Severn, Gloucestershire, in October 1512.

Trees shed instructive light on landscape variation. In Herefordshire, with its hedged fields and frequent woods, one accident in six involved a tree. In neighbouring Worcestershire and Shropshire, the figure was one in seven. In Leicestershire and Northamptonshire with their large open fields, it was fewer than one in twenty, and in Lincolnshire, with its windswept fens and rolling wolds, fewer still. There were oaks nearly everywhere, in woods, on pastures, in hedges, making up four in ten of the identifiable trees mentioned in inquests. Ash and elm, the other prime timber and firewood trees, were next most common but more concentrated: elms in Kent, ashes in East Anglia. Beech was frequent in Kent, Sussex and parts of Buckinghamshire, hornbeam and poplar in East Anglia. Willows occurred everywhere, but patchily and often on riverbanks, blackthorn and hawthorn where hedges were plentiful. Alder, birch and maple, aspen, elder and holm oak, lime, service tree and wych elm caused a few mishaps each.

With variations in landscape went variety of crops and livestock. Lake District accidents featured oats and peas, tolerant of conditions that would defeat frailer seedlings. The more versatile agriculture of the Midlands and South added barley, rye and beans. Wheat, the most sensitive grain, was concentrated in East Anglia and the chalky downs. Cattle were ubiquitous as a source of domestic milk, but some areas specialised in stock raising or dairying. In the Yorkshire hills, there was trouble with cows and bulls at Coverham, Grinton and Marske, at Castleford, Hemsworth and Norland. Sheep were almost as widespread as cattle. They could prosper in the uplands of Yorkshire and Derbyshire, in the downlands of Oxfordshire or Gloucestershire, and on large open fields, converted from arable, in the Midlands.

Sharp contrasts in landscape and farming were possible even in a single county. In the south and east of Warwickshire lay the Feldon, an area of well-ploughed open fields. There, as the traveller John Leland put it in the 1530s, the land was 'somewhat barren of wood, but very plentifull of corne'. In the north and west rose the hilly, woody Arden. Here, as Leland learned, the ground was 'muche enclosyd, plentifull of gres, but no great plenty of corne'.

The large fields of the Feldon were worked by horses and grew wheat, like that stacked so high at Chadshunt that Thomas Clement fell off a fourteen-rung ladder trying to reach the top. Ambitious gentry landlords could turn them to profitable pasture. The cart that overturned on Martin Clerke as he drove it through the common fields of Princethorpe on 9 August 1561 was carrying seventy-three tods of wool, some 146 stones. At £24, the wool was worth more than ten times as much as the cart and its horses. Its owner was Clement Throckmorton, esquire, who was shortly to serve as MP for the county.

In Arden, life was more varied. The patchwork of enclosed fields made for many stiles, like those Nicholas Saunders and John Kelyng fell off at Haseley and Great Packington. Trees were felled or lopped and carts full of wood, drawn by oxen not horses, came to grief on the roads. Coal was dug in perilous pits from Tamworth to Nuneaton. There were gentlemen's parks with angry stags and restive horses. Herdsmen and milkmaids drowned crossing the Tame. Livestock needed hay, piled into unstable haystacks and loaded onto unsteady carts. Leather industries used cattle hides and accident victims from Atherstone included a tanner and a glover.

Similar contrasts can be drawn in Wiltshire. On the chalk downlands of the south-east were nucleated villages surrounded by large open arable fields manured by the sheep pastured on the higher slopes. In the clay vales of the north-west were hamlets dispersed among irregular hedged fields. Dairying was so dominant there that contemporaries spoke of the chalk and the cheese.

The fields of the chalklands were worked by labourers and servants who died ploughing, rolling crops, falling from barley-mows, driving carts full of harvest grain. The trees were in managed and named copses, 'Easter Bushe Copice' at Chilmark or 'Brinckeridge Copes' in Fosbury. The sheep, moved between fields and downs, were boated across the Avon. Hay from the river meadows kept sheep and plough-horses fed through the year. Up on the downs, conditions could be inhospitable. At Charlton Down, north of Downton, John Potter, riding on his master's orders from Upper Burgate to Salisbury, died in a February storm so calamitous that it drove the coroner to purple prose: the vigour of John's soul was diminished by the fury and sudden indignation of the airs.

The cheese country was very different. Juries described roads enclosed with banks or stony hedges running between pastures and enclosed fields. The clay soil demanded oxen for tillage, of the sort that killed ploughmen at South Marston and Rowde. Hay was even more important here than on the chalk, and haycarts and hayricks were to the fore. The cattle coexisted with pigs, their diet topped up with whey. At Calne, Jane Fosbury and her baby daughter lived in a ruinous building belonging to John Tinnes. When Jane went out in the morning to milk Tinnes's cows, a sow suckling her piglets in an adjacent room attacked the baby in bed. Children here faced other dangers. Faith Benett played on a cheese mould in her father's house at Highworth and fell off holding a knife. At Westport, just outside Malmesbury, Joan Vizer drowned in her father's tanning vat.

Different field forms were characteristic of different landscapes and farming systems. It is not always easy to tell fields apart in the inquest reports, but jurors made distinctions sufficiently often to draw some conclusions. While most counties had a mixture of open fields and enclosed, the balance varied. Enclosed fields, which might be called closes, crofts or pightles or, if near houses, termed yards or garths, accounted for one in twelve accidents in Cornwall, Devon and Somerset and open fields fewer than one in four hundred. The disparity was almost as great in Norfolk, Suffolk and Essex. In Leicestershire and Northamptonshire, the balance was reversed. Here, at the heart of open-field farming in what some landscape historians have called the Central Region or Central Province, one in eight accidents occurred in what were probably open fields while enclosed fields saw fewer than one in twenty.

The descriptions and names of enclosed fields in the reports show their variety. Specified sizes ranged between two and eight acres. Some enclosed land by a house or outbuilding, 'Home Close', 'Parsonage Crofte', 'Dovehowse Close' and so on. Others catered for livestock, 'Oxe Close', 'Cowe Pasture', or 'Connye Close' for rabbits. Some were ploughed up as arable land. Many included trees: 'Asshe Close', for example, 'Wilowes Close' and 'Peretree Close'. Sometimes ownership lent a name. Margaret Crompe, wife of Roger Crompe, drowned washing linens in the pond at 'Crompe Croft' in Pencombe, Herefordshire.

Enclosure might be done with hedges, fences or stone walls, any of which might sit atop a bank. Which farmers chose depended on the livestock involved and the materials available. Quickset hedges and fences of dead wood are not always easy to tell apart in the reports. Sometimes the jurors made it clear that they were discussing a 'quyck hedge', a bushy hedge or a brambly hedge twelve feet thick. Sometimes they described a fence with posts and rails, most often used in rural areas, it seems, around bodies of water, like one millpond closed off with a fence on one side and a hedge of thorns on the other. In most parts of the countryside, stone walls were built round churchyards, homesteads or gardens rather than fields. Only in Westmorland, where Roland Skayffe and John Shipparde injured themselves getting over walls at Asby Grange and Stane Ridding, did accidents with walls outnumber those with hedges.

Hedges were the default option for good reason. They provided firewood, berries and browsing, and they grew naturally once set. Yet they needed to be made and repaired, and hedging accidents recurred between December and May. Hedgers had trouble cutting stakes of oak or branches of willow or uprooting saplings to build or strengthen hedges, carting 'rise' or brushwood for filling gaps, driving stakes into the ground or working on banks by ditches.

Hedges were controversial. Over centuries they spread across the countryside in a process that might be exploited by landlords or big farmers to appropriate communal resources or convert tenanted arable land into profitable pasture. Accidents suggest a crude measure of the speed of change in our period. The proportion involving enclosed fields nearly tripled over the century, from one in forty before 1540, through one in twenty-five in the middle decades, to one in seventeen in the 1580s and one in fifteen in the 1590s. Meanwhile the proportion occurring in probably open fields fell from more than one in forty between 1540 and 1580 to below one in sixty in the 1590s. No wonder the century saw enclosure riots, legislation to limit enclosure, and enclosure commissions sent out by opinion-conscious statesmen.

Hedges, fences and walls could be considerable obstacles, and several victims fell from them or landed heavily when jumping over them. Gates were a help in getting through, but they might collapse and their ironwork was sharp. Stiles were welcome but a lot could go wrong as walkers crossed, blown off by the wind, tripped by a thorny hedge, falling into a ditch or onto a pointed stake. Carrying knives across stiles caused trouble from Coulsdon in Surrey to Darley in Derbyshire, and scythes were just as bad. It is particularly unpleasant to contemplate the fate of John Oyler, who slipped on a stile and tore his 'codd', dying twelve days later of a putrefied scrotum.

The most extreme form of enclosure, marked off by great banks or sturdy fences, was the private park. While created primarily for deer and other game, they also furnished timber and grazing for livestock. Parks clustered where they had always done, in the wooded parts of the Midlands and south-east. Parks were status symbols. Great owners whose parks saw accidents included the earl of Sussex and Lord Rich at Woodham Walter and Little Leighs, Essex, Lord Bergavenny at Birling, Kent, and the bishop of Norwich at Hoxne, Suffolk.

In contrast to closes and parks, jurors sometimes spoke of the fields of a village, of open fields, or of common fields. The last name made sense because although lands were held by individual tenants they had to farm them collaboratively under the regulation of the manor court to prevent weeds spreading from fallow landholdings, or one farmer's animals eating another's crops. Sometimes it is clear that the fields surrounding one village stretched to the fields around another. In Leicestershire, for example, John Trovet, the shepherd who watched over the flocks of Medbourne, fell chasing two Slawton men who were trying to drive the sheep away across the fields to their village.

The names jurors used for fields in central England were often suggestive of large fields around a settlement ('Northe Felde', 'Southe Feld', 'East Fyeld' or 'Westfield') of fields planted by agreement with a single crop ('the Wheate Fielde', 'the Barlye Fyld', 'Pease Feilde') or occasionally of fields with distinctive soil ('Claye Fielde' or 'Stonylondes'). These contrasted with the more varied names used in the more complex systems to the west and east. There, even when apparently discussing large or open fields, they distinguished 'Highfeld', 'Upperfylde' and 'the Over Fyld' from 'Myddlefeld', 'Lowfeld' and 'Netherfeld', 'Brodefylde' and 'Longefelde' from 'Greatefyld' and 'Oldefyld', 'Sandefeld', 'Blackelande' and 'Mill Hill Feld' from 'Heyfeldys', 'Bromefeld' and 'Thornyland Field'.

Many accidents in open fields involved ploughing, harrowing or the carting of crops or manure, though animals pastured on fields left fallow for the year or brought in to eat stubble and leave dung featured too. Spots in open fields catered for many other activities, with pits for digging marl, clay, gravel, chalk, stone and coal. Villagers knew whose land was whose, and jurors sometimes picked out individual furlongs within a field, with names like 'Longfurlonge', 'Sandfurlonge', 'Hunger Hill Furlonge', 'Longdane' or 'Melbridge Furlonge'. Such furlong names could persist even when enclosure carved out private sections in the open fields. One enclosed field at Corsham, Wiltshire, was located inside a larger field called 'Gasterd' and was called 'Lyde Furlonge'.

The open fields were navigated using the greenways that traversed them and the headlands and balks or boundary ridges created by repeated ploughing. Bedfordshire provides vivid examples. At Wilstead, the headlands were so high that Nicholas Astlyn's cart was caught by the wind and overturned as it sat on one. At Chellington, fifteen-year-old Jane Wright was hit by a cart as she walked along a green headland taking two pots of drink to her master's harvesters in the August heat. At Turvey, a cart ran over eight-year-old Walter Stevenson as he slept by a hedge on a 'warde balke'.

Farming used land beside closes and open fields. Riverside meadows or leas, enriched by periodic flooding, were a feature of most lowland landscapes and saw accidents in two-thirds of counties. They made good livestock pastures as their names suggest: 'Cowleyse', 'Oxe Leasowe' and 'Pig Leas', 'Wyke Somerlease' at Ditcheat, Somerset, for grazing only in summer, 'the Fattynge Lease' at Lacock, Wiltshire, for fattening up stock. The alternative was to mow the grass for hay, and one in four accidents in meadows came in the hay harvest.

Common lands too had an important economic role. While they varied in appearance, from moors, marshes or woodlands to less cultivable corners of lowland villages, they had features in common. They provided grazing space, firewood and mineral resources, as ever with attendant risks. Sometimes space was allotted within them, 'Hurdesman Dole' at Findern in Derbyshire assigned for the herdsman's use. As village greens, alongside roads or surrounded by houses, they were especially prominent in some regions. Half of all our accidents on greens happened in just five counties: Suffolk, Essex, Bedfordshire, Hertfordshire and Kent.

LANDSCAPES

The names with which jurors identified the sites of accidents sometimes tell us more of how they related to the landscapes in which they lived. Some were already old, some more recent, some mentioned for the first or only time in our inquest reports. Some were colourful. Elizabeth Awse was crushed by falling clay as she dug in a pit called 'Cattysbrayn' at Eynsham, Oxfordshire, in 1519, a term applied in various places to deposits of clay mixed with small stones resembling the brains of cats. Fruit trees or wildlife gave their names to spots like 'Appultree Hill' at Manton, Rutland, 'Damasyn Fyld' at Foleshill, north of Coventry, or 'Squyrell Pole' at Bishopstoke, Hampshire. Rabbit farming marked out the 'Cunnyngrey Lane' at Fulfen, Staffordshire, and the 'Coninger Poole' in Maisemore by Gloucester.

Other names had social significance. 'Galowe Hyll' at Litlington, Bedfordshire, and 'Galowhyl' at Selborne, Hampshire, were places of execution or of the gibbeting of felons' bodies. Between Billington in Bedfordshire and Slapton in Buckinghamshire ran 'the Shyre Dytche', marking the county boundary, into which eight-year-old Richard Townes fell. The 'bekyn' at Stone in Kent near which John Lull died digging sand was one of a chain kept up to spread warning of invasion, and was shown, with sightlines running out to Whitstable in one direction and Allhallows on the Hoo peninsula in the other, in the map of Kentish beacons published by William Lambarde in 1596. 'Gospelfeld' at Coleshill in the Chilterns, where the labourers John Grene and John Crowcheley were crushed in a collapsing marl pit, would have been where the annual procession to mark out the parish boundaries stopped for a gospel reading.

A few spots had folkloric associations. In Wiltshire, the large stones assembled into circles and avenues by the prehistoric inhabitants were known as Saracens' stones, the Saracens standing in for the pagans of distant antiquity. It was on 'a sarason stone' that Thomas Stronge of Kennett landed when he fell headfirst from a walnut tree in September 1580. In Norfolk 'Marions Ponde' in Rising Park was perhaps associated with

Maid Marian, the versatile female lead in May games, morris dances and Robin Hood plays. Somewhere between myth and history stood ancient landmarks like the 'Grene Barrowe' in Huish, Wiltshire, and the Fossdyke, the old canal between Lincoln and Torksey on the Trent.

Wayside crosses were widespread and often referenced in locating cart accidents or roadside drownings. At 'Woodhey Crosse' in Sutton Courtenay, Berkshire, Thomas Whittyngton stopped on the way from East Hendred to Abingdon, fearing to lose his bearings amid December floods, only to die of exposure overnight. Wayside crosses came under attack in the Reformation as graven idols, but many survive, if only as stumps, and some place-names long outlived the monuments. The names of religious houses, like their ruins, were equally persistent. Dissolution was recent when jurors mentioned Marrick Priory Mill, Missenden Abbey moat and a narrow road called the 'Priours Gutte' at St Augustine's Abbey, Canterbury. The abbeys were still within living memory when there were drownings in 'the Covent Poole' at Merevale and on the River Bure between St Benet's and Oby. The monks were a matter of history by the 1590s, but jurors still spoke of the lands of St Radegund's Abbey in Kent and of St Andrew's Priory, Northampton.

The experience of living in the landscape was shaped by the weather. Those caught in storms might be blown over or hit by falling objects. Edward Wyn was driving cattle to Helwith in the Yorkshire Dales in November 1541 when he was overcome by a great rainstorm. Shelter might not help. Robert Moreton, Christopher Petre and Henry Grene were killed when sheds in which they sought refuge fell on them. Eight-year-old William Strange lay under a felled tree to keep out of the rain, but it rolled over him. Those on the water faced perils too. William Wheler was blown out of his boat as he fished on the Severn at Sandhurst near Gloucester, and William Browse's boat capsized in a storm on the Avon at Tewkesbury.

Lightning storms, coming mostly in July, August or September at the peak of the farming year, presented unique challenges. Some caught in the open were killed by direct strikes, at Tottenham, in Cumberland, picking peas in Norfolk, walking between villages in Yorkshire, where Jane Smythe had her hat, hair and clothes set on fire. Standing under a tree for shelter was no help to Thomas Lewys and Mary Morrys near Hughley in the Shropshire hills, or to Richard Ostler at Athelington in Suffolk.

With prolonged or intense rain any river could flood, sweeping pedestrians and riders off roads, causeways and bridges. John Howson and Robert Newton, riding together on one mare, tried to cross the flooded bridge over the Wensum at Lenwade, Norfolk. They asked John Curtyse, presumably a local, to guide them, but then rejected his advice, gambling on a route that, in the end, led into deep water. Rivers in torrent could demolish or scour out houses. A beam of Margaret Atkensone's house at Croft-on-Tees fell on her head as the river swept through, and at Kendal, Nicholas Yanson's two sons were washed out of his house in their bed.

Snow and ice were lethal in the uplands. Winter 1542–3 was especially bad, with three deaths in snowstorms in Westmorland and a terrible day on the Welsh borders on 23 December. In Shropshire sudden wind and snowfall left lying dead by the roads two women in Trefarclawdd, a man at Cockshutt and two sisters aged twelve and six at Whittington. In Herefordshire, three women fell into snow-covered pits as they took the road south-west from Hereford towards Eaton Bishop, Didley and Kilpeck. February 1572 was grim too. In the Peak District one traveller fell into a snowy pit between Nether Haddon and Edensor, and in the North York Moors one lost his way in the snow between Old Byland and Thriston.

It was not only in the hills that people were caught in blizzards or missed their footing in the snow. At Riddlesworth, Norfolk, in January 1571, Robert Crane was asleep in bed with his three-year-old son, John, when one wall of their dilapidated house collapsed under the weight of snow. At Ranworth in the Broads in January 1574, Catherine Awsten was walking the mile and a half to Panxworth with her six-month old daughter Anne when a great snowstorm broke over them. They died sheltering in a ditch under a hedge. At Mitcham, Surrey, in February 1579, Margaret Russelles went out to check on her master's livestock, tripped on ridged ploughland and lay in the snow until dead.

Ice held peculiar perils. It clogged rivers and made surfaces of all sorts treacherous. Ice cracked too easily under Elizabeth Halley, dipping for water in the frozen River Soar, and William Maste, trying to find his step-father's horses in the frozen Cambridgeshire fens. Ice would not break to release five-year-old Joan Samborne, who fell from the back of Philippa Reed as they climbed a stile at Baltonsborough, Somerset, and was swept under the surface of a frozen stream.

When it obstructed work, ice had to be dealt with. William Marshall and Thomas Carter fell to their deaths breaking the ice off mill wheels. Alice Monsell went out at six on a December morning to wash some clothes in a pit of water. She used her washing-beetle or 'batteldore' to break the ice but lost her balance and drowned. Playing bowls on ice must have been a thrilling test of skill, but high-risk. Henry Skelbroke, an Oxford miller, was taking on Roland Cowper and his four servants on the frozen River Cherwell in December 1534 when his bowl slid into the water. When he went to retrieve it, the ice would not bear his weight.

Sunshine could be troublesome too. In July 1566 young Richard Foxe sought shade in a gravel pit only to be buried in a collapse. In June 1575, irritated by the heat, the bullocks drawing a coal cart jerked it forwards and dozing Richard Lister fell out. The greatest danger of a heatwave, however, was the way it drove men into rivers and ponds to cool off. Thirteen bathers drowned in June 1583 alone. Lack of sun or moon, conversely, made night-time travel or work perilous, bringing mishaps as early as six or seven in the evening in winter, around eight or nine in spring and autumn and after ten in summer. Horses might be as little able to see their way as their riders and even those provident enough to carry a candle might find that the wind blew it out.

Landscapes, then, shaped lives, in farming, housing, industry and travel. This is hardly surprising. The balance of population between town and countryside was roughly the reverse of today's and people were more thinly spread, with a total population around one-twentieth of ours. The lie of the land, the quality of the soil, the forms of fields, the distribution of water, hedges and trees made for the contrasts that so struck travellers like John Leland. Landscapes shaped communities and the lives of their residents in ways we can hear in the jurors' descriptions of fields and copses, meadows and commons, hills and stepping stones. The people of the fens were not the same as the people of the fells, the people of the Arden not the same as the people of the Feldon. Now landscapes determine lives less than they used to, but open downs and wooded hills, wide plains and serried mountains still feel very different. Tourism may have overtaken cattle and mines in the Lakes, flowers and vegetables supplanted willows and wildfowl in the long-drained fens, but no one would mistake one for the other.

The deadly snow of December 1542 or the risks of lightning in open country show how the state of the weather was a constant issue. We may be less at its mercy, but we still have to take care with floods, ice and heatwaves. The darkness threatens us only when our many means of artificial light fail, but then Tudor travellers found their way with candles when they could. Deaths by snow and lightning not just in the hills, but at Mitcham and Tottenham, remind us how much even varied landscapes had in common. Different regions were also interdependent. Chalk-country folk ate the cheese from the cheese country, and cheese-country folk brewed with chalk-country barley. Later we shall have to think about the trade and travel that tied the regions of England together. First, we must ask how those in different farming systems navigated the rhythms of the agricultural year to grow the wheat and barley, hay and straw, apples and pears, timber, hemp and hops to feed themselves and keep their economy moving.

# 9

## Seedtime and Harvest

For the many employed in agriculture, somewhere between half and three-quarters of the workforce, the rhythms of the crop-growing year shaped daily life profoundly. The pattern was set out in the farming handbooks of the age. They increased in complexity and literary ambition from John Fitzherbert's *Boke of Husbandrie*, printed in 1523 and at least twenty more times before 1598, to Thomas Tusser's *Hundreth Good Pointes of Husbandrie*, published in 1557 and at least seventeen more times to 1599, expanding on the way to *Five Hundreth Points of Good Husbandry*. We can match the advice of the handbooks to what went wrong on the ground.

Both Fitzherbert and Tusser began with ploughing to ready the soil for crops. Fitzherbert devoted his first nine chapters to ploughing, for the plough was the farmer's 'moste necessaryest instrumente'. Tusser started his farming year with September, the first of three months of autumn ploughing which accounted for one in three ploughing accidents. Rather more mishaps came in the spring, when Tusser advised a second session before sowing barley, peas or beans. Plough-teams for heavier soil – what one jury called 'the longe land in the heighe cley' – and predominantly in the western counties, from Somerset through the Welsh borders to Cumberland, used oxen. Those for lighter soil, clocking up twice as many accidents, used horses. Teams might be as large as six and occasionally mixed horse and ox.

Most problems centred on management of the team. Animals kicked or gored the ploughman, often in response to excessive use of the whip or goad. The jurors who described fifteen-year-old Henry Hyde furiously beating a bullock clearly thought he had gone too far. Some animals grew restive when caught and harnessed or attached to the plough. Others were distracted in more unusual ways, a horse by the noise of a harness chain, a team of oxen by fighting dogs. Ploughing was generally work for men, but women helped by fetching horses.

Some ploughmen slipped when turning the team at the end of a furrow or in a rainstorm. Robert Lakes died despite the best intentions of his workmate, Robert Ramsey. Lakes was at the head of the horses, Ramsey guiding the plough, when one horse turned fast towards Lakes. Thinking it would knock him over, Ramsey threw a plough-staff to stop it. The staff missed the horse but hit Lakes. Lakes fell and the startled horse trampled him. The unluckiest victim of this sort was John Harvy, whose father's staff bounced off the horse and hit John in the head.

Gruesome injuries came from falling in front of the plough. The lucky were hit only by the coulter, which broke the soil ahead of the main ploughshare. Even that could go in up to five inches deep and an inch or two wide. The ploughshare was worse. Wounds could be eight inches long and up to six or eight inches deep. Hugh Sandwich was ripped open four inches wide the whole length and depth of his torso.

In addition to ploughing, Tusser advised autumn harrowing to uproot weeds or bury sown seed, with a repeat in spring and added rolling to break up lumps in the soil. Together, harrowing and rolling caused about a quarter as many accidents as ploughing. Harrowing seems to have been almost as much women's work as men's, presumably because the equipment was lighter and the need less urgent for powerful steering to keep the furrow straight. The dangers were similar. Horses became unsettled when hitched up or unhitched or whipped, when drivers paused to clear mud from the blades of a harrow, or a bystander grabbed the traces. Falling roller-drivers were hit on the head or crushed. Falling harrow-drivers were raked by the harrow's iron teeth, Jane Knappe wounded in fifteen places from leg to ear.

Tusser harped on the importance of manure or compost, heaped up in the farmyard, carried out in carts and ploughed into the fields, enriching the soil and multiplying crop yields. 'Lay compas up handsomely' he advised, for

> One aker well compassed, passeth some three,
> Thy barne shall at harvest declare it to thee.

Manuring caused as many accidents as ploughing, but getting the muck to the fields was more hazardous than spreading it. Carts overturned on their drivers, on passengers, on bystanders, on watching children. Drivers fell from the carts or the cart-horses. Loaders mishandled their pitchforks, children came off wheelbarrows, spreaders fell beneath torrents of dung.

Dung-carts went, as Tusser envisaged, from farmstead to fields. Richard Snowden, husbandman, was driving his from his house at Sparkford, Somerset, to his arable land when he ran over a toddler. Farmyards, where manoeuvring might be tight, could be as dangerous as the open road or the fields, where piles of unloaded compost made extra obstacles. Where river transport was easier, boats carried manure: there was a drowning as one was unloaded on the Wensum at the western edge of Norwich. Tusser dwelt on dung from August to May, leaving out only the harvest months of June and July, but in practice the summer saw as many mucky mishaps as the spring and autumn.

Where seaweed or 'ware' was plentiful, that too might be spread. John Thurston of Frinton, Essex, drowned with three helpers in his boat coming back from South Wood in Holland loaded with 'bundles of ware roddes'. Another aid to fertility was marl. Though it did not loom large for Tusser or Fitzherbert, digging and spreading marl cost almost as many lives as ploughing or manuring, mainly in the chalky counties of the South and East: it was a Buckinghamshire jury that called marl 'chalkdung'. June and July were the busiest months. Husbandmen and labourers did the digging, working in teams – sometimes two diggers died, once three – with pickaxes, mattocks and shovels. A few female servants joined in, loading carts, sometimes digging. The great hazard was the collapse of overhanging earth and rock in pits that might be ten feet or more deep. Three or four cartloads fell on Robert Tykhull, eight cartloads on John Crowcheley and John Grene, ten cartloads on Robert Smythe.

Occasionally land required other preparation. Estate mapping was newly fashionable among profit-seeking landlords and farmers, and William Clarke met his end measuring a meadow at North Muskham, Nottinghamshire. More sensational was the fate of William Serjeant at Wistanswick, Shropshire. Aiming to clear space for cultivation and perhaps fertilise the soil in the process, he set fire to a field of gorse. The wind stirred up the flames and soon the surrounding hedges were also alight. He tried to douse the hedges but died from burns and asphyxiation.

Once the soil was ready, crops could be sown, last year's harvest providing the seed. In autumn Richard Skott fell off a ladder taking wheat seed out of the pile in his barn. In spring James Kinge was dragged by a horse as he went to collect beans for sowing in his master's field. Immediately sowing was done, birds became a threat. As Tusser reminded his readers,

> With sling or bowe
> Keepe corne from crowe.

At Patching, Sussex, in April 1556, Thomas Branches did just that, using a leather sling to scare crows off freshly sown barley. Richard Sowton was standing right by him when one stone 'sudenlye slypte owte of the slynge backewarde'. At Revelstoke, Devon, in March 1564, Andrew Wylloughby scared off birds with a gun but inadvertently hit a field-worker.

Weeding seems to have been low in risk and so was monitoring growth, though trips to check on grass and beans led Thomas Playte to fall in the river and Jane Haler to trip on a stile. The next great burst of accidents came with harvest, claiming around one in sixty of our victims. Hay was cut first, causing mishaps from late May into July and August. Then came the cereals, peas and beans, concentrated in August but tailing off into September. In each harvest, working at speed in the uncertain English weather, there were three prime moments of danger: reaping the crops, loading them onto carts, and driving them out of the fields. The days were long, with accidents from five in the morning till ten at night, and tiredness risked misjudgements.

Scythes were lethally sharp. Labourers and husbandmen hit themselves while working or on the way to work. Some tripped over scythes left lying around, but the unlucky were hit by fellow-mowers. Men worked closely in teams, walking to and fro across fields in a staggered line, as one report explained, to keep out of range of swinging blades. But after hours of work – in one case four hours – mowers blundered into one another, or stumbled on a furrow, or stepped unexpectedly backwards, or stopped and started suddenly.

New reapers were a liability. Thomas Strynger asked to borrow Richard Wyghtwyk's scythe and then caught him with it. John Richardson came over from another meadow to tell John Furnys he was cutting too slowly to keep up with Thomas Jackson, took up the scythe and hit Furnys with his first stroke. Almost every wound was in the legs, up to four or six inches long and two inches deep, but scythes could go deeper. Humphrey Willinge slashed himself six inches deep when he grabbed the shaft of

William Clyfforde's scythe. William Robins fell from a horse with a scythe over his shoulder and cut off his right arm. Pitchforks were dangerous at harvest time too, but scythes were the real menace.

Harvest carting killed at least a hundred victims, doubtless more, as we cannot always tell how closely summer accidents related to the harvest. Half of these deaths resulted from a fall from the cart. Some loaded in haste, some stood on carts jolted by restless animals or on top of slippery crops. As carts carried the harvest home, they met all the usual mishaps: overturning, shedding loads, running over drivers and passers-by. But driving in the fields presented special problems. Half a dozen drivers came unstuck when they hit cocks of stacked corn, newly piled haystacks, or sheaves of wheat that jammed under their wheels.

In harvest, almost everyone turned to field work. Whole households took part: masters and servants, husbandmen and labourers, fathers and sons. Yeomen worked with carts or hay or wielded a 'reepe hook', and even gentlemen sometimes worked up a sweat, climbing on a haycart or scything. One in ten harvest victims was a woman. Many were servants, loading haycarts, making haycocks, collecting reaped barley or cutting peas, but there were also wives working with husbands, sons or servants, and a Lincolnshire widow, Elizabeth Cowper, who fell from the hay in her cart. Harvest work was exhausting. Several of those killed in cart crashes were lying on top of the harvested crops, resting from their labours. William Godfray was tired out when he went for a wash at eight in the evening and drowned. John Williamson sneaked into William Pereson's hut for a six o'clock nap and suffocated under the hay.

The trouble did not end when all was safely gathered in. Stacked crops killed more people than firearms. Problems began in harvest time, as carts came back to farmyards top-heavy with hay and toppled onto children. Unloaders and stackers fell from carts or ladders, out of the window of a hayloft or while climbing up to the 'pytch hole', through which grain was thrown into the barn.

William Tey tripped in the yard, running to get his servants to help unload his peas. Carts in tight spaces jammed workers against barn posts. As hay and other crops were stacked, they had to be trodden down at the risk of falls from the top. This was mainly work for young women, but housewives, husbandmen and labourers took a turn.

Barn storage was best, but Tusser recognised that not everyone had space, and ricks in yards or fields or flimsier wooden structures, hovels, might have to do instead. Nearly half of accidents with stored crops happened in barns, others in dedicated yards, a 'stacke garthe' in Yorkshire, a 'reeke yarde' in Cambridgeshire. Wooden scaffolds and hovels collapsed, and not all barns were as solid as they looked. Some were too solid. Henry Stallan fell off a stack of barley and landed painfully on top of an open barn door. High up, there might be tallets or lofts, good for storing produce away from rats and mice, but perilous to reach.

Stacks were high, up to eighteen feet for barley, twelve feet for hay, thatched against the rain if built outdoors. Ladders were useful to climb them, but they could slip or break. Stacks collapsed on those working, playing or sleeping nearby. Many fell on those pulling out crops to feed livestock, causing accidents all year as hay was eked out through the winter. Others were fetching down one kind of produce stored safely on top of another: peas on top of rye, barley on top of hay, apples on hay or barley. Some mishaps involved tools used to handle the crops, usually pitchforks but sometimes hay-crooks or mattocks for turning the pile, or a 'cuttynge knyffe' for peas. Falls onto pitchforks with two long tines produced eye-watering injuries: a prong under the right arm and through to the heart, a prong through the lip and nose into the brain, a prong in the fundament to the depth of a foot.

Straw too had many uses, for bedding, stabling, kindling, thatching and animal feed. John Pyle was sent into the fields at Hoo in Kent as late as November to collect stubble and others came unstuck gathering, loading or stacking straw in the harvest months or later. Threshing began after harvest, and accidents were mainly spread between August and December. Most involved stack collapses and falls, but Richard Rogers managed to hit himself in the head with a flail.

Many other crops were grown. There were accidents with onions in Rutland, leeks in Somerset, vetches for cattle feed in Suffolk and Kent, and hops for brewing in multiple counties. There was hemp cultivation for rope-making, often in special closes called the 'hemp yard' or 'hempehay'. Some herbs were collected from the wild, others grown in gardens, watered in the evening or picked before dawn. James Gryme was well-equipped for gardening, carrying a 'paire of gardiner sheres'. They went five inches into his chest when he fell.

The last waves of harvest in the fields coincided with the season for picking fruit and nuts. Fruit was roughly as deadly as firearms. Pears, found in more than half of counties, caused most fatalities, apples rather fewer, though they were equally widespread, with predictable concentrations in Herefordshire, Somerset and Kent. Plums and nuts killed a dozen each, and other fruit a handful. Cherries, strawberries and raspberries were picked first, in June and July, then came pears, running from July to October with a peak in August, also the main month for plums. Apples ripened last, mainly in September or October. Walnuts and hazelnuts were September delicacies, as were the grapes on the only 'grapetree' implicated in a fatality, growing at Prittlewell in Essex.

Trees grew in orchards, gardens or yards, with a smaller number in closes or fields. Some were temptingly accessible. One morning Jasper Freeman and James Yott were driving their master's cart from Yalding to Maidstone. At Barming there was a great stony bank at the side of the road, topped by trees with plums and nuts. Jasper climbed up it in search of a quick treat as the cart rolled on but slipped down in front of the wheels. Most were more private. John Kettell tried and failed to swim across a moat to scrump some of the cherries in Sir John Goodwyn's orchard. They could be tall: pear trees thirty or forty feet, walnut trees thirty feet, plum trees sixteen feet. They were cared for – pruners fell from apple and walnut trees – and some were marked out by the jurors with distinctive names: a Somerset 'bullon tree' with small plums, a Suffolk 'wardeyn tre' and an Essex 'margaretpeare tree' with special varieties of pear, and William Smithe's Bedfordshire 'Frenche costard tree' with its large, ribbed apples.

The great hazard was falling. Trees were not as strong as they looked, and many pickers sat, stood or leant on branches that broke. Aware of this fragility, many used ladders and others reached up from blocks or piles of wood. Pickers came from all ranks of society, and a quarter were women and girls. Some were well-equipped. Several had poles or hooks, and one had a rake for retrieving windfall pears from a pond. Thomas Rase had a bag around his neck to put his apples in and Katherine Campion loaded hers into her skirt. But it was impossible to think of everything. In Derbyshire a plumpicker and an apple-picker were attacked by furious deer, the same fate as a Gloucestershire nut-gatherer.

Coastal plants lent variety. Rock samphire was spicy, succulent and nutritious, but risky to harvest from the cliffs. In June 1576, John Pantridge fell 170 feet onto the rocks below 'Peppers Mede' at Freshwater, Isle of Wight. A month later John Turle cracked his skull at Fairlight, Sussex, and in May 1587 at Weston-super-Mare it was Joan Davys who broke her neck practising what Shakespeare in *King Lear* called for its dangers a 'dreadful trade'.

Other vegetation served as fuel or feed, animal bedding or spiny fencing. Bracken was widely cut in the autumn, soft but slippery. Richard Martyn used some to cushion his saddle, but Ellen Inwood slid off her brother's cart when trampling down their load. Gorse or furze was cut in heathlands from Dorset and the Quantocks through the Midlands to the Peak District. Broom played a similar role in the scrubbier parts of the South and East. It was gathered in quantity by farmers and their men, bundles piled high on carts, but was accessible to the disadvantaged too. Alice Upcotte, an eighty-year-old widow, fell into the River Barle on the edge of Exmoor as she walked home with a 'burthen of broome' in November 1590. Holly, ivy and mistletoe were useful not only as Christmas decorations but also as fodder. Thomas Cleygate fell from a tree cutting mistletoe to feed his sheep in February, and Roger Russell met a similar fate in May.

Reeds, rushes and sedges were also versatile, ranging from basket-weaving and thatching – one jury called sedge 'fenne thack' – to floor-coverings and simple rushlight candles. They were mainly cut in summer, and it was often work for women. These were plants of the fens and riverside. Two-thirds of accidents came in East Anglia or marshland Kent, others by the Derwent, Cherwell and Wiltshire Avon. Cutting and transport were predictably dangerous. There were mistimed jumps from overloaded boats, carts bogged down in marshy ground, suffocations under piles of sedge. Again and again, there were drownings.

One accident in thirty involved cutting trees, roughly half felling the tree entirely and half removing branches while leaving the tree standing, what jurors called 'loppinge' or 'croppynge of trees'. Such work fell mainly in the winter months and early spring.

> Now season is good
> To lop or fell wood

wrote Tusser of January, adding a reminder for March. The six months from November to April accounted for three-quarters of tree-cutting mishaps. This was practical, for trees without leaves were easier to handle and labour was not needed for the harvest. It also fitted the seasonal need for fodder and firewood.

Hay stocks for wintering livestock were supplemented by lopping leafy boughs from trees, or indeed by slicing off the growing tops – 'oke heddes', one jury called them – to make the tree a pollard. Tusser set such work, pruning 'the superfluous bows' for beasts 'to go brows', in January, but timing must have depended on the state of the weather. It was in February 1565 that the keeper of Castle Camps park in Cambridgeshire sent John Spycer out to cut branches to feed the park livestock, in what the jurors described as extreme and snowy conditions.

Most of those working on trees were labourers, husbandmen or yeomen, busy with their farms, but there were also craftsmen and tradesmen. The occasional gentleman took a turn, cutting oak boughs in the Westmorland woods, digging up an ash tree in Kent. It was almost entirely men's work, but Jane Pyamore climbed a birch tree to lop it, and other women fell from ashes or oaks. For specialised purposes craftsmen sourced their own timber. A wheelwright, a ploughwright and a cooper died felling ash trees, and half a dozen carpenters lost their lives among ashes and oaks. It may have been those who needed special varieties who went into the woods to buy it, as John Coke was planning to do in Bilsthorpe Wood when he fell off his mare at Mansfield, Nottinghamshire, in August 1534.

The tools used were dangerous. A dozen accidents involved axes, hatchets or thinner-bladed and perhaps longer-handled implements, a 'handebyll', a 'heggebill' or a 'cobyngbill'. The blades glanced off the wood – what one report in a mangle of English and Law French called 'le slydyng de le axe' – or were dropped to the ground, where one unlucky tumble ended forehead-first on an axe blade. Much more dangerous were the trees themselves. One in three lopping accidents came when branches fell unexpectedly onto the worker or a bystander below. Half came when the lopper fell from the tree. Occasionally a ladder slipped, occasionally there was a gust of wind, but the commonest cause was a snapping or falling branch. Loppers fell onto stones, cut branches and tree stumps, and into ponds and flooded pits. In a few freak accidents, cut boughs pinned climbers by the neck high in trees until they died.

When felling trees, climbing was less necessary. Some aimed to tie a rope to the treetop to steer the tree's fall, especially away from a house. More clambered up to clear a snag as the tree fell. But in the great majority of deaths, the tree, in whole or in part, came down on the victim. The details sometimes suggest incompetence – juries talked of thoughtlessness, of negligence, of insufficient care – sometimes bad luck or sudden wind. More often they show the inherent complexity of felling trees in mixed and closely packed woodland or in a hedgerow at the side of a field. Falling trees flattened people against standing trees or bounced off haystacks. Trees caught on others of the same kind, elm on elm, oak on oak, or on contrasting neighbours, ash on oak, beech on maple, oak on ash or beech. Entangled branches had to be cut off or trees dragged apart with levers, ropes, even on occasion horses, and timber fell in unpredictable ways. There were alternatives to the axe, but they had their own dangers. Half a dozen victims tried digging up trees and Thomas Keper met an explosive end breaking a tree trunk apart with gunpowder.

Fellers worked in teams more often than loppers. Groups of up to four are mentioned and one team of two came and asked three carpenters who were busy nearby 'squaryng off tymber' to lend them a hand. This posed problems. Conscientious axemen shouted 'beware' before the decisive blow, but assistants and bystanders were still at risk. Thirteen-year-old John Grene was digging up the roots of a tree with a spade while his father was cutting from the other side. As the tree began to topple, his father shouted to him to run, but it was too late. Sixty-year-old Robert Hilles was watching his son fell an elm when told to take cover. He tripped in the bushes under the falling tree.

For construction or boatbuilding, timber had to be split with axes and wedges, shaped with a 'brode axe' or sawn up with a 'whypsawe'. Carpenters and labourers had some mishaps with axes and wedges, but sawing accidents were more common. The problem was not the saw, but the way it was used. Logs were positioned on wooden transoms or rollers above a sawpit, so that the saw could be held by one worker above and one below. When adjusting the log, or sawing too vigorously, it readily fell on the sawyer in the pit, some struck by half an oak or a ton of wood. Pits also tended to fill with water and thus become sites for drownings. Richard Gage proved the two hazards of sawpits. As he threw water out with a shovel, he knocked a 'roller' and was crushed by the 'timber logge' it supported. Though much wood was used green, some planks were stacked to dry on a 'perch', like those that collapsed on Jane Turnor and Jane Earle, dropping thirty or more pieces of timber on each. Others were stored before use, like the 'three firr bordes', presumably imported, that fell on Thomas Badd in his father's storehouse at Newport, Isle of Wight.

Moving timber was almost as hard as cutting it. Loading whole trees or large logs onto carts or boats and positioning them so that their weight was well distributed might need pits to get the cart at the right level, or levers and windlasses to move the wood, what jurors called gins or ferns. John Cockes and his sons saw that their four horses could not draw the big curved 'tymber logge' they had got onto their cart 'untill yt were layd streight', so they set to work with levers, but it rolled off and hit John. Elsewhere levers slipped, ropes broke, wood on gins swung out of control or broke the machinery with its weight.

The ensuing journeys presented all the usual hazards of transport with bulky and shifting loads. Beams overhanging carts, sometimes twenty or thirty feet long, hit drivers or bystanders. Toppling wood crushed heads and bodies, broke legs and backs. Timber was transported in all states, but preparation did not make it much safer to handle. Nicholas Foster was killed in a gin accident hoisting 'a tun of elmon squared tymber' belonging to William Barnes, one of the masters of the queen's ships, and others died in transport mishaps with sawed boards and joists, house sills and a bedstead. Good plans could go wrong. David Thomas's neighbours at Michaelchurch Escley, Herefordshire, tried to get some timber to his house by sliding it downhill through the February snow, but it veered off course. Even trees small enough to carry, like the 'sapilling oke' William Warde put over his shoulder, could unbalance a walker on January ice.

Some woods had more specialised uses. Willow rods – osiers or withies – were collected for basket-making and use as strong but flexible ties: two boats that sank on the Severn in 1542 were bound together with willow twigs. Several victims were climbing a 'withye tre' or gathering 'withye twigges', and John Brigges drowned in a ditch at Amwell, Hertfordshire, with forty bundles of 'osyer roddes' on his back. Poles from other trees for firewood or woodcrafts were obtained by coppicing. Several accidents took place in coppices, and the tree-stump that William Cooke tripped over in 'Bollowe Coppyce' at Frome, Somerset, was likely a coppice stool from which shoots had been cut. Bark was needed for tanning. Edward Fissher was peeling the bark of a tree at Wythop in Cumberland when another tree fell on him.

Another use for wood was charcoal burning, most famously for iron and glass production. Contemporaries did not always distinguish between wood-based 'charcole' and mineral 'sea coales' and juries often spoke simply of coal. When accidents with coal carts occurred in coal-mining regions, it is probably safe to assume that mineral coal was involved, but in other counties it may well have been charcoal. The probability is greatest south of London, where one of the great charcoal-making areas lay. A labourer died in 1527 sleeping on a coal cart at Croydon, and a collier of Beddington had a mishap with a coal cart at Streatham in 1581.

We are on surer ground with charcoal manufacture, where accidents multiplied from the 1570s as the demands of industry grew. In Monmouthshire, Hertfordshire and Norfolk there was trouble cutting a beech tree with a 'coallinge bille', taking a cart to collect 'charcoles' and digging a 'call pitt'. At Tonbridge, Kent, a midnight storm demolished the hut of poles and turf that John Stace had built himself next to the stack of charcoal wood he had ready to burn. Most poignantly, Giles Lowet at Allensmore in Herefordshire and Michael Bynney at Ashburnham in Sussex slept on top of smouldering charcoal pits to keep warm. One was suffocated by smoke and the other fell through the pit to the heart of the fire and died four hours later of his burns.

Finally, huge amounts of wood were consumed in domestic fires. Firewood featured in at least one in fifty accidents, more than one in thirty if we assume that some lopped branches and much generic 'wood' were for fires. Scrubbiest was underwood, brushwood, thorns or bushes, sometimes called by jurors 'smallwoode', 'rysewod', 'tynsell', 'frith' or 'trouse', also useful in hedging and construction. In the minds of jurors, such underwood overlapped at the thinnest end with brambles and wild roses, 'thornes and breers', and at the thickest with 'bavens', insubstantial bundles of sticks. More solid but more scattered were twigs, 'stykes' or the 'chippes' left behind when timber was cut. Next came bigger bundles, 'faggotes' and 'kyddes', 'drawes' of sawn wood and 'ostry fagottes' destined for hospitality venues. Larger were cut blocks of firewood of different sorts, from 'byllettes' through 'talwood', 'clyfte', 'clogges', 'logges' and 'blokkes', to probably the biggest, identified by jurors as a whole tree trunk, the 'bonfyer blok'. The more substantial categories, harder to handle and more profitable for sale, generated rather more accidents.

Firewood was collected, moved and used all year. Husbandmen and labourers were to the fore as ever, but many women and girls also went out for wood. The work could be sociable. In the woods at Swancoate, Shropshire, in January 1531, twelve-year-old Agnes Chadok was using iron hooks to break up oak branches with other girls and women when a branch fell on her. In January 1561 at Maidstone, Juliana Style talked to Elizabeth Strong as she collected chips from under felled trees and did not notice a falling elm until it was too late. But it could be hazardously lonely. In February 1571 Jane Kendall slipped into the Trent at Gainsborough, trying to pull out wood floating in the river. In September 1584 Joan Norton was collecting sticks in Cudworth Park, Somerset, when a stag charged her.

Mishandled axes and falling boughs took their toll of those in search of firewood, and there were always trips and slips. Jane Bedforde fell on January ice carrying a bundle of wood on her head, and Joan Haywarde fell backwards onto a tree stump as she tugged at a dry branch to snap it. But the great majority of mishaps came in transport, carts in the woods and on the roads, boats on rivers large and small. Cartloads could be heavy, up to fifty or sixty faggots or mixtures of faggots and logs, piled high and alarmingly unstable. Germain Alen tipped cart and wood over on top of himself in the effort to level out his load, and Nicholas Greene fell ten feet from the top of the thorn bushes he was securing. Boats carried more, one lighter in Kent a thousand billets. Not only did many meet mishaps taking firewood home, but as population rose, town markets pulled in ever more wood for sale at ever higher prices. Wood headed for towns from Faversham to Thirsk, five miles by cart into Croydon and Colchester, six miles to Cambridge, nine miles to Hitchin, by boat along the Wye into Hereford and the Ouse into York.

Delivery and distribution caused further problems. These began with carts of wood parked in yards, shedding their loads as they tipped up or fell off their props, and continued on foot. Joyce Smyth and Mary Mawsone fell off bridges homeward bound with loads of wood on their heads. John Smalley, John Pyckworth and John Dawson stumbled with wood on their backs. Matthew Hertley's walk from Davygate in York to his master's house in Stonegate can only have taken a couple of minutes, but he still managed to fall and drop the firewood from his shoulder onto his head. Handling problems persisted from woodyard to hearth. Woodpiles collapsed or climbers fell from stacks of wood or faggots, one thirty feet high. Chopping firewood could be harder than it looked. Robert Forsett's axe glanced off a knot in a billet of wood onto John Chase's shin, cutting it down to the bone. At the last moment, wood bound for the fire fell on those carrying it or sitting nearby.

Farming handbooks codified effectively most of the lessons that farming folk usually learned from watching parents, masters, mistresses and workmates. They did miss occasional points: was it Tusser's Essex boyhood and farming experience in Norfolk and Suffolk that made him forget about marl, so important to his neighbours on the chalk to the west of those counties? At every stage of the growing year, from ploughing, harrowing and manuring to harvest and storage, there were tasks that demanded hard work, skill and sometimes good fortune. Lopping and felling trees was particularly complex and unpredictable and carried concomitant risks.

Agriculture is still a comparatively dangerous industry, though many of the reasons why it was dangerous in the sixteenth century no longer apply. Far fewer of us work in it, about one in two hundred of the total population. Fewer household members work together to produce their own food, reducing the exposure of the inexperienced to risky tasks like ploughing and harvesting. Swinging scythes and horse-drawn ploughs, carts loaded down with manure or grain, are no longer the threats they were. Haystacks and fruit trees are fewer and more controlled. Timber, firewood and winter branches for livestock browsing are no longer so essential or so accessible. What remains a major contributor to the agricultural death rate is the interaction between people and animals. Our forebears had trouble with that too.

# 10

# Wild and Tame

The lives of people and of animals were closely entangled in Tudor England. One fatal accident in four involved an animal in one way or another. People met animals in farming, hunting and travel, in homes and woods and marshes, generating different kinds of risks as the strength and aggression of the creature combined with the frequency of interaction and its site. Ducks could not savage the unwary like bears and bulls but were more likely to bring on a drowning. Yet the world of animals was never predictable. Horses or cattle might be disturbed by dogs, pigs or insects. Runners stumbled on molehills and anthills, and carts got stuck in fox-earths. Even dead animals could kill. In March 1516, at Ellerton in Yorkshire, Isabel Chamber tripped over the skull of a horse and fell into a marshland spring.

All manner of game was ripe for hunting. The high-status quarry was deer. Few died in the chase, though it did happen. John Massie tripped running after a doe in Bagworth Park, Leicestershire, and cut his thigh on his sword. William Gryffethe drowned in a pond in Wedgnock Park, Warwickshire, trying to recover a buck. Most spectacularly, Elis ap Euan was butted in the head by a buck he had just shot in Brickhill Park, Buckinghamshire. Much more common were attacks by stags on those walking or working in parks or woods. The dangerous months were September to November, what one jury called 'the rutt tyme', when stags were itching for a fight. The injuries were horrible, broken limbs, torn bowels. Derbyshire jurors liked precision: fourteen separate wounds on John Sharpe at Staveley, twenty-three on Richard Calley at Haddon.

Smaller mammals could be hunted for meat or pelts. Thomas Hatton and Thomas Welles went after squirrels. They threw a staff or cudgel to knock the squirrel from the tree, but Hatton's staff got stuck and he fell retrieving it, while Welles tripped over a tree-root as he ran, looking upwards, and fell on his cudgel. Hare coursing had to be done at speed. John Vinnicot got in a tangle with his five-foot staff and impaled himself on the sharp end as he vaulted over a hedge. John Battell hunted otters in the Lincolnshire fens but fell through December ice.

Rabbits lived in the margins between wild creatures and farmed. They bred in warrens carefully maintained by landlords who culled them for profit and protected them with devices like the pit for trapping foxes into which Margery Egeoke fell. But they spread across the countryside to feed. John Frankecheyny and Francis Stourton were hunting them in the open when they had mishaps with bows and arrows. William Potter and Richard Reyner were poaching, breaking into warrens on November nights in parties of half a dozen. Potter was shot by one of his partners in crime. Reyner, fully equipped with nets, ferrets and greyhounds, was ambushed by the park keeper and his sons in the queen's park at Langley Marish, Buckinghamshire, and hit by a crossbow bolt.

Birds caused six times as many hunting accidents as mammals. Here the pastime with cachet was falconry. Young hawks for training had to be taken from nests or caught in traps, and both involved perilous climbs up trees or over cliffs. Sir Christopher Alleyn and his sons watched as Francis Eton clambered after fledglings, but Richard Ward, John Foster and Louis Meverell, a clergyman, a yeoman and a gentleman, climbed in person. Thomas Samborne got as far as going out hunting but fell on his knife as he made a perch for his goshawk. Robert Barowe, gentleman, had a 'hawkkes perke' in an oriel window at his house, but fell out of the window as he inspected it.

For those in search of birds to eat, wildfowl was a prime target. Some were caught young, but this involved running around the slippery edges of ponds or rowing fast after ducklings, cygnets, moorhens or coots. The only professional bird-catcher among our victims, John Nycolson, may have been on the chase when he fell into the River Eden. Batfowling aimed to surprise drowsy birds with nets or staffs at the waterside on autumn evenings. But there were risks. One hunter overbalanced throwing his net over a teal, another hitting a mallard. John Shorte was on the dark side of a hedge, ready to catch the birds flushed out by Arthur Fayerfaxe's beating, when Arthur hit him through the hedge. In the 1580s and 1590s, shooting ducks began to look an easier option, but guns presented dangers all their own.

More died going after crows than ducks. Here the aim was to climb trees in spring to take chicks from the nest. Rook chicks were a particular delicacy, and rooks outnumbered their relatives at least two to one among the climbers' prey. All manner of men tried it, from a Kent beggar to a Warwickshire gentleman, but slipping holds and snapping branches sent them tumbling down, forty, fifty or sixty feet, even those who equipped themselves with a long stick to knock down the nest. Adult crows could be shot, but the usual risks ensued.

Heron and starling chicks also lured hunters into the trees. House martins nesting on buildings posed a different challenge. Alexander Hyckes fell from a bridge at Aynho, Northamptonshire, and Alan Walton from the treasury next to the gate of Pontefract Castle. Walton wanted the 'litle bird calld a martyn' for his daughter Ellen, but whether as a pet or for dinner is unclear. Pigeons too nested in buildings. Catherine Machyn climbed a ladder in a barn to catch some, but others went higher. John Emere, a monk of Sawtry Abbey, Huntingdonshire, fell from the roof of the abbey church. Richard Alworth came down sixty feet from the broken ceiling of a chapel at Over Norton, Oxfordshire. Trapping was a final option, traditional for some birds, such as woodcock. Richard Wolstanrrose hit his head on a rock as he snagged his large 'cockeshut nette'. John Skrymsher cut his leg on his knife as he fashioned 'pitfalles' for birds.

Bees, like rabbits, hovered between wild and farmed. Thomas Bradleye and Henry Moises climbed trees craving wild honey. Bradleye even took a hatchet with him to widen the crack in the tree that led to the nest but fell, surrounded by irate bees. Thomas Lowe and John Tyllam were presumably trying to stock hives as they climbed after swarms. Most intriguing was the scene at Beckley, Sussex, in June 1568, when the servants of Thomas Water rushed outside with a brass tub and a small cowbell to calm swarming bees and charm them into a hive. They left behind in the kitchen Thomas's little daughter Mary, who fell into a tub of water.

Fishing caused more fatalities than all other types of hunting combined. It killed wherever there was water, all over England, all year, though summer was worst. A quarter of fishers were in boats and the rest on foot. Most were men, of all ranks and ages. Women fished occasionally. In Cumberland, Catherine Hostill fished at Holme Cultram, and in Norfolk, Jane Coper caught sand-eels in the Salthouse Main Channel. Both were overtaken by incoming tides. Fishermen did not feature only as victims, for they were often the first finders of the drowned.

It is rarely clear what type of fish was being taken. Eels were widely trapped and lampreys caught on the Wensum. Crustaceans and shellfish appeared occasionally. Hugh Jones got stuck in a 'myre' at North Hinksey, just outside Oxford, going after crayfish. George Dilley was crushed by a mare loaded with oysters as it climbed a bank at Redcliff near Osmington on the Dorset coast. Fish could be poached like any other game. Fever-ridden William Hargate checked his ponds at 4 a.m., worried that someone was taking his fish. Thomas Archer, scholar of St John's College, Cambridge, stole small pike from a pond behind Buckingham (now Magdalene) College. George Broun and his brother William fished in a stream at ten at night. When the farmer of the fishery and his servants appeared, George drowned trying to escape.

Net, line and fish-trap each had distinctive dangers. Nets varied in form and might be spread from boats, from banks, or by wading in the water. The Lincolnshire 'tramel' had a combination of large and fine mesh, the Norfolk 'shove nette' had a frame to push along a riverbed, and the Westmorland 'podde nett' was probably narrow-necked to take eels. Some were deployed at night and some managed with ropes which might snap. Some, attached to arm or foot, could drag the user down. Others snagged on wood in the water or came up overloaded with rotten pond matter. Big nets could drown teams of fishermen, two men in the Thames, three in the Eden, five in the Eamont.

Traps, generally made of wicker, were as varied as nets and accounted for almost as many deaths. They were often sited at mill floodgates or other weirs, and one user in seven was a miller. Jurors called them by various names. There were leaps in the Midlands, hard-weels on the Severn, grig-weels on the Thames, store-weels on the Cherwell, hives in Suffolk, and a 'dochell' in a Lincolnshire ditch. The commonest problem was to overbalance, either when pulling out a full trap, heavy with fish, or when throwing an empty trap in. It could happen whether working from a boat, standing on the shore or balancing on a weir.

Fewer died angling, though those fishing while standing by rivers, sometimes on slippery rocks, may well have been using what more forthcoming jurors called an 'anglyng rodde' or an 'anglewand'. Anglers fell in when banks collapsed, or when reaching for a hooked fish or dropped rod. Mostly fishing alone, they had no one to rescue them. The most basic technique of all was to grab fish by hand, fatal to boys and girls.

Dogs were the commonest domestic animals and featured indirectly in many accidents, usually by provoking other creatures. Dogs running loose harassed horses, cattle, pigs or sheep, and humans were caught in the crossfire. William Parys threw dirt at a spaniel to stop it chasing his ducks but hit Juliana Streton instead. Dogs were present as a matter of course in hunting accidents: bloodhounds tracking deer, greyhounds chasing hares, spaniels waiting to retrieve shot waterfowl. Seven of the king's hunting hounds were in a cart crash at Campsall, Yorkshire, in 1532, presumably heading up the Great North Road.

Half the deaths directly caused by dogs were bites or maulings. Attacks happened in houses and yards, on the roads, in the fields. Some dogs were 'madd' or rabid and others were guard dogs broken loose. When Barnaby Barker's two mastiffs ran at Mary Bell as she walked out at first light to milk her master's cows, they dragged behind them the iron chains and weights that normally tied them down. Dogs hunted in larger packs than that. As eight-year-old William Marshall went by Lamer Place, Sir John Butler's house in Wheathampstead, Hertfordshire, four young dogs – three greyhounds and a mastiff – ran him down and bit him all over. Owners felt some responsibility. Christopher Ponet killed his 'mongerell mastif' after it bit Jane Cloke's arm and leg down to the bone, and Thomas Blakes hanged his fallow-coloured mastiff after it attacked John Bonate.

Others avoided a bite but still came off worse. William Collens fell to his death fleeing a mastiff, and John Jervis's guard dog knocked him into a pond when he let it out of the building it had been shut in overnight. Matthew Anderton stabbed himself in the leg fighting off the dogs in Butcher Row, Aylesbury. Perhaps he should have expected an attack, as dogs were often linked with butchers or tanners. Thomas Blakes was a butcher, for example, and Barnaby Barker a tanner.

Children played with dogs at home and lost out in the rough-and-tumble. Some boys played nastier games. Three drowned throwing dogs into rivers or pits, and one drowning a cat. Christopher Crewe the jurors singled out as moved by some fury as he flung a dog which had followed him on an errand into the River Stour three or four times in the effort to drown it. Others were kindly. On 15 February 1586 a dog fell down the vicarage well at Lynsted, Kent. The vicar's wife asked William Fyssher to go to the rescue. He tied himself to the well-rope by a belt and climbed into the well bucket. His weight broke the rope and he fell into the water beneath, presumably leaving the dog to its fate.

Further dangers came from pest control. Ratsbane was readily mistaken for other white powders. Barbara Gilbert mixed it, instead of flour, with milk in a family meal. Others tucked obliviously into bread or dough baited with it. Forgetfulness did for Richard Ferren, a Rutland yeoman. At Simon Lacye's mercer's shop in Uppingham he bought some ratsbane wrapped in paper for a penny and put it in his pocket to carry home together with some nuts. On the way home the paper broke. At home he settled down in front of the fire, asked his wife for a drink and began to eat the nuts, now thoroughly sprinkled with arsenic. John Annis found another way to get into trouble with the rats he heard in the roof of a barn. He fell to his death climbing a ladder with a pole to knock them down.

The livestock most likely to come into the house were pigs. They were involved in as many accidents as dogs and mounted more fatal attacks. Rooting anywhere for food, they posed a constant danger to unwatched babies, pulled from cradles and bitten in the head. Leonard Mascall's *First Booke of Cattell*, published in 1587 and five times more before 1610, as handy a guide to livestock as Tusser to farming, warned that pigs took 'yoong children . . . being left alone'. Boars, hogs and sows all killed, though boars most frequently. Some older children attacked were herding the pigs, others playing near them, some just passing by. Farming pigs brought other dangers. One boy was hit by a stick his father threw at a hog. Robert Longe was sufficiently concerned when he saw a piglet fall down a well that he climbed in to rescue it, only to be asphyxiated.

Four features of pig husbandry posed distinctive problems. Children and servants drowned in large vats of pigswill left standing in kitchens. Pigsties needed building and cleaning out. Beata Goodwyn drowned making a 'hoggesvate' of wood, brushwood and straw next to a pond. Acorns were a good diet supplement – Tusser wrote of 'plenty of acorns, the porkling to fat' – but autumn saw falls from trees while knocking them down. And slaughter was a tense moment. Arthur Goostree, jolted by a dog, stabbed himself just trying to mark a pig. William Pitte's 'baken hogge' bit him in the hand as he tried to kill it. On Christmas Eve 1567 at Rickinghall Superior, Suffolk, Jane Typtott was holding a pig on a bench, ready for the kill, when the pig, as the jurors put it, argued back. In the struggle her knife went into her leg.

Ducks and geese caused drownings among the women who cared for domestic fowl. Agnes Crycheley had had too much to drink when she went looking for her goslings on the orchard pond. Dorothy Cobbie kept her father's gander tied up but reached out for it holding on to a rotten stake. Doves in dovecotes, kept for eggs and chicks, demanded some dangerous climbs. Chickens were safer, though Isabel Philips hit her head on a well bucket retrieving a fallen cockerel, and Margaret Amyas fell fetching eggs from a hayloft. Sometimes predators had to be eliminated, not just a practical measure but a social duty mandated by acts of parliament designed to protect everyone's chicks and crops. John Coole succeeded in destroying a kite's nest but fell from a broken branch.

Milk was important in feeding households and underpinned major industries in cheese and butter. Leather was a versatile material and beef a desirable meat. No wonder cattle were widespread and were behind one fatal accident in thirty. Half of these involved draught oxen, but even the remainder made cattle more dangerous than pigs, fowl and sheep combined. The importance of cattle was further underlined by their value. Most bulls forfeited were worth more than £1 and most cows at least half that, while most oxen were priced at £2 or more, and the red ox of Hugh Holt of Martock, Somerset, came in at £4 6s. 8d., more than all but the most extraordinary horses. Half the bulls in accidents were owned by the gentry, while others were the communal property of villagers who could not afford a bull of their own.

Milking cows was almost entirely women's work, done above all by female servants but also by housewives and widows. The special responsibility of the housewife for her cows was sometimes brought out by the jurors, as when Margaret Pytcherde, wife of Thomas Pytcherde, gentleman, was said to be checking on her heifers by the pond next to his house. Milking was work for the beginning and end of the day, accidents falling between four and six on summer mornings, rather later in the autumn, and between five and six in the evening. There were drownings and falling trees as milkers walked to find the cows. There were heavy pails to carry the milk and sharp pail-stakes to hang them on. Unsettled cows had to be held by a halter during milking or chased across an uneven field. Restive cows struck out with their horns, and young bulls sharing the fields attacked milkers from behind. Processing the milk posed fewer hazards, though one maid met her end in a 'mylkhowse' at Westonzoyland, Somerset, when a wicker hurdle fell on her.

Herding cows and calves was shared between men, women and children. Frightened cows were dangerous. Jane Verney was gored by a cow with a broken leg, and William Bruton fell into the Avon trying to rescue a 'madde cowe' stuck on the riverbank. Cows with calves attacked people with dogs or others who got too close, like young Robert Hankyn, suddenly surrounded by all the cattle of his village as the common herdsman drove them home at dusk. Those under-confident of their ability to hang on to a cow, often children, tied the halter around their body and were dragged along if the cow ran off. Abraham Phillippes was even unwise enough to tie a calf's halter round his neck with a running knot. By goring, dragging or trampling, cows killed one and a half times as many victims as bulls, though they would have outnumbered bulls by far more than that. Leonard Mascall reckoned that a 'good and lusty' bull could cope with sixty cows.

Bull attacks killed mostly men. Some were herding the bulls or getting them out of pits or ponds, but most were just passers-by. Husbandmen, yeomen, labourers and boys, a tilemaker and a clergyman were gored and tossed. Some attacks were savage. The cleric was found with a penetrating wound to the neck, a wound to the lower left leg and a wound to the left thigh that ripped out flesh, sinews and veins. Oxen and bullocks, fattened for meat or haulage, large but docile, caused fewer deaths than bulls or cows, but in similar ways.

Cattle were worth keeping healthy. At Glatton, Huntingdonshire, in April 1530, William Cowper tried to cure his ox of the barbs, inflamed growths under the tongue, with two of his neighbours, Oliver Johnson and Alice Leverche. As Oliver held the ox's head steady, William approached it with a pair of tongs, presumably aiming to cut away the growths as cattle-care handbooks advised. The ox knocked William to the ground, then turned and wounded Oliver in the side. Beasts facing slaughter might also take the initiative. One bullock in a slaughterhouse attacked the glover trying to catch it, and another, bought by a butcher, ran off as they returned from market. The butcher gave chase and fell down a well.

Shelter and fodder posed challenges in winter. Cattle packed into barns, stables, cowsheds or ox-houses turned on visitors, but feeding in the fields could be bleak. A bundle of rain-soaked straw could swell unmanageably. Cribs had sharp staked sides, and Susan Ottye, 'gret with chyld', slipped and fell onto one. At Mansergh, Westmorland, when he went out to feed his stock on 15 January 1568, William Bower found the body of a lame man who had been seen wandering in the parish of Kirkby Lonsdale.

The sheep was, Leonard Mascall assured his readers, 'no harmefull beast', but even sheep presented dangers. They were involved in almost as many deaths as pigs and far more multiple fatalities. Farm workers tripped and fell when herding or taking feed to winter sheepcotes. Wattle hurdles were used to fold grazing flocks. Carts crashed delivering them to the fields a dozen at a time, and a pile of four collapsed onto twelve-year-old John Benett as he sheltered from an August storm. Several men fell on shears as they hurried through the countryside at shearing time.

The most distinctive incidents came when washing sheep ready for shearing. Accidents clustered in June and July across the sheep-raising counties. Any flowing water would do, though shallow places were chosen where possible, a ford, the 'the wasshen slade', the 'ship wasshyng water'. Farmers and their households worked together and one in three victims was female. Panicky sheep tried to get away or jumped up and knocked people over, sometimes into rushing water that dragged them off downstream. Then co-workers came to help, and it was this that produced multiple deaths. Two drowned at South Clifton on the Trent in 1532, three at Beanacre on the Avon in 1551, three at Surfleet, Lincolnshire, in 1570, four at Plumpton, Yorkshire, in 1557.

One tragedy we can reconstruct in detail unfolded at Slaidburn in the Forest of Bowland in June 1560. Alice Bonde of Byram was washing sheep at eleven in the morning when a wether, a castrated ram, knocked her into a 'turnepoole', a turbulent patch. Her sister Catherine, working in the river too, saw Alice flat out in the water and rushed towards her, but also lost her footing. John Swinglehirst jumped in from the bank to help, but all three drowned. Washing sheep could be not only dangerous but dull. William Hall, a twenty-four-year-old labourer, was working with an Essex husbandman, Edmund Beamont of Tolleshunt D'Arcy, and his other servants, washing three hundred sheep in a salt creek in the Blackwater Estuary. At four on a Sunday afternoon, William tried to liven things up. As a jest, the jurors reported, he rode across the stream on the back of a ram. Funny or not, he soon fell off, his body recovered some three hours later.

For utility and for danger, all other animals were eclipsed by horses. Horse accidents outnumbered all other animal accidents by nearly three to one. Two in five of these involved draught horses. Almost as many killed those riding or preparing to ride. The remainder encompassed a huge variety of interactions, from the intimacy of grooming to the sudden glimpse of a runaway coming round a corner before a trampling. Accidents with horses happened all over England and all through the year. One in three was a cart crash, one in five a rider drowned, one in eight a fall. One victim in twenty was crushed by a falling horse or dragged by a runaway. Bites were only occasional, but angry or frightened horses kicked or trampled one in seven of those they killed.

The need to identify horses for forfeiture made jurors describe them in detail, but their evidence is more useful in some ways than others. It suggests first that, while everyday horses were no doubt ridden or harnessed for draught as needed, better horses were preferred for riding. The average value of a horse used for traction was 13*s.* 4*d.*, that of a riding horse 17*s.* 10*d.*, and the figure was not unduly skewed by top-quality mounts priced at £3 and above. Such valuable horses were owned by the social elite, gentry, clergy and the occasional yeoman, butcher or innkeeper, though even they could not match the £20 great gelding, presumably a warhorse, of the earl of Pembroke.

The reports say nothing about bloodstock or gait. Mares, geldings and stallions can be hard to tell apart because the term 'horse' was used to refer both to any generic equine or to a stallion, what jurors occasionally called a 'stoned horse'. It appears that mares were put to work at least as much as geldings and were somewhat preferred for riding. On the other hand, at least half the expensive riding horses of the rich were geldings. The jurors are more help with coats, telling us about some six hundred horses, sometimes very precisely. The mare that kicked John Morlyn as he caught it was red-sorrel with a flaxen mane. The gelding that fell on John Raynold, labourer, when he cheekily asked the bishop of Ely's horse-keeper if he could ride it, was black in coat, mane and tail.

Leonard Mascall thought there was a hierarchy of desirable coats. Bay and sorrel led the way, followed by dappled and flea-bitten greys, then dun, white and black. Coal-black he put near the end, as likely to prove dangerous, but iron-grey was worst, unfit for serious work. Bays and greys were certainly popular. Bays formed the second commonest category, a quarter of all horses described, and sorrels, chestnuts and the 'kyte hewed', presumably the colour of a red kite, another one in fourteen. Greys, to which a few roans might be added, were the largest group, at more than one in three. Duns and browns were far fewer at around one in thirty, blacks one in six, whites, which Mascall thought overly delicate, below one in ten. Jurors identified only a few iron-grey or flea-bitten horses. Bays do seem to have been expensive while whites and blacks were often cheap. Bays and greys were commonest among horses owned by the gentry and the flea-bitten mounts may also have been choice, often ridden by yeomen.

Value depended on more than coat. Three of the cheapest animals, worth 2s. or less, were called debilitated. Blind horses, generally used in carts and mills but occasionally ridden, the old and the lame were also priced down. Nags were good for riding – one was used for hunting by a gentleman – but generally small and inexpensive. Foals were cheap, but colts and fillies approached the prices of all but the best adult horses. Riders tried the untamed at their peril. William Davye, who mounted his father's grey colt when told to lead it to pasture, was chancing his luck. Others were breaking horses in for their owners. Laurence French only got as far as putting a bit on a fiery but valuable colt before it kicked him in the head.

The Mantuan ambassador to England in 1557 was impressed that 'there is no male or female peasant who does not ride on horseback'. The jurors gave a social status to more than half of the almost eight hundred killed riding and confirmed his view. The largest groups, each providing one victim in five, were labourers and male or female servants. Next came yeomen, their wives and children at one in seven, husbandmen and their families at one in eight, and artisans or traders and their families at one in ten. Only one victim in thirteen was a gentleman or cleric, the same proportion as otherwise unidentified boys and girls under fourteen, many of whom were probably labourers or servants like the hundreds to whom the jurors did not bother to attach a social description. More men than women rode, but the ambassador probably took that for granted. Male victims outnumbered female by seven to one.

What the ambassador did not point out was that poorer people rode cheaper horses. The average horse ridden by a labourer or husbandman was worth 15s. The average horse ridden by a gentleman or esquire was worth nearly twice as much, £1 8s. And while husbandmen and yeomen often owned their mount, labourers and servants were far more likely to be riding someone else's horse. Some rode a cart-horse while driving or a plough-horse returning from the fields. Many others were riding on their master's errands. Horse use was thus spread differently from horse ownership. A quarter of identifiable owners were yeomen, a similar number husbandmen, one in seven an artisan or trader, one in twenty a widow. More than a quarter came from the peerage, gentry or clergy.

Many falls came when horses stumbled, bucked or bolted. Some mounts were blamed as headstrong, impetuous, ill-natured or wild, but most reports were matter-of-fact. Horses were startled by noises – a carter's whip, horse fetters jangling in a bag, grain pouring from a sack – or worried about slippery mud. Occasionally they fell asleep. Falls were made worse by a hard landing, a kick or a dragging. Some riders were guilty of poor horsemanship on borrowed mounts, like young Alexander Fetherstonhalgh of Willimontswick, Northumberland, who fell fording the Tyne, or John Asplyn, a clergyman who tried too tight a turn at a gallop. The dozen victims who were either drunk or fell asleep on horseback were equally at fault. So was John Dowe, who urinated from the back of his horse rather than dismount.

Mounting was tricky. A makeshift mounting-block might roll away or too vigorous a jump carry the rider right across the horse. Tack and baggage could be troublesome. Reins, bridles and girths broke. Riders found it hard to keep their seat on top of packsaddles, sheepskins or sacks. The more elaborate harness required for ploughs, carts or panniers entangled and dragged those who fell even more readily than stirrups and stirrup leathers. High saddle pommels ruptured those who crashed against them.

The side-saddles used by women may have been particularly unstable. Emmeline Shirley fell into a pond from an 'an olde saddell for a wooman' as she watered a gelding on the way back from market. Extra problems faced those doubling up, women behind men, children behind relatives or servants, even three children together on one mare. John Fawcett tied ten-year-old Mary, probably his niece, to him with a towel, but it just meant that they drowned together, whereas fourteen-year-old Thomas Stott survived to give evidence of what happened when he and John Cragge, the clergyman with whom he was riding pillion, came off their horse crossing the Cumberland Derwent and Cragge was swept into a whirlpool.

Anything that took horses to water was dangerous. Dozens of accidents involved horses led or ridden to drink or for a wash, in rivers, streams or ponds. Simple kicks, falls and drags into the water were complicated by horses that panicked or swam unexpectedly or got tangled in their harness. Even recognised spots – 'the horse pole' at Bishop's Castle, Shropshire, 'the wateringe place' at Eaton Socon, Bedfordshire, 'the horse leyz' at Burton on the Wolds, Leicestershire – were not always safe. Often the victims were boys or young men caring for their masters' mounts.

Shoeing was another perilous moment. Tethered horses kicked out, both at professionals like Richard Stabler, the earl of Arundel's horse-keeper, and at passers-by. The fresh nail in a horseshoe caught on Thomas Hatche's hose, and as he and the horse tried to pull free his leg was broken. Horses kicked servants and owners grooming them in stables or yards or checking on them in the fields. One man cut himself on his knife bending over to examine his horse's legs, another on scissors when trimming a mane. Tails were a danger area, whether untangling a twig or tying a knot. Winter feeding indoors with hay, barley and lentils led to more kicks. Injured horses were sensitive. A guest's horse with a wound on its back kicked William Dyce as he tended to it at the Cardinal's Hat Inn in Ware, Hertfordshire. Specialist veterinary care was available but might be distant. John Lay walked five miles so that Laurence Foster, 'horseleche', could cure his master's colt of a fistula.

Horses, ranging far and wide and ridden to round up livestock, encountered many other animals. Alice Bothe's mare was bitten by dogs, and William Marchall's gelding unnerved by barking. Jane Hewe was thrown when her mount was startled by a hog. The bull that Henry Ellergil was leading charged his horse. Admittedly it may have been over-excited, as he was taking it to mate with his cow. Rabbits were no problem, but their holes were, John Hugill's mare tripping on them on Gilling Moor in Yorkshire.

Interactions between horses caused trouble. Those who rode one horse and led others might find them heading in different directions. Andrew Brusted and Henry Wyant were kicked by fighting horses. The horse that jumped at the mare Richard Alyn was leading may have had amorous intentions. And even a dead horse could be awkward. Thomas Chapman's mare threw him in the fields of Billingborough, Lincolnshire, as he dragged a quarter of a horse's corpse back to his master's house.

Jurors recognised characteristic mistakes in dealing with horses as victims approached them silently or from behind. They did not condemn the violence that some used to bend horses to their will but did note its effects. Dozens of horses reacted to beating or to objects thrown at them. Usually these were cart-horses or plough-horses, but some riders overused the spurs, whip or bit. A couple hit horses they were trying to mount. Even a calculated blow from an experienced horse-keeper was risky. William Erington drowned in Sir Richard Southwell's pond, kicked unconscious by his master's valuable bay after forcing it into the water with a punch in the side.

One might sympathise with those who hit horses by accident, for example when dismounting from another horse, but perhaps not with William Kyrsbye, who struck his master's mare so hard with the handle of a pitchfork that he stabbed himself under the ribs with the prongs. Crueller still was David Morrys, servant to John Jones of Trefeglwys, Montgomeryshire. Sixty miles from home, at Adeney in Shropshire, he made mischief on an August evening. Seeing a mare locked up in the common pound he picked some stinging nettles, lifted its tail, and stung it. The result was dramatic but also fatal, a mighty kick in the chest.

One last practice would certainly raise eyebrows today. The majority of those killed leading horses were dragged by runaways, sometimes for a quarter or a third of a mile, until their bodies were, as one report put it, totally demolished. Three dozen died because they had tied the halter to their body, rather than holding it in a firm but releasable grip. The arm was the most popular place, more often right than left, but one in three tied it round their waist or even their neck. Those holding the halter in their hands were dragged far less often, and indeed several lost their grip on the horse and chased after it only to be kicked. Conversely three victims who had been leading a horse and then mounted it still had the halter tied to their arm when they fell off.

A third of those who did this were boys or girls under fourteen and several others not much older. The jurors made little attempt to explain the practice. Two reports called it childish behaviour and one did suggest that the victim wanted to leave his hands free to wash his face while his charges drank. Perhaps others needed their hands to carry things. But it seems most likely they were just frightened of losing the horse and unsure of their own strength to hold it.

Tudor interactions with animals could be bloody on either side. Humans posed a threat to almost all creatures, though less deliberately to those they set to work like horses, oxen and dogs than to those they killed to eat or, as we shall see, those they baited for entertainment. Guard dogs, hungry pigs and rutting stags killed people regularly, but were overshadowed by unsettled cattle and horses. Environmental factors entered the equation as water came into play with fish and wildfowl and tall trees for nesting birds. People complicated the situation for one another as they quarrelled over poaching, rode without due care and attention or misplaced the ratsbane. But they also developed the expertise that usually kept them safe when setting a fish-trap, milking a cow or washing a horse.

Dealings with animals still kill people, just as there is still human cruelty to animals, though we find it less acceptable. Nowadays in England cattle, dogs, horse-riding and angling each account for a similar share of human fatalities. The same creatures were dangerous in Tudor times, but at much higher ratios to the human population. Currently there is about one sheep for every four people in England, and then there was one person for every three or four sheep. Now there is about one horse for every eighty people, and then there was perhaps one for every ten. Today people outnumber cattle about seven to one, and then it was about three to one. Deer, pigs and the ingredients for rook pie barely register as threats, and sheep-washing in rivers is a thing of the past. Now when we think of deaths at work, unless we are cattle farmers or work with horses, we probably do not think of animals. We may have industrial machinery in mind, or the great pit disasters of the last two centuries. Such things also worried our ancestors.

# 11

## Places of Work

While farming, timber and domestic tasks accounted for most work accidents, and building and transport for significant slices, other employments presented major dangers. Mining has always been dangerous, mills were powerful, and other industries had distinctive hazards. Meanwhile the inquests allow us to glimpse on occasion the social dynamics of work alongside its practicalities.

Though coal-mining was at an early point in the expansion that would fuel the Industrial Revolution, it generated many more deaths than any other extractive industry if we add transport troubles to those at the pits. Pit deaths occurred in almost every coalfield then in operation. In Cumberland and Westmorland, they came at Bolton and Stainmore, in the north-east at Newcastle. In Yorkshire, with its many scattered collieries, accidents clustered around Leeds, at Bradford, Beeston, Roundhay, Seacroft, Scholes and Whitkirk, and around Rotherham, at Greasbrough, Rawmarsh and Wentworth, with a handful in between. As the seams ran into Derbyshire and Nottinghamshire, there was trouble at Dronfield, Chesterfield and North Wingfield, at Belper, Shipley, Stanley and Eggington, at Strelley and at Wollaton.

In Leicestershire the pits around Coleorton saw mishaps as did those in the Warwickshire Arden. In Staffordshire there were three at Wednesbury, already a significant mining centre by 1500, and others to the west at Wolverhampton and Sedgley and to the north at Arblaster Hey, Beaudesert and Leycett. In Shropshire calamities struck near Coalbrookdale at Dawley Magna and Wellington, but also to the south in Bitterley. The only major coalfield without recorded mine accidents was the south-west, but carts loaded with 'sea coles or mendipp coles' got into trouble at Priddy and Mells. Everywhere transport accidents shadowed those in pits, with carts in the mining counties and boats on the Severn and Tyne. There were trips into Leicester from the Coleorton workings and loads of 'smythes cole', small-cut bituminous coal for iron-working, destined for blacksmiths. Many coal wagons must have been substantial, drawn by large teams, but coal was also carried in sacks on shoulders.

Almost all mine accidents were caused by either a fall down the pit or a collapse. Some who fell were not working in the mines but walking past them, home from Rotherham fair, back from a day's begging, or across fields scattered with pits like 'Fernelye Crofte' at Heath. Those who fell at work were often climbing up and down ropes that snapped, but Hugh Massye was using his rope to pull out 'a baskett full of yearth' when he lost his balance, and John Archer was digging while standing on a board. Occasional reports mentioned the wheel round which a rope was wound at the top of the mine or the hook to which it was attached. Victims of collapses were usually digging out coal when anything ranging from a single stone to a 'shelf of see coole' fell on them. Both falls and collapses were made worse by the depths to which pits were sunk. Some were twelve feet deep, presumably bell-pits, but others much deeper, sixty or even eighty feet at Coleorton in 1549.

Flooding was a regular problem, and some victims were baling out the mine or digging a 'soughe' to drain off water. Some drowned when they fell, and Richard Judson was inundated when his digging broke through into another, flooded shaft. The final peril was suffocation as gases collected in the pit, what jurors called 'erthe myre or dampe' or 'yearthe dampe'. It afflicted not only diggers but even Richard Shafton, who was merely supervising. It is not clear whether the 'trunke planke' that William Porter died checking at Strelley in 1540 was part of a wooden water pump or of a ventilation pipe to combat damp.

Accidents mining metals were rarer. There were pit collapses digging for 'irenstone' near Chesterfield and Leeds, for 'leydhure' in Westmorland and North Yorkshire. Robert Bowes, gentleman, met his end at a more famous venture, the royal copper mines at Newlands in Crosthwaite, Cumberland. He fell to his death when a ladder chain broke as he was inspecting the mine in 1600. In Cornwall and Devon, it was tin mines that peppered the landscape. Margery Taperell may have fallen into a tin pit near Plymouth in 1504, Oliver Hannaford injured himself digging with a 'tynhoke' at Ashburton, and Thomas Hicke, tinner of St Stephen-in-Brannell, drowned in the tinwork pool at Polgooth mine after an accident with the 'wynder wyndinge rope'.

Building stone came in a wide range of qualities, from rubble for foundations to the finest freestone. Excavation sites ranged from small pits to well-known quarries. Occasionally working practices misfired, but most accidents were rockfalls. Even John Moore, who was trying to break a stone with an iron bar, impaled his forehead on the bar only when a large mass of earth fell on his back. Skilled workers were hit by falling stones in places like 'Dene Quarrey' in East Farleigh, Kent, where Thomas Wysynden was exercising his 'mason crafte' in 1510, or 'Colyers Pyttes' in the same parish, where another mason, Thomas Cheseman, died sixty-six years later. Wysynden and Cheseman both lived at Loose, a focal point of Kentish ragstone mining. The neighbouring village was West Farleigh, where Stephen Leche, a priest, fell down a quarry in 1511.

The Cotswolds were another centre, with accidents at Prestbury, Sudeley and Black Bourton, while Cambridge's building stone came from the border of Northamptonshire and Rutland, where there were collapses at King's Cliffe and Ketton. One way or another, stone was dug almost everywhere. To the south there were accidents at Gatcombe, Isle of Wight, and Cuckfield in Sussex, to the west in a quarry 'neare by the sea cliffes' at Bideford, Devon, and at Over Stowey in the Quantocks. To the north Robert Marshall, a waller, went to 'Edwarde Dale Ende' near Bakewell to source stones, Mary Partryk fell into an old flooded 'stone pytt' on Pilley Hills south of Barnsley, and Nicholas Sheperd sought stone at 'Kytt Knott' in Longsleddale.

Some stones had special purposes. Chellaston in Derbyshire, where John Huttet died in a pit in 1532, was famous for its alabaster, carved and polished for tomb effigies or religious images. Slates and shingles were good for roofing, like the 'healing stone' that John Graye was after at Tilland in Quethiock, Cornwall, in March 1582. The pit was full of water and to empty it he stood on a 'flacke', or wattle hurdle, suspended from four ropes. One rope broke and he drowned.

Chalk was widely dug and generated more accidents than any other stone. It was excavated from Dorset and Hampshire to Norfolk and Suffolk, with incidents commonest in Hertfordshire and Kent. The harder sorts could be cut for building, like the Bedfordshire 'hurrocke stones' of Totternhoe and Harlington. Softer chalks were burnt for lime, used in mortar and lime-wash. Unlike most other digging, women as well as men dug chalk. Margaret Darby at Crockenhill, Kent, and Margaret Spinke at Coddenham, Suffolk, were gathering chalk for lime-kilns, the latter wielding a pickaxe, when a bank of chalk fell on each of them. The kilns were also hazardous, as Christopher Wyldman found when he fell into one in operation and was, as the jurors put it, consumed by fire. With chalk came flint, hard to work – John Dobson merely shattered a block into fatal shards when he heated it in a large fire to break it up – but handy for striking sparks and used for building where other stone was short. John Grove was digging in a chalk pit when he met his end, but he was looking for 'flynt' and 'pybble stones'.

Sand and gravel were also essential for building, and as many accidents happened in a 'sande pytte' or 'gravell pytt' as in chalk pits. Collapses when overhanging earth or sand 'did calve', as a Norfolk jury put it, were again the problem. It must have been tempting just to scrape away a bit more where others had already dug. The jurors even said that John Gyles was not thinking about his master's command to dig in a flat place when he got himself buried. As in chalk pits, women worked alongside men, and in major collapses they died together: Jane Grace and Edward Hall at Little Stukeley, Huntingdonshire, Jane Felkyn, Agnes Smyth and Thomas Knolles at Stone, Staffordshire. Tools for digging looser or lighter material – shovels, spades, mattocks and hoes – were presumably more familiar to women than those that masons used on freestone. Other women were helpers, throwing sand out of the pit or loading carts.

Varieties of earth and clay together generated rather more accidents than chalk. The 'wallyng erth' dug out at West Chisenbury, Wiltshire, must have been for constructing wattle-and-daub walls, like the clay for making a wall dug at Burmington, Warwickshire, while the 'lome' that featured in several accidents was probably similar. Yet again overhangs were the great danger, up to sixty cartloads of earth falling on the unwary. Thomas Kyng and Stephen Edward even sat down for a rest in the cavity they had cleared out. Clay, more often mentioned in the eastern counties, might also have been dug for brick-making. Though brickmakers and tilemakers had accidents unrelated to their trade, only one incident illuminates their industry. At Stoke, outside Coventry, in 1517, William Gosworth was making tiles in a 'tylhouse' next to William Ruyley's house. He playfully threw a lump of clay at

Ruyley's servant Alice, but it missed her and killed Ruyley's five-year-old son, John.

Other deposits had industrial uses. Robert Osborn died in the 'fullers pyttes' at Wavendon, Buckinghamshire, digging for fuller's earth, fine clay for cleaning and thickening woollen cloth. Thomas Egborne and Nicholas Gyles were crushed by a fall in the 'playster pyttes' at Newton-on-Trent, Lincolnshire, digging gypsum for high-quality plaster. William Redioughe may have been digging for potash at Outlane in Huddersfield when a great stone fell on him. Salt was invaluable. Inland it was obtained by evaporation from saline springs, on the coast by flooding pits with sea-water and boiling the brine in pans. Droitwich had one of the great salt springs and it was there that Peter Chaundeler filled his wagon with salt before driving back to Worcester. On the Wash, Thomas Mychell was driving his cart to Holbeach Hurn to load up with salt when it overturned. On the Solway Firth, ageing John Carr was working at the salt-pans or 'saltcootes' at Whitrigg in Bowness when he fell and broke his neck.

Peat was dug as a fuel across the northern moorlands and in the fens. There were accidents carrying it by cart in Northumberland, Yorkshire and Lincolnshire, by boat across Windermere, on horseback in Westmorland, and on foot on the common moor at Goole. At Thursby, Cumberland and Ashwicken, Norfolk, it was stacked dangerously high in yards ready for burning, while at Holme-on-Spalding Moor, Yorkshire, John Welshe kept his peat in a cart in the yard, which overturned on his servant Alice Madderson as she pulled off turves to make a fire.

Watermills and windmills were far more dangerous than mines, accounting for one in twenty-two of our victims. They were widespread. We have watermill accidents from thirty-five counties, windmill accidents from twenty-one and horse-mill accidents from fifteen. They were vital for milling grain for baking and malt for brewing, and efficient for fulling cloth to make it durable, and for sharpening metal blades. Every aspect of their operation was laced with danger. Some claimed multiple victims: two, five months apart, at the corn-mills at Sudbury, Suffolk; two, twelve years apart, at Clifton Mill, Westmorland; two, both millers, twenty-four years apart, at Burford Mill, Oxfordshire.

The sources of milling power were perilous. Windmills were best sited high to catch the wind, and their ladders and sails were hazardous to climb. Watermills needed a smooth channel of water to drive their wheels, and a reservoir in a dammed millpond or behind a weir to fill it. Millponds made good places to bathe, to wash clothes, to fetch water, to pick flowers. A quarter of all mill accidents were drownings apparently unconnected with the mill's operation. Millstreams worked best when they flowed fast, and even the outflow through a 'waste poole', like that, twelve feet deep, in which Thomas Bocher drowned washing his horse, could be alarmingly powerful. Crossing-places might consist of a single plank, while the splash of the water on the wheel could make the surroundings slippery. Even maintaining millponds and millraces was hazardous. Richard Gobert died digging gravel to line a mill channel, while one boat sank as John Carter and Richard Shutt tried to shore up a millpond's banks, and another as Silvester Goore and Mary Wright used 'ramming claye' to mend the 'bracke' through which water flowed from the stream to the mill.

Three times as many millworkers died in millraces as millponds because it was there that they controlled the flow of the water into the mill. It was easy to lose one's balance when opening or closing a floodgate with a lever, but Edward Hall's solution was no better. One Saturday evening he did as he had often done before, pushing down the shuttle that regulated the flow by jumping onto it, but this time his feet slipped and he fell between floodgate and wheel. Waterwheels were fearsome things, armed with protruding ladles or float-boards, and a third of those who fell into millraces died from hitting the wheel. Those who tried to slow the wheel down by putting a foot on it found just how powerful waterwheels were.

Windmills posed similar problems in managing the power supply. Sails caught the wind best when covered in canvas sail-cloths, and half a dozen millers fell putting them on or taking them off. Thomas Folly of Mucking, Essex, for example, rushed out in a tempestuous wind to 'withdrawe the sailes' of his mill, but forgot to secure the 'gripe' that would stop the mill turning. He climbed one sail to pull down the rope that spread the sailcloths, but the sail turned beneath him. And wind was harder to control than water. If the breeze strengthened while the miller was at work, things might suddenly start to turn.

The power and intricacy of mills' internal machinery brought further perils. Half of all those who died operating mills were caught in the workings. The most dangerous spot was where the cog-wheel, turning on the same axle as the wheel or sails outside, transferred power to the trundle or lantern-pinion, rotating in the horizontal plane to drive the upper millstone. All too many millers ended up like John Palmer, a boy found sitting with a broken skull between the cog-wheel and the trundle in a windmill at Oakington, Cambridgeshire. Other parts of the mill played their part in accidents too: the 'cogge pitt' or 'cogge hole' in which the cog-wheel revolved, the axletree on which it turned, the spindle that joined the trundle to the millstones, the bridge tree on which the base of the spindle sat, the loucher that enclosed the millstones, the hopper that sat above them to feed in the grain. Even the hoist for raising sacks of grain to the hopper could pose problems. It was this that Elizabeth Dodd fell against in an epileptic attack, causing a heavy 'mold for a pulley' to fall onto her head, while the sack of wheat that John Statsbury was hoisting swung towards his wife and knocked her to the ground.

Juries could often work out the sequence of events in macabre detail. William Gullocke went down into the cog pit at a watermill in Compton Martin, Somerset, but fell and grabbed the cog-wheel with his left hand to steady himself. The wheel pulled his hand, then his arm, then his body in between the cogs and the rungs of the trundle until his arm was broken and his body crushed. Alice Chadweke put her right hand between the cogs and the trundle of a windmill in the fields of Carlton-on-Trent, Nottinghamshire, so that her hand and then her head were pulled in and the back of her skull shattered.

One reason so many were caught was the need to lubricate wooden gearing with grease or tallow while it ran. Others were braking the mill by putting a wedge between cogwheel and trundle or tying the cog-wheel to a post. Another hazard was loose clothing. Men were caught by the sleeves of their shirts, jerkins, jackets and coats, women by the sleeves of their gowns, the hems of their petticoats or the kerchiefs on their heads or necks. One man was caught by his dagger, one by his hair, John Hoigeson by his frayed clothes, John Taylor by his fashionably slashed pair of 'cutt brechys'.

There were other temptations. To start a sluggish mill, one might try to push it round, as Nicholas Dyckenson did, only to catch his sleeve on a cog. Or if all was going well one might start fiddling with the machinery. Fifteen-year-old Elizabeth Fuller, having loaded a mill with grain, played with a cog-wheel and ended with her body crushed and torn apart. And woodwork needed mending just as earthworks did. Millers and joiners died fixing waterwheels, windmill sails, floodgates, cog-wheels and trundles.

Windmills, light enough to turn into the wind, might be dangerously frail. A rod snapped off one sail, a five-yard section off another. At Wimbotsham, Norfolk, in November 1543, two men milling at midnight to take advantage of a mighty wind were killed when the whole mill collapsed, leaving only the cross trees that stood on the ground and three supporting spars. At Ayston, Norfolk, in February 1561, a miller grabbed the 'pyetree' to swing the mill round and catch the westerly wind, but much of the mill-house fell over.

Horse-mills, commoner in areas where water power was less practicable and often used to grind brewing malt, posed problems of their own. The horse might run faster than expected and the driver lose control, an issue especially when children were left in charge. Susan Blomfylde was seven when she came to grief 'dryvyng ... the myll horse', and at eight William Bowes had three horses to manage. Many parts of the machinery could pose problems, from the cog-wheel, spindle and millstones to the 'nogge' or peg to which the horse's head was tied. Simple accidents saw operators or passers-by hit by the sweep, draught or 'sword' that the horse drew around to turn the wheel. More often victims were caught between moving elements and the fixed posts that stood around the mill.

Mills had problems not only with their power source and transmission, but also with the output. Millstones were heavy and awkwardly shaped and caused one operating accident in ten, most often when they were being changed over. Once lifted they could fall on people or crush them against a beam. John Bankes was hit in the head when a piece of wood slipped out of the knot of the rope suspending his millstone, Matthew Jeffrey battered when his feet slipped and the stone he was manoeuvring pinned him to a 'bayerd', a heavy transport barrow. The grooves that channelled the grain had to be regularly re-cut, but such pecking required the upper stone to be raised. Thomas Taylor propped it up with a hammer and a wooden wedge but nudged them while his head was between the stones. Roger Danver's small staff worked no better. Stones might break while running and pieces fly off, hitting those nearby.

Fulling-mills, tucking-mills, thicking-mills or walkmills fed their power not into millstones but into wooden 'fulling stockes' that beat the cloth. The mills were as widely distributed as the industry they served, so while some accidents occurred in famous cloth-making centres such as Reading, Newbury and Hamstead Marshall in Berkshire, in Dursley, Gloucestershire, Keynsham, Somerset or Edington, Wiltshire, they ranged from Surrey to Northumberland and from Monmouthshire to Norfolk. The victims included both fullers and those who gathered the 'myll flockes or puffes' – excess wool – from among the moving machinery. Those who fell into the 'knee pitt', cradle or cistern were smashed by the 'knee' or other parts of the stocks. There were lacerating iron hooks and crushing beams. Alice Wheler's end shows most clearly the workings of the mill, in which a trip mechanism caused the stocks to rise and fall onto the cloth: as the water drove the millwheel, it made a 'tappet', presumably on an axle, raise and drop the 'shanke' and 'brace'. The shank hit her on the head and the brace in the mouth.

The availability of power when wind or water flow was favourable tempted millers to work through the night and killed a dozen or more as they did so. At five in a late November dusk, John Fell left his workmates in Lord Cobham's windmill at Cooling, Kent, to get a candle so they could carry on working, as the mill was running fast. He walked within range of the whirling sails and was hit on the head. At six on a December morning, Thomas Ladde needed a lamp to make his way safely from his work at the mill to his master's house, but the lamp blew out and he stumbled into the river. Thomas Chetley, a loader or miller's assistant, was at work in a watermill at Watford between 1 and 2 a.m. when his wife, Jane, went to the millpond to wet a broom. Not seeing that a familiar plank lying over the water had been removed, she missed her footing and drowned.

All this makes clear why mill work was so very dangerous compared with other occupations. Not only millers but their wives died at an uncommonly high rate, and most of their deaths were work related. Whole households shared the risks, for millers' homes doubled up as places of work like so many others. Millers' children and servants drowned even when they were not working the mill. Fourteen-year-old Jane Morton, servant of the miller at Castle Mills in Goldington, Bedfordshire, slipping off the bridge into the millpond on her way to feed the pigs in the miller's pigsty in April 1535, can stand for many others.

Other mills, though rarer than grain- or fulling-mills, presented similar dangers. There was a cider mill at Dartmouth and an 'oylemyln howse' with an 'oylepres' at Deeping St James in Lincolnshire. Commonest were those processing metals. In the iron industry, mills drove furnace bellows and forge hammers: one jury described in detail how a waterwheel was connected by a beam to the 'great hammer' which beat the newly smelted 'bloome' of iron, held in place by clasps. Accidents clustered in the Sussex Weald. There the industry was expanding fast, at Catsfield, at 'Hoodlye hammer' in Lamberhurst, on the 'hammer ryver' at Salehurst, at 'Baxhame Forge' in Frant, 'Beache Furnace' in Battle and 'Paylersfurnace' in Wadhurst. The workings stretched into Kent, where the son of a foundryman drowned in a 'furnace pond' at Horsmonden.

There was innovation as well as growth. Cannon-founding was new, and in 1579 and 1590 there were accidents with big guns on carts at Chelsfield and Yalding, perhaps on their way to the naval bases on the Thames. At Dartford, Godfrey Box set up England's first iron-slitting mill. One of his servants was killed in 1600 when a cartload of iron on its way to his 'iron myll howse' overturned. The most alarmingly novel technology was the blast-furnace, as John William found out at Tonbridge in March 1565. He climbed onto the top of his master's furnace and being, in the jurors' opinion, idle and moved by wantonness, began to play and jump on the charcoal and kick it around. The furnace was already lit and as the fire took hold the charcoal sank. A hole opened beneath John's feet and the smoke and dust blasted up through it and suffocated him.

Metal-working thrived among the furnaces. Cutlers from Horsmonden, Tonbridge and Cranbrook and locksmiths from Benenden, West Malling and Lewes featured in accidents, and there were grindstone mills to sharpen blades at Horsmonden, Maidstone and Guildford. The West Midlands was another centre, where craftsmen from Birmingham, Bromsgrove and Rowley worked on horse-bits, tools and nails. Thomas Burnefford, scythe-smith of Belbroughton, died sharpening scythes at Stone in 1564, while there was a 'blade mylne' at Moseley, 'Fundsley Smythie' in Baggeridge and a workshop powered by water from a 'smythie fleame' at Trentham. The Forest of Dean was active too, and a Gloucester cutler died heading for Mitcheldean on business in 1529. Famous for its knives was the Sheffield area, where a furbisher from Rotherham drowned in the Don and a cutler from Darnall in the Sheaf. Yet another zone was Exmoor. At Horner Wood, where archaeologists have found evidence of iron production in earthworks, buildings and slag, Jane Jordaine, wife of William Jordaine of Luccombe, 'iren man', died washing clothes in the 'iren mill poonde', forty feet wide and ten feet deep.

Some lines of metal-working were concentrated in big towns. London goldsmiths met mishaps, a Gloucester brasier, and a York founder. But blacksmithing to repair tools and shoe horses was ubiquitous. Accidents with smiths happened in fifty places large and small. They give a glimpse of village smithies like Christopher Ellyse's 'black smythe forge' at Waddesdon, Buckinghamshire, or those described with their open 'bulke' at the front and anvil inside at Willey, Herefordshire, Coton, Cambridgeshire, or Slindon, Sussex.

Another expanding trade, mostly found in substantial towns, was commercial brewing. Work with large volumes of hot liquid was hazardous and Ralph Bicardike's brewery in Cambridge seems to have been particularly bad. On 1 May 1525, Clement Ferror was standing on a bench there to stir the malt in a boiling mash-vat, fell in and was badly scalded, dying next day. Just eleven weeks later Thomas Brankeston and William Bicardike were carrying a barrel of boiling wort across the brewhouse to empty it into a tub when Thomas fell backwards into more hot liquid. He took nine days to die. Similar accidents with vats and furnaces of lead and copper or the boiling water needed to expand barrel hoops happened in breweries at Taunton, Kingston upon Thames, Thetford and Milton Regis by Sittingbourne.

Three significant and widespread industries generated surprisingly few accidents. Pottery manufacture registered no deaths, though well-known potting areas saw transport mishaps. At Ingatestone, Essex, in 1584, John Richeardson, a potter from nearby Stock, was taking 'earthenpottes' to a fair at Brentwood when his packhorse was swept away. At Low Toynton, Lincolnshire, in 1531, Thomas Bukke and William Rowe were carrying a whole cartload of pots when Rowe fell asleep at eleven at night, fell off the cart and was run over.

The leather trades were more visible. Tanners and the tanyards where they turned hides into leather appeared in accidents in a score of towns and a scatter of villages. Whittawers, who treated the skins of sheep, goats and deer, featured in accidents at Cambridge and Coventry. Curriers, who prepared the leather before it passed to the craftsmen who would use it, cropped up at Coventry and Leicester, at Southwark, Chertsey and Harrold in Bedfordshire.

Tanneries were often on the edge of town. This made sense when tanning involved soaking hides first in various mixtures of lime, dung and urine and then, for up to a year, in oak bark. The 'tanne pitt' and 'tanne fates' where hides were immersed were the major hazards of the 'tanne yarde'. Almost all the dozen victims who fell into them were small children. In contrast to brewers, few tanners seem to have died at their work and when they did it was not actually when tanning. John Dymoke apparently cut himself trimming ox horns from hides. John Huffyld fell from his horse carrying five tanned hides from Bordesley to Coventry. The only accident with a tanning tool killed a girl who tripped and hit her head on a 'barkers rym'.

Even more striking is the absence of danger in the textile industries. By some calculations one in six of the adult population were involved in cloth-making, and yet even when weavers and others did feature in accidents it was rarely a matter of their work. Fulling-mills were dangerous and so was dyeing. Dyers, their apprentices and their children fell into cauldrons and casks of hot woad, madder and other liquids. They worked in a range of towns – Minchinhampton and Leominster, Norwich and Boston, Newark-on-Trent and York – but were most prominent at Coventry. There were a couple of drownings washing wool and cloth and a handful of deaths from falling looms and spinning wheels. George Waterhous dropped a 'tenter barre', part of a wooden frame for stretching cloth, on his head as he carried it out onto the 'Tenter Grene' at Leeds from the house of Augustine Wilkynson, gentleman clothier. But it was hard to get killed making cloth.

Accidents incidentally involving textile workers or related to transport and marketing show us something more of the pattern of cloth-making. There were weavers and the shearmen who trimmed the cloth in the old cloth towns, Coventry, Gloucester, Worcester, Shrewsbury and York. Clothworkers and the big clothiers who employed multiple women to spin and men to weave were also present in zones of burgeoning rural manufacture. Wiltshire was one key area, at Melksham, Whaddon and Westbury, at Bishopstrow, Edington and East Chisenbury. The Weald of Kent was another, in a string of villages around Horsmonden and Cranbrook, including Benenden, where there was a field called 'Wurkhowscroft', presumably the site for a cloth workshop. Central Suffolk was a third textile zone, from Mildenhall to Lavenham, the boomtown of early Tudor cloth-making, and south to Bures, Wissington and East Bergholt. The West Riding of Yorkshire was a fourth, at Warley, Sowerby and Skircoat, Dalton, Halifax and Wakefield. But cloth-makers were almost everywhere, mentioned in twenty-four counties. Some were specialised – John More, worsted weaver, Richard Davy, haircloth maker – but most made the standard cloths mentioned in reports: kerseys, narrow cloths, and broadcloths.

Some accidents enable us to situate weaving in the wider economy. Wool moved all over England, fleeces lugged on a back in Berkshire or loaded on a cart in Wiltshire, sacks passed from the window of an Oxfordshire house or carried on horseback to market in Norfolk, packs manhandled in Hertfordshire or taken by cart to Lavenham. John Hewett, the 'wolman' who died in a fall in Leeds, was presumably a dealer. It was already valuable in its raw state. A crashed cartload in the 1550s might be worth up to £30. Some moved again as yarn from spinners to weavers, from Bury St Edmunds to Lavenham, from Little Hereford to Buildwas Bridge, perhaps heading for Shrewsbury. Spinning raised its worth, to £1 for a forty-pound bundle or 6*d.* a pound, where the raw wool in one crash worked out at less than half that. Woven but not yet fulled, the cloth was carried by packhorse to and from fulling-mills.

Once ready for customers it was on the move again. Margaret Moyne fell into the River Crimple at Pannal carrying a large load of it on her head from Harrogate to Follifoot. Marmaduke Bowes fell into the Ouse at York trying to lever a pack of it through the door of the 'Commune Crayne' for loading. Much of it headed for London, domestic hub and centre of the export market. Cartloads of cloth met trouble all around the capital, coming in from Bures at Writtle, from Kent at Strood, from Harpenden at Chipping. It was doubtless for London that cloth from Halifax was bound when the packhorse driver carrying it fell into the River Soar in Leicestershire, halfway there.

Mishaps in various industries give a closer insight into working relationships. Workmates or fellow-tradesmen played games or swam together. Four shoemakers found a drowned body at Uffington, Shropshire, in 1542. Some larked about at work. At Staplehurst in the Weald of Kent in November 1525, James Kyng and William Fermor were sitting by the fire eating bread and cheese for breakfast, the first meal of the working day. James playfully nudged William with his shoulder and William's food knife went into James's thigh. They were in a workhouse belonging to William Scranton, presumably an ancestor of Thomas Scranton, a Staplehurst clothier of the next generation. Others did not get on so well. At John Bradburye's brewery, Dierick Jonson and Roger Nyckson exchanged opprobrious words before one gave the other a smack on the ear. They fell to the ground and wrestled, and their master's dog bit Dierick in the arm.

The relationship between master and apprentice was central to many crafts, but unpredictable. Teenaged apprentices varied between the diligent and the reckless. Robert Cowcheman, apprentice clothier, pressed on with work, concealing from his master the illness that left him too weak to struggle out of a well after a fall. William Griffin, apprentice dyer, was doing his best to get the lid back onto a boiling vat of woad when he fell in. John Wall, apprentice cutler, was stretching as hard as he could to get a piece of brass off a shelf when he toppled over onto a sword. But Willliam Addison, apprentice glazier, had too much time on his hands. Apparently loaned out by his master in Southwark to another glazing workshop in Dartford, he decided, working alone one Friday afternoon, to explore the nooks and crannies. He found a mysterious sweet powder, wrapped up in some paper, of which he ate a spoonful or more. He did not realise that it was sugar mixed with arsenic.

Coal-mining was already showing in Tudor times the lethal dangers that would haunt it into the twentieth century, but it had not yet established its deadly preponderance over all other forms of mining and quarrying. Chalk and clay, sand and gravel, freestone and slate collectively outweighed it for pit disasters, though the need to distribute it widely from the sites of its production made coal transport a killer. More distinctive in the sixteenth century were the extreme hazards of harnessing the power of water and wind for industries as old as milling grain and as new as cannon-founding. For the economy, wind and water were a transformative addition to the power of human and animal muscle, but power supply, internal machinery and the grinding or hammering tools they drove all posed terrible risks.

The contrast with other industries is clear. Brewing, tanning and charcoal claimed some lives, but pottery and that huge employer cloth-making were very safe. The ironic effect is that we can use accidents to track textile manufacture, but only by looking for its shadows, in the misadventures of off-duty weavers and the transport of wool, yarn and cloth. The process is a useful reminder that the woollen caps and waterlogged clothes, the knives and scythes, horseshoes and guns that featured in accidents usually came from somewhere else in the country and someone else's work. So did the intoxicating beer brewed in steaming breweries and the leather for horse-harness tanned in stinking tan pits.

Later we shall have to turn to the trade and travel that tied them all together. For now, we should pause at the close of the working week or the end of the working day and prepare ourselves for faith and festivity.

# 12

# Faith and Festivity

The church was everywhere in Tudor society. Accident reports mostly tell us of its social and institutional life, but glimpses of piety do appear. The church's buildings, often the most substantial in a village or the most spectacular in a town, recurred as landmarks in jurors' narratives, as did associated places, Church Lanes, Church Fields, Church Meads and Church Ponds. The clergy featured not only in their pastoral role – sometimes to the satisfaction of coroners, as witnesses or first finders of bodies, sometimes to their frustration, performing hasty burials – but in many other areas of life.

Men, women and children met hazards walking or riding to church, often alone: slippery banks, gusts of wind, rising floods, falling trees. In company things could get more riotous. William Cloke jumped playfully on Michael Colbrand's back as they walked home in a group but fell on his knife as they tumbled over. For morning services, the journey could be as early as six, while evening services clustered at four. The pattern of the church's year called people not just on Sundays, but on Christmas Day, Ash Wednesday, Holy Rood Day, or indeed other weekdays for a regular service or special event.

What happened at church changed over the century as the Reformation introduced Protestant ideas and practices. Until the 1530s jurors referred instinctively to going to mass, but by 1550 it was divine service and in the 1560s and 1570s morning prayer and evening prayer. Earlier on, calendar customs lent variety. On Palm Sunday the boys of Chippenham, Wiltshire, climbed onto the church roof to throw small cakes to the crowd below. In 1507, Francis Gore and Nicholas Hulkebere were scrambling to collect the cakes when two stones dislodged from the south aisle's battlements fell on them.

By the 1590s, especially in areas of Protestant enthusiasm like the Weald of Kent, sermons were central. At Rolvenden in 1598 a butcher, Henry Siesly, was sitting close to the pulpit as William Reade, the vicar, was, as the jurors put it, preaching the gospel. A volume of the works of Heinrich Bullinger, the Zurich theologian popular among advanced Elizabethan clergy – Reade was probably a Cambridge graduate – fell from the pulpit and hit him on the head. He never recovered and died four weeks later. Not everyone was rapt by the new style of worship. On Tuesday in Whitsun week 1596, Thomas Gryffyn of Orsett, Essex, labourer, was disturbing evening prayer. The parish constable, William Garreth, the churchwarden, William Bright and others tried to put him in the stocks. They secured his right leg, but he resisted with all his might, dragging the stocks out into the road. He died next day from internal injuries.

Church was a communal experience. John Hirst was said to be walking among his neighbours in Huddersfield church on Passion Sunday 1562 when a ceiling beam fell on him. But private prayer was encouraged and others were sitting praying when misfortune struck. Christopher Conyers, a gentleman of Brotton on the Cleveland coast, sought the grandeur of God in the open air. On 22 November 1531 he spent the morning walking around his land to watch his servants at work. At around eleven he reached the seaside cliffs, where he sat down to pray with a book in his hand. When it was nearly noon and time to go home, he got up, but the tussock of grass under his feet gave way and slid down the cliff. He tried to cling on, but fell about 150 feet, breaking his right arm, his left leg, his whole body. At the top of the cliff those who came to look for him found his reading glasses.

Rites of passage were important. Dead newborns might be noted as unbaptised. Henry Kente had been gravely ill for ten days when he called in his confessor to give him the last rites in July 1512. That night he rose in agony from his bed as his exhausted carers slept, stumbled out of the house and drowned. Others, like John Stedeman who crushed his leg in a riding fall in 1518, had time for the last rites in the days after their accident. Bishops had a unique role in ordaining clerics and confirming layfolk. Their celebrity status was evident from the fate of Walter Knyght of Warleggan, Cornwall. On Monday, 8 September 1595, he was waiting near St Leonard's Chapel, on the downs outside Bodmin, for the arrival of Gervase Babington, the new bishop of Exeter, on his first local tour. The crowd was 5,000 strong and Walter was trampled by a restless horse.

The clergy were a larger and more diverse group before the Reformation than after. There were monks, like those from Woburn and Bolton Abbey who drowned on short journeys. There were nuns, like those at Barking Abbey, where the abbess's butler cut up her bread with a dangerously large knife. There were friars, like the Gloucester Dominican who fell off a causeway heading for the village of Over to collect alms. There were teams of priests at collegiate churches, like Tattershall College in Lincolnshire or Attleborough College in Norfolk, where there were accidents with restless horses and wandering ducks. Lower in the hierarchy were chaplains. Ordained but underemployed, some of them clearly needed to get their hands dirty, like James Bynson, who fell stacking peas with a pitchfork. There were also religious professionals who were not quite clergy. In Kent we find William Umfrey, parish clerk of Wilmington, killed by a collapsing cart, and John Hastyngs, the aged hermit who fell into a ditch near his hermitage by the chapel of St Anne at Boxley.

The parish clergy mainly persevered through religious turmoil, their lives bound up with their parishioners in play as at prayer. Arthur Greneacres, rector of Whitchurch, Shropshire, was enjoying a little archery in the parsonage close in 1587 with his respectable neighbours – a gentleman, two yeomen, a draper and a mercer – when an arrow went astray. Watching archery proved no safer for Henry Newton at Egerton, Kent, in 1581 or Thomas Watson at Carlisle in 1600. Thomas Jameson, rector of North Piddle, Worcestershire, perhaps rejoiced in his neighbours' company a little too much. At seven in the evening of Monday, 6 March 1570, he was on his way home from Upton Snodsbury, two miles away, when he stumbled into a stream, very, very drunk.

Parish clergy ran the usual perils of village life. The rector of Welsh Bicknor came out of his boat on the River Wye and the curate of St James, Isle of Grain, fell into a garden pond. In Bedfordshire the aged vicar of Westoning tumbled backwards off a toilet seat and hung, suspended by his hose, until he expired, while the even more aged curate of Potsgrove was blown into a pit by the wind. Good social connections might not protect them. Anthony Harleston had been presented to the rectory of Stifford in Essex by his relatives and was staying at their manor house, South Ockendon Hall, when he drowned bathing in the moat in 1569. Once the Reformation allowed them to marry, their children suffered the common tragedies.

Rectories and vicarages could be substantial buildings. They had stairs down which servants or indeed clerics themselves – Baldwin Hamlett, vicar of Wilmington, Sussex – had fatal falls. They had halls and kitchens, lofts and barns, yards, ponds and wells. They contained the paraphernalia of comfortable life with their attendant dangers: chairs, candlesticks, even guns. If they caught fire, the results could be drastic. When Dr Thomas Wodeward's house at Wingham in Kent burnt in 1518, one teenage labourer died on his bed upstairs and two of those working to extinguish the blaze were killed by a collapsing chimney. They housed servants and visitors – an esquire died in his bedroom at Souldrop rectory, Bedfordshire, when the roof collapsed – and they were the centre of considerable economic enterprises. The fields, crops and livestock of the clergy, the fine horses, palaces and parks of the bishops, feature in dozens of accidents.

Parish churches were solid, but they needed constant repair. A dozen accidents widely spread in space and time show workmen in trouble. Sheets of lead roofing snagged on timbers and parishioners got too close despite warnings to stay away. Doubtless more work was needed, as bits periodically fell off. Robert Michell's admiration for the fifteenth-century fan vault of Sherborne Abbey cost him dear. As he stood in the belfry looking at it on 17 May 1589, the eve of Whit Sunday, a weighty stone fell out of the vault and hit him on the head.

Work often focused on towers or steeples and this fitted the prominent role of bell-ringing in parish life, claiming two dozen victims. The commonest mishaps involved bell-ropes. They tangled around the ringer's legs or arms, lifted and then dropped him, often head-first or onto paved stone floors. John Smythe at Stoney Stanton, Leicestershire, was swung out of the nearest window. Others were hanging, inspecting or repairing bells or simply standing around when heavy bells or bell-stocks fell on them. Enthusiastic ringers or resonating bells broke the wooden floors or ceilings of belfries, causing terrifying falls, sixty feet in the case of John Gusten at Egham, Surrey. Unconventional techniques also ran into trouble. William Taylor tried to teach Nicholas Lyne to ring a bell without a rope by climbing into the steeple and ringing it on the stock. He misjudged the swing of the bell and crushed his head between bell and bell-frame. John Robinson stood on a bench to ring because his rope was too short, only for the rope to catch on the bench and turn all upside down.

Ringing often served to summon parishioners to church, sometimes to mark a curfew. Other occasions changed over the century. In 1519 the bells at Bramham in Yorkshire were commemorating deceased parishioners, but three sets of ringers in the 1580s and 1590s had a new purpose. They chimed on 17 November, the anniversary of the queen's accession, for what the jurors called joy for the happy reign of Queen Elizabeth. Participation was also recreational and nearly all our ringers were ringing in company with their neighbours. Their occupations were diverse, including a yeoman, a butcher and a painter. So were their ages, younger men mixing with those in their sixties.

Other recreations were no better. Archery practice was understandably lethal, but it was a loyal duty as well as an entertainment. Football was as bad as bell-ringing and so was wrestling, each laying out two dozen dead. One basic problem was that men did not take the knives off their belts before playing, so fifteen wrestlers and four footballers stabbed themselves in collisions or falls. Both sports were ubiquitous, football played from Cornwall to Cumberland and from Herefordshire to Essex, challenges to wrestle ringing out in at least twenty different counties. But where wrestling was evenly spread across the year, football was heavily concentrated in February and March, when three-quarters of all accidents occurred, the time of year when the ground was firm and there were no crops to trample or to tend.

Football had alarmingly few rules, though some jurors were keen to stress that it was not a mere brawl but a traditional recreation. In Cornwall it even had its own name, 'whurlyng'. Players, up to sixty strong, ran fast holding the ball or chased after it, then threw it or kicked it towards the goal. In tackling they grabbed each other, crashed into each other, pushed each other away, or kicked each other while 'strickeinge at the football', as they were, as one report put it, contending in the game and struggle. Isaac Faller even called out 'Let us make work for the surgeon' as he charged into the fray. The results ranged from battered bodies and internal injuries to broken legs and a shattered neck.

Football might lack proper balls – at Ettington in Warwickshire in 1552 they made one from an old shoe – and it usually improvised pitches. Players played in enclosed fields, on meadows and common greens, often near churches, at Outwell, Norfolk, in the churchyard itself. They fell over molehills or furrows and onto stones and tree stumps. When the ball went onto the porch of the parish church at Empingham, Rutland, Robert Judkin had to fetch a ladder to retrieve it. Boys in their mid-teens played. So did working men of all sorts, many labourers, but also husbandmen, yeomen and a range of craftsmen: weavers, tanners, a fuller, a tailor, a mason, a brewer's man. They were often described as neighbours, but at times they were surely local rivals: in 1509 the Cornishmen of Benbole and those of Bodieve met to play at Tregorden, in between their villages. Sunday was the commonest match day, seeing nearly half the accidents, but games might crop up anywhere in the week.

Wrestling even more than football was a test of masculine prowess. When Stephen Kayngham found three of his neighbours wrestling on a Sunday afternoon in the churchyard at Skeckling in Yorkshire, he told them he was a manly man who could throw all three of them over the churchyard wall. John Homler said he doubted it and got picked up and dropped over the wall. Friends and brothers wrestled, out of familiarity, or sociably and lovingly, as reports put it. Fulk Wyghtman found William Hochynson asleep in a field at three o'clock on a July afternoon and pushed him until he woke up and started wrestling. The aim was to throw one's opponent to the ground and injuries came when one contestant crashed down on top of another, or fallers landed on something sharp. Occasionally the jurors even described the decisive move, lifting up an opponent's leg in one's hands, or leaning backwards while holding his arms and neck to kick his legs away from under him.

Wrestlers, like footballers, numbered many labourers, some husbandmen and servants, and a scatter of artisans. They wrestled outdoors, in churchyards and closes, on top of haystacks, on the way home from the pastures. They wrestled indoors, in barns, in the rectory hall at Kneesall, Nottinghamshire, over the Christmas holidays in 1549–50 or, unwisely, in a dye-house where both wrestlers fell into a tank of scalding liquid. They wrestled at many times of day, though again mainly on Sundays or other major holidays.

Beyond wrestling lay all manner of horseplay. John Ildesley and William Bucke were sitting in a field eating when John jokily kicked William's right hand and cut his foot on William's knife. Walter Barnarde's idea of jesting with William Byrde was to throw dust down his neck while William was holding a horse by the foot. In kicking dust back at Walter, William kicked up a sharp tool that hit him. Men walking down the road or on work breaks playfully pushed their companions over, sometimes onto knives or pitchforks. Gambling added a further edge. On a late February evening in Bedford, half a dozen craftsmen were playing dice. John Clapham and Thomas Philips quarrelled over the game and Clapham snatched off Philips's woollen hat. Philips tried to grab it back and Clapham, drawing a dagger, cut himself in the leg.

This sort of tussling overlapped with boyish boisterousness. Lads between eleven and fourteen wrestled fatally. One eleven-year-old grabbed another by the coat sleeves and pulled him into a pond. A third, Anthony Dyvett, played with Edward Lunkeslowe, four years younger, by hitting him with a leather satchel – perhaps a school bag? – through which his knife poked Edward three inches deep. Some adolescents played around with cartwheels like younger children and some victims of apparently childish accidents whose age was not given may just have been adults having a laugh.

Young women messed about too. Jane Barnefild and Elizabeth Piersall were at the hemp yard in Newport, Shropshire, when one playfully grabbed the other round the neck and pulled her over. At seven in the evening perhaps it was the end of a long day. Agnes Thorneton was in the kitchen chatting to her fellow-servants and the son of her master, John Knell, when Thomas Clarke suddenly jumped up on John's shoulder and pushed him backwards onto Agnes's knife. Even at the age of thirty, Cecily Johnson was making merry with many others in a common pasture in Roydon, Norfolk, in May 1575. Fleeing John Platfott's attempts to throw a pail of water over her, she fell onto stony ground.

More recognised pastimes might be no safer. 'Cristmas playe' caused John Sanway to fall off a bench and 'Christenmas games' gave John Hypper crushed testicles. Running games might or might not have set rules, but one which clearly did was 'base' or 'prysone bace'. Players tried to catch members of the opposing team when they ran outside a safe area, but William Warter, playing at Dartford, Kent, at seven in the evening on St George's Day 1545, did not understand. Told to stand near a stony road-bank, he moved, against the game's rules, and ran across the bank towards another player, who collided with him. These running games were unusually mixed, as young working men played with boys and girls. Such games might involve a ball, like the 'cacche ball' played at Wheatley, Oxfordshire. They might have a designated venue, like 'the forstall or playeng place' at Benenden, Kent, where twelve-year-old John Kyte fell fatally while running.

Some games produced incidental fatalities. In tip-cat or 'catt', a wooden peg was flicked up and hit with a stick, but Nicholas More fell onto a dagger while playing. Thomas Wright had problems with his tennis ball only when it landed on a wall. He climbed to retrieve it but fell backwards into a cauldron of boiling wort. In bowls too, it was not the bowls themselves but where they went that was the problem. Robert Williams lost his into the river when playing in a meadow by Magdalen Bridge in Oxford and drowned fetching it. Stephen Jones abandoned his on a riverside meadow at Allington, Dorset, to rescue two boys in trouble in the water. It is not clear what 'masteryes' were in prospect at the 'game' held on Hurst Common near St Ives, Huntingdonshire, on St Bartholomew's Day 1530. Nor did Thomas Ive, a labourer from Swavesey, get to find out. The crowd swelled as folk flocked in from nearby counties. As the press got denser, Thomas fell and cut his thigh on a sword with a broken scabbard.

Other sports were more intrinsically alarming. The summer substitute for football, generating accidents from June to October, was throwing the sledgehammer. This was so lethal that safety arrangements were required. The competition on Dallow Mead at Luton in 1572 was part of a 'comon game' announced through nearby villages. It was licensed by the county justices of the peace and there was a safe area for spectators, though John Dawson left it just as Reginald Foxe, a miller from Ickleford, Hertfordshire, was throwing. Throwers were expected to warn those watching and we might feel particular sympathy for six-year-old Amias Byckner, who was minding his own business when Robert Woode practised throwing his hammer over a house and hit him. Alternatives to sledgehammers were available. Bystanders or participants were fatally injured in the casting of an iron bar at Faxton, Northamptonshire, a plough coulter at Holme Cultram, Cumberland, stone quoits at Milton, Berkshire and Chipping Sodbury, Gloucestershire, a horse's leg bone at East Witton in Wensleydale, and a pikestaff, thrown at a wheel in the road, at Midgley in Calderdale.

Surely dancing was safe. That depended where and how one danced. We have already met reckless young men who danced too long in drunken crowds. Kitchens were risky too. William Lamley was drunk when he tried to dance on one leg in Andrew Lemyng's kitchen, stumbled into the fire and was drenched in boiling water. William Westbiche was apparently sober when he danced in Goodleve Baker's kitchen while John Norington and Alice Lull cooked dinner, but he still managed to spin round and impale himself on the roasting spit. John Segrewe was in the hall rather than the kitchen at Robert Gyllett's house, but dancing while holding a dagger was not a good idea. Dancing round a maypole was safe enough, but the pole itself was another matter.

From late April to the end of May and across the country, maypoles were killers. In June and July, the very similar summer poles took over. Standing by roads and on greens, erected by yeomen, husbandmen and labourers, joiners, shoemakers and servants, they fell when they were being put up, when they were being taken down – even though the workmen shouted 'Aware, aware, avoide' – and when they were meant to be standing still, but the wind was blowing. They caused cart crashes on delivery and shootings when the jollity was enlivened by gunfire. Birch or ash trees up to forty feet tall, they could do terrible damage, in one case a head wound seven inches long, four inches wide and two inches deep.

The natural world provided a range of other recreations. From April to August, girls and boys, often around the age of four or five, picked flowers. The usual peril was drowning, though one boy was kicked by a horse. The biggest expedition – seven single-women, two housewives and a male dyer – may also have been in search of edible bilberries. Variety was wide: roses, primroses, privet blossom, paigles (probably cowslips), kingcups (probably buttercups), gales (probably bog-myrtles) and yellow boddles (probably corn marigolds). It was the last that little Jane Shaxspere was picking when she fell into the millpond at Upton Warren in June 1569, twenty miles from Stratford, where William Shakespeare was five years old at the time; but how they were related, or whether family memory of her fate had anything to do with the making of Ophelia, we cannot say. At Christmastime other plants came into play. Jane Jenden fell off a table decorating her home with branches for Christmas 1561, but whether Walter Gouter and Anne Atkinson, who fell from trees collecting ivy in December, had yuletide or hungry cattle in mind we do not know.

Animals provided varied entertainment. Horse racing might be organised or impromptu. Jane Jonys, a Wiltshire housewife, was watching a 'ronnyng game' at Dauntsey on Sunday, 2 August 1534 when one of the horses ran her down. Ellen Rotlyffe, a Lincolnshire servant, was trampled among the thirty or so horses racing in the fields at Blankney on Sunday, 29 June 1561. Henry Hedlam and Brian Newton just felt like racing, galloping their horses up and down a narrow path at the London Charterhouse in January 1540.

Newton's horse drew ahead and to catch up Hedlam switched onto another path, where he crashed into an elm tree and broke his neck.

Most animal attractions were bloodier. There was cock fighting in the 'cockpitte house' built by Ralph Donington, a Coventry mercer, until the building collapsed in 1596, killing a spectator. There was bull-baiting in which, supposedly to make the beef taste better, a bull was tied to a 'bulstake' and owners set their mastiffs to fight it. The ropes broke at Wellington, Somerset, in 1571 and Chawleigh, Devon, in 1582, and the escaped bulls gored a servant and a widow. Other victims were closer to the action. Philip Syky, labourer, was setting his dog on a red bull at Woolstone, Buckinghamshire when the bull went for him instead. William Alford was pulling his dog away from a bull at Kilmington, Somerset, when the bull caught him. Peter Singleman alias Tucker, a Bridport sailor, waited for his dog and Nicholas Warren's to get their turn with the bull, but was disappointed when his dog bit the bull in the legs. As he stepped in to drag it back and tell it to attack from the front, the bull ripped open his thigh.

Bear-baiting was yet more sensational, worth the investment to build stands for spectators like the ones that collapsed in Southwark in 1583. Bears that 'dyd breke louse' from their iron chains, whether in public – the marketplace at Carlisle – or in confined spaces – the hall of Lord Bergavenny's house at Birling in Kent, the old Austin Friars building just outside the city wall at Oxford – could deliver a terrible mauling. Bergavenny's bear, said the jurors, wounded Agnes Rapte rapidly, furiously and gravely, as it 'did bite and teare' her head, body and legs. When David Northe's bear got out at Hereford, it broke into Dafydd ap Rhydderch's house through the window at 1 a.m. and pulled his wife, Agnes ferch Owen, out of her bed and into the street, mangling her ferociously and tearing apart her throat with its claws. No wonder horses were wary. Robert Clark's mare panicked and threw him off when they met some bears on the road.

The biggest draw was bear-baiting with added bull-baiting and the organisers knew it, among them Simon Poulter, greatest showman of the Southwark bearpits. On 4 June 1567, his servants came past Charing Cross between ten and eleven in the morning, proclaiming that bears and a bull were to be baited with dogs at Paris Garden in two days' time. To make sure they got noticed, they had with them a drum, a bull and a bear. Understandably startled, the horse drawing a collier's cart bolted and five-year-old George Jeames was run over.

Only a lion was scarier than a bear. Naturally, Roger Sheppard took the chance to see a lioness when it was on show at his father-in-law's house at Loughborough in August 1579. It was tied to a beam with a rope and chains, but its keeper had, as the jurors laconically put it, done this in too relaxed a way. The lioness, as they explained, violently took hold of Roger, and with its teeth and claws dreadfully bit, tormented and devoured him. With wounds in his forehead, neck, right side and left side up to six inches deep, he lasted half an hour.

Less stressful fun was provided by minstrels. One distracted Thomas Dakyn when he was meant to be watching archers. But Thomas Talior of Scarborough suffered for his art. At nine on a May evening in Malton, twenty miles from home, he was playing – maybe juggling? – with two daggers when he fell and one of them caught him in the neck.

Plays performed on crowded streets required more dramatic effects. On the Clothmarket at Newcastle in June 1552, it was time to enliven the annual Corpus Christi plays with a big flash and a bang, perhaps for Doomsday or the Harrowing of Hell. A keelman and a yeoman set off three removable chambers of the type used in shipboard guns. One chamber exploded and the shrapnel hit Jane Smyth, servant to a merchant, and Edmund Fenwycke, a boy lying on a scaffold to watch. Gunpowder and drama did not mix well at Usk, Monmouthshire, either, where Thomas David was shot in the chest by a handgun propped up ready for a 'stache playe' on Good Friday 1555, or Brookland, Kent, where a gun burst at a play about St Erasmus in 1519. In other cases, it was the crowd that was the problem. In the busy churchyard at Gloucester Cathedral on the evening of 28 June 1592, John a Thomas got a better view of the play by climbing up 'the preaching place or crosse'. He dislodged a stone which fell on eight-year-old Thomas Johnson, son of a weaver, who was watching with other boys.

Maybe it was easier to make one's own entertainment, but even that had its perils. Six-year-old John Colkyn fell into the River Sherbourne in Coventry cutting reeds to make 'pypes'. Ten-year-old Richard Jepson cut himself falling off a pile of firewood in the 'woodhowse' of the vicarage at Cranbrook, Kent, having climbed up with a knife to cut a small piece of wood to adjust an instrument – a musical instrument? – so he could play.

For company and drink there were always alehouses, inns or taverns. Wherever one drank one had to get home. William Stratford, a labourer from Cerney Wick in Gloucestershire, drank all night in Ralph Right's inn after a day's business in Cricklade, Wiltshire. Wandering home drunk at six in the morning, he fell into the Thames. Thomas Beettes, a butcher from Brentwood in Essex, tried to be more careful. He had a few drinks with Benjamin Colthurst, George Greathead and others at William Shorloke's alehouse. They jested with the landlord for an hour or more, at which point Thomas realised that he was getting drunk and had better walk home. He was wearing 'a payer of slyppers', which may have been good for relaxing, but not for an unsteady walk. It ended with him face-down, drowned in a ditch.

Roughly one in a hundred of our victims was drunk. Men outnumbered women, but not dramatically: one male victim in a hundred was intoxicated, one female in 116. The men ranged across society and included a brewer, who should presumably have known the risks. The women divided evenly between spinsters and wives. Alcohol – usually ale or beer but sometimes wine – was consumed all year, but drunkenness was an evening problem. Only a quarter of these accidents had happened by four in the afternoon. A third came between four and seven, a further third between seven and eleven, and others as late as midnight or beyond.

Some victims were drunker than others, described as entirely drunk, very drunk and lacking control over their bodies, or greatly taken with drink and not able to rule themselves. Two died just from being drunk, suffering what the reports called a 'paraclisim', perhaps a paroxysm. Some were so drunk that the jurors vented their disapproval. William Creswyke, a Kent weaver, they thought, had been in John Hardyng's inn at Newington with other idle people from morning till evening, conducting himself badly and in a disorderly way. Others got the benefit of the doubt. John Cook, a yeoman farmer of East Hardwick, Yorkshire, fell off a stile into a ditch on his way home from Ackworth. But he had been spending his time eating and drinking in the company of many honest men, said the jurors, and they made no mention of inebriation.

Loss of coordination led to numerous falls and drownings. John Sterre blundered into a cauldron of boiling water while trying to warm himself by the fire. Some felt sleepy. Margery Leyght drifted off on a washing stool and slid into the pond. John Harres fell asleep riding home on his master's horse. Margery Westall meandered dozily through a field near her home in Wolvercote, outside Oxford. Others felt sick. John Weley collapsed and choked on his own vomit after drunkenly attacking a neighbour. Robert Collen felt unwell crossing a bridge on his way home at midnight, tried to empty his stomach into the river below, and ended up falling in.

The sorriest victims just miscalculated their intake. On a challenging journey home after a long day at market they succumbed to exposure or tottered, disorientated, into streams. Hugh Hudson, aged sixty, spent the day selling bread and fish in Newport, Shropshire, but lost his way on a cold March night on the five-mile walk to High Offley. Jane Whyte, a Dorset widow, got fatally chilled sleeping under a hedge on Rampisham Down after drinking too much at the market in Evershot. Mabel Elcokes had been busy all day, and drinking all day, in Much Wenlock. She made it almost all the three miles home to Atterley before she fell one time too many. William Borman at least had the excuse that he was on the way home from a wedding when he fell from his stumbling horse, stupefied with drink, and broke his neck on a cart-rut.

Drunks did some odd things. George Hewet tried propelling his boat down the Tyne by paddling with his feet, one on each side. Ralph Powlaye climbed a ladder to the top of a house chimney and jumped onto the turf roofing, which could not hold his weight. Thomas Edwards hit his cart-horse so hard that it overturned the cart and killed Anthony Vahey, who had given him the drink in the first place. Alice Wyse picked up a sword from where two men were practising their skills, wandered off with it, tripped and wounded herself in the leg.

Some were fighting drunk. William Philippes, a regular toper, started hitting Thomas Wynter with the end of his hedging bill – apparently in jest – and drew a knife when Thomas grabbed the haft. Robert Rogers of Rowley Regis kept beating Thomas Cartwright of Halesowen with a staff as they walked from Birmingham to Edgbaston. Richard Eliott pulled out his sword in great fury amid a crowd and swung it about, then fell over and stabbed himself in the cheek. When he started uttering malicious and reproachful words, Thomas Carpinter was taken out of the house of the courtier Urian Brereton at Evesham. Outside, ready to fight anyone, he shouted 'Cum to me, man for man, who will' and was told to keep the peace. He refused, fell over and hit his head on a stone.

In the sixteenth century church attendance was part of social life, but in the world of accidents there were those who went enthusiastically beyond the conventional piety of mass, common prayer and rites of passage and those who dissented from it. The clergy were familiar figures in the community, though their roles changed somewhat as monks, friars and hermits departed, an increasing premium was placed on learned preaching, and parsonages began to fill with clerical wives and children. There was some effort to keep churches in repair but perhaps more to keep the bells ringing.

Recreations that we might count safe now, such as bowls or tennis, were only incidentally risky then, but others were dangerous in their Tudor versions – not just football, wrestling and throwing the hammer, but maypole-dancing, playgoing, Christmas games and flower-picking. Animal baiting killed people as well as bulls, bears and dogs. Alcoholic drink was much more widely and continuously drunk than today and brewing techniques made it hard to predict its alcohol content. As a result, it complicated all manner of activities for women and men alike, though the end of the day was when it took most serious effect. Leisure activities that distracted from godliness could meet with disapproval, as could the loss of self-control induced by drink. But beyond high jinks lay both a realm of disorder and the structures of control ready to suppress it.

# 13

# Crime and Control

For all the richness of its faith and festivity, Tudor England was not the merrie England of myth. Neighbours quarrelled and fought. The law could bear down heavily on those who stepped out of line. And the threat of invasion from Scotland, France or Spain kept weapons ready to hand.

Dozens of accidental deaths occurred in violent disputes. Quite how many is hard to say, because deaths judged accidental by Tudor jurors might look to us more like self-defence or indeed the quiet dismissal of a fair fight. Consider the confrontation between John Harford and William Mundye, one a yeoman of Ramsbury, Wiltshire, and the other a royal gamekeeper from nearby Aldbourne Chase. On a Sunday morning in November 1574 William was on his way home after morning prayer in Ramsbury parish church. He was followed by his hound and carried his forest bill, a combined agricultural tool and weapon.

On the road between the villages John lay in wait for half an hour, ready to match William's eleven- or twelve-foot forest bill with a pikestaff three feet longer. John hit William in the left hand, injuring his fingers, then rushed at him with murderous intent, but ran into the bill's sharp point, wounding his forehead three inches deep and dying three days later. The jurors, who included four gentlemen, attributed considerable blame to John – he waited for William with malice aforethought and attacked him feloniously and by instigation of the Devil – and concluded that he killed himself by his own assault but did so involuntarily and by misfortune. The King's Bench clerks tidied this up into death by misfortune, but the rambling verdict captured the event's ambiguities.

Others planned similar attacks. Two Gloucestershire gentlemen lured their neighbour into an ambush at the village marl pits. Richard Shirley made sure he was going for the right man: before hitting John Mastyr, he asked him, 'Is thy name John Mastyr?' But most assaults were more spontaneous, many beginning with a chance meeting on the road. All too often trouble started with abusive words, as encounters turned into quarrels and quarrels into bloodshed. When Nicholas Morles accused John Horner of taking his master's horse without permission, John replied, 'By Goddes body, thow belyest me; ytt were almes to thrust a dagger through both thy chekes.' No wonder matters escalated. Most explicit was William Johnson's challenge to William Raunson on the road from Aylesbury to Walton: 'Stand vyllayn and defend thyself, for I wyll thrust ye throwght with my swerde.' Drink often played a role. There were fights in alehouses at Newark, Wakefield and Ripley, Derbyshire, at the Lion Inn in Guildford and outside the Hart Inn at Warminster. Many quarrels broke out between 8 p.m. and midnight when drink had doubtless flowed.

Men fought however they could. Commonest were fists, stones, knives and staffs, grappling with the arms or grabbing by the hair.

But some carried daggers, swords, bows or pikes. Daggers, with strong blades of ten inches or a foot, were much more dangerous than everyday knives and jurors valued them accordingly, six times or more as much as a knife. Swords were longer still, perhaps three feet, and around twice the price of a dagger. The spontaneous reached for tools: billhooks, reaping hooks, pitchforks or wood-knives. Some were more inventive: a firebrand, a hazel stick, an earthenware pot.

Youths scrapped readily. A fifteen-year-old threw flour in the eyes of a fourteen-year-old as they worked in a mill at Horsham and then jumped on his back. Older men fell out while ploughing or reaping wheat. Sometimes there were other grudges. Robert Wyborne and Thomas Digge argued over the rent for a house. Digge, an esquire, drew his rapier and Wyborne, defending himself with his hedging bill, poked himself in the head. Taking matters to law might not help. Richard Jete, enraged that Edmund Taillour had brought a summons for him to appear before the Archbishop of Canterbury's Court of Arches, grabbed Taillour's dagger and unintentionally stabbed his own son.

Friends and relations tried to keep the peace but could make things worse. Neighbours pulled Robert Goderich away from John Jerves so hard that he crashed into a stone wall. When Brian Redman's dog joined in his assault on Roger Welles, Roger Marshe tried to beat the dog away but hit Welles on the head. Some peacemakers were stabbed as they separated combatants or collapsed as they rushed to intervene. Thomas Brice, parish constable of East Pennard in Somerset, fell in the line of duty. In the febrile summer of 1549, as revolts broke out all over England, he separated three men who were fighting and took away their knives. When two of them resorted to fisticuffs, he ran over to break them up, tripped on an anthill, and stabbed himself in the groin with one of the confiscated blades.

Criminals were not immune to accidents. Richard Smyth broke his neck climbing in through the window of a Birmingham house at 1 a.m. and several burglars got into knife fights when confronted.

Alexander Robson and Henry Stocow, rustling sheep in Northumberland, drowned at midnight driving their prey across the Tyne. Henry Sisson, stealing fruit from a Northamptonshire orchard, fell into a pond. Twelve-year-old Andrew Dedynham slipped into a tanyard in Bungay, Suffolk, to steal tanner's bark at four on a Sunday afternoon, when everyone in the household, except for one inattentive maidservant, was away at church. He had not reckoned with the three guard dogs and two days later he was dead from their bites.

Swashbuckling villains met dramatic ends. John Hollande rowed out in a skiff with a crew of seven to plunder a ship in the harbour at Shoreham-by-Sea but drowned as he disembarked. Nicholas Jurden, a Westminster fishmonger, sailed his sons and servants to Limehouse on a January night to intercept fishing boats heading for London. They robbed a Dunkirker of two baskets of turbot, but the London customs officers gave chase, running them down at Banaster's Stair on the Surrey bank. Jurden brazened it out, saying he was taking fish for the king, but the customer called his bluff, inviting him to explain himself to the mayor. Jurden refused and they began to detain him. He grabbed a bill from his boat and Richard Nasshe, leading the arrest party, hit him on the head with a halberd.

Neighbours banded together to follow thieves and not just in wild Cumberland, where John Cowper wounded himself chasing robbers in the night in 1565. In quiet Brightwell-cum-Sotwell, Berkshire, two servants of William Yate of Long Wittenham were held up in 1534 by armed men who took 12s. 4d. from them. The whole village of Brightwell joined them in a two-mile pursuit to Clapcot, where the raiders rode into the Thames to evade capture and drowned. In busy Reading in 1554, Henry White caught up with William Grenway, a fugitive offender from Burghfield. Grenway refused to surrender, White hit him on the head with his staff, and Grenway died twelve days later.

It was every subject's duty to keep the peace. Hearing several men beating up James Dobyson in York's Walmgate, Robert

Warrom dashed out of his house to restore order, though being very drunk he fell over backwards and hit his head on the cobbles. At times of tension householders took turns to stand watch. Watchmen could be dozy. Thomas Wever, on a night watch at Ackleton, Shropshire, in October 1538, was crushed by falling earth as he rested beneath an overhanging hill. They could be overzealous. In May 1556, at nine in the evening, Richard Browne, Thomas Knyght and George Amler were keeping watch at the request of the village constable in the highway at Fundenhall, Norfolk. When William Wetynge appeared, Browne, the local tailor, told him sternly to go home. Wetynge, enraged, rushed at Browne and impaled himself on Browne's pitchfork.

Legal officers had bailiffs to execute their arrest warrants. Suspects drowned evading the under-bailiff of Leeds, the deputy bailiff of Dudley hundred, the bailiffs of the sheriff of Worcestershire. John Watkyns's plunge into the Wye did get him away from the mayor of Hereford's bailiffs, but he drowned in a stream later in his escape. William Hutt's getaway was more elaborate still. He was a Northampton poulterer, accused of counterfeiting in 1550, when the English coinage was in a dire state after years of debasement to fund the king's wars. He ran when the mayor's men came for him but crushed his side leaping from a high wall. He pressed on, jumping into a millpond from which his pursuers pulled him out and took him to gaol. Under interrogation he confessed to forging nineteen or twenty groats – coins worth 4d. each – which were duly discovered. Next night he died of his injuries. Far away in Cornwall, Michael Tapnell had a better idea. When Walter Carlyan of St Blazey came with two neighbours to a tin works at St Neot to arrest him in a suit over a £10 debt, he lowered himself down the mine on a rope to hide. His grip failed and he fell to his death.

Arrest generally brought imprisonment, though there might be one last bid for freedom. Richard Syngledaye slipped the clutches of the Somerset bailiffs on the causeway at Street while under escort to prison in Somerton, only to drown in a stream.

Tudor prisons, often housed in ageing castles, were not for long-term incarceration, but for holding suspects awaiting trial or execution. Conditions were grim. Griffin Jones and Daniel Biddell each fell from the rope on a windlass by which the gaoler's men lowered prisoners into 'the dungeon' or 'the pitt' at Warwick. Escape was tempting. Roger Segens's rope broke as he abseiled out of Norwich Castle. At Maidstone gaol Ralph Gooder tried a woollen blanket, tying it around the iron bar of a window grating and crawling out at eleven one night. His hands slipped and he fell to the stones below.

The great escape was plotted by twenty-eight prisoners, including one woman, Agnes Scalys, kept in the 'doungeon' of Colchester Castle. The dungeon was thirty feet long, fourteen feet wide and twelve feet high. Its stone walls were seven feet thick and nineteen of the inmates were chained to a wooden beam for extra security. But they had a plan. They had hidden some firewood, some sulphur, and the means to strike a light. On Christmas Day 1502, perhaps hoping that festive distraction would help their getaway, they broke the bolt on the chain, then set fire to the wooden door on the entrance, two feet three inches wide. The burning door filled the dungeon with smoke and all were suffocated.

There were many places of imprisonment beside county gaols. Town prisons at Hereford's Widemarsh Gate and York's Kidcote saw escapers fall to their deaths. At Ramsey Abbey, errant clergy like Thomas Sadd, who broke a leg in a nocturnal escape attempt, were kept by the porter. Justices of the peace had powers of arrest and held suspects in their homes. In Warwickshire Roger Fynche, a carpenter from Packwood, was put in a chamber of Edward Greville's house at Milcote. He made it out of the window but fell onto a wall and broke his neck.

Given the dangers of escape some adapted to prison life. William Holloswaye, held in Stafford gaol on suspicion of felony, drowned drawing water from a well. In Nottingham gaol, John Boothe took advantage of the exercise facilities. On the afternoon of 23 March

1593, he was in the prisoners' 'sporting place', enjoying some 'leaping'. Wishing to jump further, he took a few extra steps backwards and fell over a 'lowe hedge' into a pit.

Men knew they might have to fight and so they practised combat, wounding one another fatally when things went wrong. They used traditional weapons, swords and bucklers, or spears and bucklers, and sometimes chose significant times and public places. It was on St George's Day 1521 and on the 'Churcheplayn' at Gillingham, Kent, that John Coksegge and Richard Chellifeld showed off their sword skills in what the jurors thought an unrestrained manner. Others mixed things up, short sword against staff, dagger against unarmed man, wooden cudgel and wooden shield against iron-tipped staff.

There could be a competitive edge. George Lawner met Walter Churke outside Walter's master's house between Great Chart and Ashford in 1552. Walter admired George's staff and banteringly asked for it. George declined but took a six-foot staff from a boy, handed it to Walter and started amicably 'staffpleyeing', offering to teach Walter a thing or two. The fun ended with a fatal blow to George's head. More sophisticated polearms may have been harder to manage. Elis Gruffudd noted the novelty weapon of 1544, the Italian 'pardisan' with its 'gallantly carved and engraved' head. The 'partessetten staf' that John Smyth wielded at Wishford, Wiltshire on May Day 1555 was valued at 3s. 4d. rather than the few pence of a plain wooden staff, so may have been one of these smart Italian models.

The weapon with which all Englishmen were supposed to train was the longbow. Archery practice was enjoined by law, increasingly fiercely so under Henry VIII amid fears that its neglect would bring military and moral decline. Towns and villages constructed butts, communal targets, and fined men who did not own bows. Accidents show that men shot all over the country, in thirty-one counties. They shot throughout the century, but the decline in the proportion of fatalities caused by the longbow shows that the pessimists had cause for concern. Between 1500 and 1520, one in thirty accidental deaths was the result of archery practice. Between 1520 and 1560 it was one in a hundred and between 1560 and 1600 fewer than one in two hundred.

Men practised in groups of two, four, even ten or more. The social range was wide. One in three archers was a labourer or servant, one in four a yeoman or husbandmen, and a similar number craftsmen and tradesmen. One in ten was a gentleman and some were boys between eight and thirteen, the age at which enthusiasts thought practice was vital if one were to handle heavy bows in adult life. Shooting was a sociable affair and neighbours shot together. There were often spectators, women as well as men, and sometimes experts supervising: at Sutton Veny, Wiltshire, in 1592, William Pyttes, gentleman, stood by the targets 'to geve ayme'. Men borrowed bows and arrows from each other. At Bildeston, Suffolk, in 1556, Thomas Curtyes asked Richard Lycence if he might 'se whether he colde drawe the bowe or not' and tried a shot.

The winter with its cold and winds and August with its heat and harvest were generally avoided. May and June were the intense months, with a smaller second peak in the autumn. One in three accidents happened on Sundays, the traditional practice time, Whit Sunday and Trinity Sunday proving particularly popular. A similar number came on holidays or holiday eves: Easter Monday, Whit Monday, Michaelmas, All Souls' Day. The remainder were scattered through the week, often in late afternoon or evening, presumably after work.

Butts were set up in fields, parks, greens or closes, sometimes near the church as a suitably communal venue. At Dudleston and Whitchurch in Shropshire they used 'the Chappell Grene' and 'the Parsonage Crofte', at Appledore in Kent 'the Church Lease', at Great Malvern the field by the church. In towns, it was tempting to use gardens, yards or roadsides, and there were mishaps with confined fields of fire at Oswestry, Oxford and Southwark. It made more sense to find accessible open spaces, such as the Pitchcroft, by the river, at Worcester.

The commonest targets were marks at 240 yards range, 'twelve-score prickes' as jurors called them. Such distances gave plenty of room for shots to go astray, especially if caught by the wind or misfired, and spectators might be hit fifty or a hundred feet from the target. It was good form to warn those around when one shot, especially if the arrow was heading their way. 'Ware, Ware,' shouted the archers, 'Ware, Ware, Ware,' or 'Beware the pryk.' Some did not hear, some were blasé, some ran in front of the targets. Arrows deflected off trees, posts or mounds of earth. Sometimes those who had already shot went forward to pick up their arrow or check on the targets, forgetting that others were still shooting. James Key, for example, 'shotte fyrst at the butte' and 'fowlode hys shote', then 'movyd hys hed ... to loke uppon the marke of the seyd butte' just as Oliver Bestow's arrow caught up with him.

Some shots were inherently perilous. Arrows aimed at the side of a house could go through the wall. Worse was the challenge to hit something small. John Wryghte shouted to Richard Hall, 'Shote at my bylle.' He missed and hit John in the eye. Having returned Richard Lycence's bow, Thomas Curtyes suggested, 'Nowe let me se howe thou canst shott at my hatt.' Richard hit it, Thomas tried and missed, and as they ran out of arrows Thomas insisted Richard try again with a last arrow with no feathers to steer it. 'Trulye that arrowe wyll flye madlye,' said Thomas, and it did, straight into his head. Thomas Pert, gentleman, did not even get that far. He drew the bow too wide and got his arrow stuck between string and bow. As he tried to free the arrow, he leant over the bow and somehow managed to shoot himself in the eye.

It was guns that displaced bows. Over the century, about one accidental death in a hundred involved guns and gunpowder, but they remained few until around 1580 and then increased in the 1580s and 1590s to around one death in fifty. Guns reached almost all parts of the kingdom even before this acceleration. Accidents happened in and around large towns like London, York and Newcastle, but also in the deep countryside.

The users were almost all men. Women owned and handled guns, but the reports give no explicit account of a woman shooting, though Katherine Amner, who was in a boat with a loaded fowling gun, may have been planning to fire it. Men with guns ranged across the social scale from gentlemen to labourers, but three groups stand out. Soldiers and sailors used them professionally. Henry VIII's campaign to fortify the English coast increased the number employed as full-time gunners and they had to practise. In August 1542, five gunners from Hurst Castle, one of Henry's forts in Hampshire, were training when they hit someone they could not see behind their target. By Elizabeth's reign militiamen too carried guns. Privately owned ships as well as those of the royal navy were armed. There were accidents with the cannon of the *William of King's Lynn* at Newcastle in 1589 and the *James of Ipswich* at Harwich in 1600.

Artisans seem to have been early adopters of the new technology, and before 1560 they made up half of identifiable users. This matched the higher rates of urban gun ownership than rural shown in muster records. Some of those involved in accidents worked in skilled manual crafts such as bookbinding and others were smiths, the metalworkers who repaired guns in the absence of more specialised technicians. Some were probably foreigners – a Cambridge shoemaker had the Dutch name Gerard Johnson and a Hull bookbinder was called Peter Franchman – and this fitted the way that guns spread into England from the nearby continent.

The third and numerically largest group of gunmen over the century were yeomen. They had a taste for consumption goods that marked out their social and cultural superiority over poorer farmers and labourers and guns may have been must-have gadgets for the upwardly mobile. Familiarity with guns was something they were happy to show off to their neighbours. When John Judson, a Westmorland labourer, was trying without success to fire a gun in December 1597, Edward Lancaster, a local yeoman, came to help him. When it still would not work, they carried it home, but as Lancaster held it, it suddenly went off and Judson was hit. Maybe Lancaster was less of an expert than he thought.

Many accidents happened at shooting practice, but three other uses stand out. One was home defence. Thomas Thornton, yeoman, for example, kept a gun, the jurors said, to defend himself and his property from felons; Agnes Sargeaunt, widow, had one to protect her house. Guns were also fired in celebration. In July 1587 at Benenden, Kent, his neighbours set up a volley of shots from multiple gun chambers, linked by a trail of gunpowder, to mark the homecoming of Thomas Guildford esquire. By far the commonest use was hunting for birds. To increase the chance of a hit and to avoid blowing game to pieces, hunters used hailshot. Described in the inquests as many small balls or pellets of lead, this featured in at least a score of accidents.

Different firearms developed to meet different needs. Before 1560, terminology was simple. Jurors called most guns a handgun. Occasionally they spoke of a 'hackebussh' or arquebus, or a shorter half-hake. The only other identifiable guns were the larger guns on ships or fortifications. After 1560, specific names came in for these large guns, such as falcon and saker, and six new types of handguns emerged. There were short guns, sometimes called pistols but more often dags. The caliver, the currier and the musket were descendants of the arquebus. Fowling pieces or birding pieces sometimes had a very long barrel for increased accuracy. Lastly there was a type named for its firing mechanism, the snaphance, a type of flintlock.

Guns were alarmingly widespread despite legislation to limit their ownership and victims were diverse. A quarter were female and several were children. Passers-by were at risk, like little Abigail Parkyns, shot by the old caliver William Revell put down on a bench outside his house. Household servants and visitors met loaded guns in the hall, in the kitchen, in the bedchamber, hanging on the wall or lying on the table. Some hunters felt safely remote, in marshes, woods or fields. Yet they hit their companions or people they had not spotted. Bullets could even ricochet off water. One missed a crow perched on a buoy on the Thames and killed Agnes Acrehed, who was washing linens in the river from the King's Bridge, or landing stage, at Westminster.

While guns sometimes burst or shook so much that they were dropped and the shot went astray, by far the largest category of accidents involved unexpected discharges. Matchlocks needed a burning match to be applied to the powder at the right moment to fire. Premature ignitions were caused by sparks from ill-controlled matches, from smith's forges, from a kitchen fire or a candle too close to a gun on a table. Delayed ignitions were an equally lethal problem as powder refused to catch, often because it was damp. Sometimes they were delayed long enough to bring a gun indoors, sometimes just long enough to look down the barrel to see what was wrong.

Sensitive spring-driven mechanisms like the snaphance posed different risks. They fired when carelessly touched, snagged or put down. One was set off by a small dog jumping onto a table. A hunter fouled his on briars as he crept towards his prey, and the nonchalant young esquire John Norton caught his on the wire of his window when trying to shoot a pigeon from inside his bedchamber. Thomas Barber slapped his down on a table at the Swan Inn in Cirencester in 1549 and shot himself in the bowels.

To minimise cumbersome muzzle-loading, guns were kept charged for long periods, in some cases a month or more, and this caused misfires. It also seems to have been hard to judge whether a gun was loaded. Weapons were carried, cleaned, mended, even overloaded by those oblivious of the powder and shot inside. Cleaning guns was important to keep them working well, but difficult. A favoured technique was to fire out a wad of paper, but some put hot metal rods or scouring sticks down barrels and set off residual powder.

The wounds guns inflicted show both their effectiveness as weapons and their dangers around the house. Direct hits from shot or fragments of barrel did terrible damage, passing right through bodies or penetrating up to twelve inches deep, reaching the heart or the brain and breaking bones, while powder burns blackened and charred flesh. Two-thirds of victims died instantly, three-quarters by the end of the day of the accident. The contrast with archery accidents is instructive, for in these only one death in six was instant and wounds were rarely more than an inch or two deep.

People realised the dangers and tried to be careful. One man stood behind a tree to watch another shooting, one shooter warned bystanders, and those practising sometimes used powder but no bullets. The jurors rarely condemned those involved in accidents for negligence. On the other hand, guns were novel, tempting and unpredictable. George Harvey picked up William Kynge's loaded gun to pass it to him and shot his sister Truth Harvey in the head. William Bloxom tried to clean the rust out of a loaded caliver and shot his wife Alice Bloxom in the side. Two days before Christmas in 1582, William Rotton found a gun in the kitchen at Francis Harrold's house at Braunstone, Leicestershire, where forty-year-old Elizabeth Fraunces was sitting by the fire. He pretended to fire it, as the jurors put it, 'cheerfully and in play', and nothing happened when he touched the mechanism, so he touched it again. This time it fired and blew off the top of Elizabeth's head.

Tudor society was more violent than ours, though its homicide rate was not high by the standards of the medieval past, or of its contemporaries on the continent, while our rate looks low because medical help turns many potential murders into attempted murders or assaults. A significant degree of communal self-policing drew many men into confrontations where suspects, law-enforcers or peacekeepers might get hurt. Prisons were grim but escape was hazardous. In a country armed for defence both personal and national, under orders to train for war and rapidly acquiring guns for hunting and home security, weapons presented a more familiar risk than today. As in so many areas of life, miscalculation by one individual or poor coordination between several could bring disaster out of what was meant to be a safe way to get something done, but when using technology designed to kill the stakes were very high.

Those who used violence to get what they wanted, robbers on the roads and pirates on the water, aimed to prey on the significant numbers of people moving around with money or goods worth taking. The communities and activities we have been examining were tied together by networks of trade and travel. We should therefore examine them next.

# 14

# Trade and Travel

It is easy to imagine that sixteenth-century society was static, but in fact people moved a good deal. Of those victims whose residence we know, three in ten met their end away from their home parish. They moved on foot or on horseback, in carts or in boats. Gentlemen and their servants travelled on business private and public, but so did men of all sorts, for work of all kinds and sometimes for entertainment. Women, housewives, widows and spinsters alike were almost as mobile as men. Their journeys were usually in and out of towns, often to market or to mills. Some were with husbands or brothers, others with workmates, neighbours, children or servants. But quite often they were alone. After all, one in six accident victims were found by women, not just in homes or nearby streets, but on the roads, in the fields, in the woods, by the river.

A walk of half a dozen miles or a ride of a dozen seems to have been normal and might often have involved a return journey the same day. These were trips of two hours or more at a time when mounted royal post messengers reckoned on seven miles an hour in summer and five in winter. A walk of a dozen miles one way was not unusual but could be taxing. Thomas Fletcher, a seventy-year-old butcher, suffered a stroke on the edge of town as he reached Newcastle from Bedlington. Some went much further. Agnes Law drowned at Alconbury, Huntingdonshire, while walking from Elton to St Ives, some twenty-four miles. John Becke, a labourer from Hutton, Westmorland, drowned at Askrigg in Wensleydale on the twenty-nine miles from Bainbridge to Kendal. Each perished before nine in the morning, for it made sense to set out early. John Hayward had already done three of the seven miles to Evesham market from his home in Broadway by eight on a December morning when he drowned in Childswickham Brook.

Journeys of any significant length were easier on horseback. Rides of around twenty miles were unexceptional: Beckington to Wells via Frome, Ely to Cambridge via Willingham, Rowsley to Fairholmes in the Derbyshire Dales. Thirty miles was feasible and did not require an exceptional horse. William Dymmok, riding from Braunstone to Nottingham, was a gentleman, but Richard Woode, riding from Hertford to Mountnessing via Lambourne, was a husbandman on his own inexpensive mount. Very long journeys demanded overnight stops. When William Whyte rode to the market at Maidstone, twenty-five miles from home, he left it till early next morning to return.

Some jobs necessitated wider travel: sailors, bargemen, pedlars. Craftsmen of a sort that not every village possessed covered an area surrounding their home. Carpenters, for example, travelled to work or source wood. Thomas Ryngstede of Cardington, Bedfordshire, was mending a wooden bell-stock in the church at Shillington, eleven miles away, when it fell on him. Thomas Bell of Whashton, Yorkshire, was lifting a beam in the watermill at Marrick, eight miles away, when he fell under the waterwheel. Richard Godfrey and John Hartley each travelled about four miles to fell timber. Masons ventured even further. John Lee of Shrewsbury died building a church tower at Lapley, Staffordshire, twenty-six miles away, Robert Thirketyll of Tittleshall, Norfolk, a house at Stratton St Mary, thirty-one miles away. They might find labouring assistants nearer to the job. Roger Elston, who died at Lapley with Lee, came from Wheaton Aston, the neighbouring village.

Tilers, plasterers and thatchers, joiners, sawyers and brickmakers also circulated for work. So did surgeons and minstrels, tinkers and smiths. The jurors even called Richard Rowthe of Hitchin, Hertfordshire, a wandering smith when he drowned twenty miles from home. Butchers journeyed to stock up on animals. Occasionally there are signs of mobile agricultural labour. Two wage-labourers scything a meadow at Stafford in 1541 came from Compton, Staffordshire, and Stockton, Shropshire, each around twenty miles away.

Some were a long way from home without explanation. We find a Dorset butcher at a Gloucestershire ferry, a Cornish surgeon in Dorset, yeomen from Sussex, Derbyshire and Monmouthshire in Bedfordshire, Wiltshire and the Mendips. Perhaps they were away on business, like Richard Malfelde. A husbandman of Morton, Nottinghamshire, he was at Killamarsh, Derbyshire, thirty miles into a trip to Lancashire to see Sir John Byron, a Nottinghamshire landowner who held crown offices around Manchester and Rochdale, when he drowned in April 1549. The vagrant poor, with pressing needs but no obvious destination, occasionally wandered much further.

Travel put a premium on the state of the roads. Those leading to major destinations were well known. Jurors talked of the 'London Hie Waye' at Wendover, Buckinghamshire, of 'London Strete' at Faringdon, Berkshire, of 'London Bridge' at Trowbridge, Wiltshire, of 'Notingham Gate' at both Cotgrave and Stoke by Newark. More locally, there was 'Lestar Wey' at Market Harborough and 'Henley Wey' at Thame, while at Bodham, Norfolk, there were both 'Thernyng Strete' and 'Morgate Strete'. Roman roads continued in use. Watling Street was the distinguishing feature of 'Weedon in le Strete' in Northamptonshire and of 'Watlyngstrete' in Shropshire. Christopher Strundall, a gentleman of Frodingham, Yorkshire, must have been on Ermine Street, the Old North Road, when he fell from his mare at the High Cross in Standon, Hertfordshire, rushing to overtake another traveller. So significant was the northward route that by 1576 the queen kept a stable at Biggleswade, where a rider was injured mounting a horse.

Some roads, even those in regular use, were clearly in a dangerous condition, especially in the wet winter and early spring. Carts got into difficulties with mud on the 'Portwaye' between Wells and Wookey, on the main road out of Dover at Buckland, on the queen's highway at 'Fryers Hole' in Gravesend. Away from the major routes it could be worse. William Peers was crushed by his horse as it tried to drag itself out of a deep muddy pool in the middle of 'Henherst Lane' in Staplehurst, Kent. Peter Cowles set out to walk the three miles from Sandhurst to Gloucester, but wandered off the certain road, as the jurors put it, into a muddy lane called 'Bearde Lane in Sandhurst'. He fell into the mud and struggled to get out. Late in the evening he managed to scramble into a field but died from cold and exhaustion.

Wheel-ruts were everywhere. Jurors spoke regularly of carts in trouble with 'a grett rutt', 'a carte routte', a 'deape carte route'. On the road from Aveley to Wennington in Essex, they reckoned the drop from a high part of the road to a rut filled with liquid mud, even in June, was a foot or more. Ruts were a danger even to those on foot. Francis Turner jumped off his cart, fell backwards into a place worn hollow in the road and broke his neck. John Rusey stumbled on a 'carte rote' and fell onto the knife hanging at his belt. He was found, dead on the road, by a neighbour on the way home from market. Equally difficult were roads lined with high banks, like the 'hollowe highe waye' between Bedmond and Potters Crouch near St Albans, or the hollow road from Bristol to Wells where Richard Anstey's horse fell from a bank at Chew Stoke.

They were a particular challenge for pedestrians who met carts and tried to edge past them, like Thomas Barrett on the hollow way called 'Asshelane' in Higford, Shropshire, or Margaret Blovell on the 'holow lane' at Gedling, Northamptonshire. Some hollow roads were so narrow that drivers jammed themselves between their cart's wheels and the bank.

Concern at the state of the roads brought legislation in 1555. As the highways were 'nowe bothe verie noisome and tedious to travell in and dangerous to all passengers and cariages', surveyors of the highways were to be elected in every parish. Quarterly they were to summon carts and workers from among the inhabitants to labour with shovels, spades, mattocks and other tools to mend the roads leading to the nearest market town. As the act proved 'verye beneficiall and most necessary to bee continued' it was regularly renewed or clarified thereafter. Road-repair accidents were not unheard of earlier, but they accelerated in response to the statute and ten inquests composed between 1556 and 1587 mentioned it.

Half the fatalities involved carts loaded with stones, as they ran people over or tipped up onto them. Almost all the rest were collapses in sand, gravel and stone pits or road cuttings. The workers were husbandmen, craftsmen and those we might expect to be sent out on behalf of their households, servants and sons, but also a spinster and the wife of a tailor. Some may not have been very practised diggers. At Poulshot, Wiltshire, in 1556, Thomas Pollard, a cloth-fuller, was digging with a mattock while Thomas Ilys was shovelling gravel. Ilys bent forward for the next shovelful as Pollard swung his mattock, straight into his forehead.

The road surface was not the only hazard. There were many gates across or alongside roads. Travellers had trouble with them, on foot, on horseback or driving carts. Several riders tangled with falling or flap gates, hinged for easy opening but liable to swing and unhorse them. The jurors at Nettlebed in Oxfordshire pronounced firmly that William Whelar, a brickmaker from South Stoke, died because he did not bother to dismount and pass the gate on foot. William Longe, a Somerset gentleman, was taking no nonsense and spurred his gelding on. It leapt the gate but fell on top of him. Occasionally gates may have regulated access in crowded spots. The much-used road from Gravesend through Milton to Rochester was already called by jurors 'the Turnepykewaye' in 1568, though there is no sign of the road toll familiar from later turnpike acts.

Bridges were the sites of almost one accident in thirty. An impressive network had been inherited from centuries of building in stone, timber and brick, and many were wide enough for carts. Some jurors gave bridges names redolent of scale or solidity – 'the great bridge of Brampton' over the Nene north of Northampton, the stone bridge at Winterbourne Steepleton, Dorset – or names that survive to this day, like Somerset's Pill Bridge. Those over streams, on the other hand, might be no more than a 'wodden planke or byrge', 'a foot planck' or a tree trunk. The bridge from which five-year-old Margaret Lansdon fell was nine feet long and six inches wide. In hilly areas even the bridge approach might be difficult. Matthew White had to go down a set of slippery steps to the bridge over the river on his way to the common pasture at Well in the Yorkshire Dales.

All bridges were vulnerable to the weather, treacherous in floods, ice and wind and on dark winter nights. Some were not in the best of repair. There were holes in which horses caught their feet, larger holes through which pedestrians fell, or unstable planks over gaps. Rotten side-rails let horses and riders plummet overboard and fishermen plunge to their deaths. Dereliction might be worse still. At Houghton, Sussex, on Christmas Eve 1580, Joan Jackson faced an unnerving combination of decayed wooden bridges, an old 'arche of a bridge', wobbly stones in the riverbed and fast flood waters; an unknown man drowned at the same place two years later. Solidity was no help to Thomas Fawne, who slipped and hit his head on the wall of a stone bridge, while some bridges had swinging gates that knocked the unwary off balance.

Carts in trouble on bridges imperilled drivers and unwary fishermen below. Reckless riders who rushed across got into trouble.

So did cautious riders who tried to turn back, or dismount and remount, or carry the horse's pack over the bridge themselves. Bridges were pinch points where horses might push pedestrians off. Similar issues afflicted the causeways built to carry roads in low-lying areas, not just the fens and the Broads but, for example, the marshes around Malton where the Derwent met the Rye, or Crankley Causeway near South Muskham on the Trent.

Fords often provided a suitable alternative, but their use demanded careful judgement and they saw a third as many accidents as bridges. Some rivers had many. There were half a dozen deaths each at fords on the Eden, the Avon and the Severn. There were two dozen at nineteen different fords along the fifty miles of the Trent from Walton-on-Trent and Stapenhill to Farndon and Kelham. Some thought fords a good shallow spot for a wash, a swim or to water animals; carters and pedestrians used them; but most who died were travellers on horseback.

Fords or waths had well-known names. Some were taken from the nearest village, others presumably from a nearby landmark, 'Longe Mede Ford' at Towcester or 'Castelwath' near Brougham. There was an 'Olde Forde' at Stepney, Middlesex, 'the Grene Forthe' at Thrumpton, Nottinghamshire, and one or more Peatwaths on the Eden. The way across was not always obvious. In Derbyshire William Nicholson, almost home on the long ride from London, came off the right road in the ford at Longford and Felicia Halsope did the same fording the Dove between Marchington and Sudbury. Jane Shaklowe did not know the right passage as she tried to ride over the Don at Mexborough, and Lawrence Bower was convinced that there was a passable ford over the Trent near the Great Wilne ferry, but he was wrong. Even at accustomed fords, the unwary met hazards: slippery stones or sudden pits, hampering mud or 'quycsande', eel-beds or matted plants such as 'rayte', water-crowfoot. Most often the trouble was a current too strong for horse and rider or weary tramper on foot.

For those who wanted to keep their feet dry and did not have far to cross, pole-vaulting was an option. Snapping stakes brought disaster for John Tydde as he jumped the River Witham at Stoke Rochford, Lincolnshire, to check on his cattle; for Laurence Helme, an elderly labourer crossing the 'Tossett sike' at Slaidburn, Yorkshire; and for Robert Bakar as he tried to clear 'the parson's pond', short-cutting from the parish church at Croxton, Cambridgeshire to the rectory on Christmas Day 1521. The same fate almost met Henry VIII, leaping a ditch on a hawking trip in Hertfordshire in 1525, but he had a servant with him to pull his head out of the mud. Others tried to jump over streams without any aid but found they fell short or landed too heavily.

Where bridges, causeways and fords were impracticable the answer was a ferry. Many of the ferry sites where mishaps occurred were long established and some survived into the twentieth century. Those on the Wye included Bredwardine, Eaton Bishop and Monnington, those on the Adur Henfield and Shoreham. On the Trent, Barton ferry was well enough known that the jurors called it the 'Barton Boote', Dunham ferry that they spoke of 'the greit fery botte of Dunham'. Nearly all deaths came from sinkings, but at Beachley, where the Severn ferry ran to Aust, William Webber slipped on the stone wharf.

Drowned ferry passengers give us a snapshot of those on the move. One in three were female, wives and single women in roughly equal numbers. There were a few gentlemen, clerics and servants, and then roughly equal numbers of yeomen and husbandmen, of labourers, and of a wide range of craftsmen. Those on boats travelling along rivers were a similar mix. Some passengers were impatient. A crowd rushed the Littleborough ferry over the Trent at five in the afternoon on Saturday, 14 October 1564, maybe at the end of a hard week's work, and two men drowned when it sank.

Passengers' homes show catchment areas. Men on the Malton ferry lived on either side of the Derwent. West Tarring, Offington and Sompting were between four and seven miles west of the Shoreham ferry, but Rye was fifty miles to the east. The same combination of short- and long-distance travellers could be found on the Combwich ferry in Somerset: two men from Stockland Bristol, the next village, and one from Brompton Ralph, sixteen miles away on the far side of the Quantocks. Those caught up in the Wilton disaster came mostly from the western side of the Wye – Aconbury, Bridstow, Goodrich, Hentland, Llangarron, Pencoyd, Sellack and Much and Little Dewchurch – but also included a shoemaker from Much Marcle to the east.

Much travel was for trade. Local trade in small items was carried by pedlars with packs on their backs. A glimpse of their activities comes from the death of Jane Iron. She came from Bristol but died at Isleworth in Middlesex, strangled by the straps of her wicker basket as she sat down on a stile to rest on her alcohol-fuelled evening walk from Syon. The goods in her basket were worth £1 13s. 4d., a tidy sum. Other itinerant traders could afford a horse. Henry Manby, a pedlar of Eye in Suffolk, had two geldings, and Eustace David, a badger or itinerant dealer from Clifford, Herefordshire, drowned riding across the Wye. David John Baker, who came to grief mounting his horse loaded up with hampers full of hats at Newport, Monmouthshire, may have done a similar trade.

England's hundreds of markets were prime sites for commercial exchange. Two dozen of our travellers certainly met their end on the way to market to sell their produce or buy what they could not grow or make. They walked and rode in equal numbers. They headed for markets throughout the year and across the country, and a third of them were women. They were selling grain, wool and cloth, and buying grain and malt.

Many others moving goods were presumably heading for market or some more private sale in town. We find cartloads of barley heading into Gloucester and Thetford, cartloads of wheat into Cranbrook and Melton Mowbray, cartloads of malt out of Banbury, Northampton and Southwark, cartloads of beer around Horncastle, Hornchurch, Witham and Reigate. Some of the timber and firewood on carts and boats must have been intended for sale. John Herd fell off a pile of timber in a yard in Nottingham as he checked it before he bought.

Smaller quantities travelled on horses with packsaddles or panniers, apples into Taunton, butter into Norwich, beer at Bedford, cheese at Bury St Edmunds and Towcester. The smallest loads went on foot. Henry Geale was carrying a small sack of wheat on his shoulders, walking the three miles to market from Bower Hinton to South Petherton in Somerset, when he slipped into a flooded ditch and drowned, weighed down by the grain. Consumers took their cash into town and their purchases home. Elizabeth Chambers had 17s. 4d. in her purse as she walked from Blackhall to Carlisle. Robert Steyll fell off a footbridge on the way back to Redmain with the shoes he had bought in Cockermouth.

Fairs were more occasional but again we can catch people coming and going. Distances travelled were larger. Labourers might walk or ride a few miles to their local fair, but others would come up to fifty miles for a famous event, from St Johns by Worcester to the fair on the Cross Green at Shrewsbury, or from Halstead in Essex to the Stourbridge Fair at Cambridge, with a cart carrying 1,300 lb of hops worth a lucrative £19 10s.

Some more specialised dealers moved around to buy and sell. Henry Clerk was a poulterer. His home was Raunds in Northamptonshire, but he came off his horse when the strap holding his panniers full of eggs and doves broke between Royston, Cambridgeshire and Tempsford, Bedfordshire. James Forth was a fishmonger, carrying his wares on three horses from Loughborough through the Leicestershire countryside. His trade must have been like that of the mackerel seller from whom Anne Middelton went out to make a purchase at Hingham, Norfolk, leaving her infant daughter alone to fall into a pail of water. Robert Consborowe, a Cambridge fishmonger, and Thomas Hedyng were royal purveyors, sent out to buy pike for the king's household in the fens north of Cambridge around Hedyng's home at Benwick, only to capsize their boat. What business Roger Leese was travelling on when he fell from his horse at Lockington, Leicestershire, in December 1572 we do not know, but he had an impressive £4 15s. 11d. in his purse to accomplish it.

Waterways and roads interlocked to move bulky loads. Imported wine was carried in barrels up the Severn to Gloucester and onwards into Shropshire, where Edward Browne told his family rather optimistically that he would cross the river to join the wine boat's crew and make merry drinking their cargo with them. It made its way in carts from London into Hampshire and through Middlesex towards Coventry, where an ironmonger's order of two barrels of malmsey was valued at a mighty £8 13s. 4d. Salted or smoked sea fish went in barrels on boats up the Parrett to Bridgwater, up the Thames to Windsor, across the fens from King's Lynn, and on carts inland from the Norfolk and Sussex coasts. It must have been a seriously large fish that rolled off Henry Walytt's cart at Exton in Rutland wrapped in a canvas cloth, fell on top of him as he slept, and suffocated him. There was lead on the road between Henley and Thame, perhaps unloaded from a barge on the Thames, iron and salt on the Severn and the Parrett. Wharves, busy with carts and boats exchanging goods, saw accidents at Dartford, Newark and Rainham.

The most intriguing cargoes show the variety of shopping to be done in well-supplied towns. Richard Hynkeley was a husbandman of Ashby St Ledgers, Northamptonshire, whose cart crashed with his day's purchases at Coventry, forty-six timber spars and 500 hats. John Richerdson dropped a barrel of prunes on his leg while unloading a cart at Newark. George Haywarde fell out of a cart on the way from Stowmarket to Haughley, apparently carrying goods bought by his neighbours: 600 lb of iron, five measures of bay salt and white salt, a pair of wicker baskets, some barley meal and a barrel of red herrings. Most varied was the merchandise carried from Appledore by the cart of Stephen Sayer of Canterbury, gentleman, when it overturned at Chartham just outside the city. In total it was worth £4 18s. 4d. There was linen cloth, coarser cloth tilts or coverings, a roll of four mattresses and a pack of upholstery ware. There was a hamper of brass kettles, two hampers of pewter ware and a pack of small metal hardware. There was a bundle of plant lantern, which may have been rushlights, and a final hamper full of hats.

Equivalent glimpses of the rural economy can be seen in accounts of carts taking hay from one farm to another, or of grain, malt or peas carried to the mill. Sometimes we can see the role of individuals in transactions. Mary Brown was sent by her mother to sell butter to a neighbour, only to be attacked by a furious cow. Richard Adcok was sent five miles by his yeoman father to sell a calf. Ill and weak in 1559, a bad year for epidemics, he fell from his horse at the gate of a field.

The trades of villages and market towns were tied together into national networks on land and water. The growing dominance of London in those networks was evident in the Londoners who met accidents far from home: a merchant at Newcastle, a pewterer in Gloucestershire, a salter in Buckinghamshire. The long-distance packhorse trades of areas without good roads are not well represented among the accidents, but there are hints. Jurors identified as carriers Roger Bateman of Old Hutton, Westmorland, and Robert Sawod of Hipperholme, near Halifax, whose horses got into trouble on their travels. Elsewhere packhorses suffered mishaps in slippery winter weather. In January 1538, Robert Boche was at Staveley, Derbyshire, riding one horse carrying grain to which two others were tied. All of them toppled into the River Doe Lea from the High Bridge between Netherthorpe and Woodthorpe. In January 1579, Robert Radley, a carrier from Bradford, was at Nottingham, heading over the Trent for London with two horses loaded with packs. One fell off the causeway into the floods beneath and he drowned in his efforts to save it.

Most carriers operated with carts on routes connecting provincial towns to London. A Norwich carrier was taking Margaret Snyers and her little daughter Mary to the capital when they fell from the cart at Wymondham. Cambridge carriers overturned their carts in Jesus Lane and on the road into Suffolk. Carters carried loads for others whether formally identified as carriers or not. Heading into Wiltshire on the London–Marlborough highway were barrels of tar for a cloth-maker of Whaddon and hops for a customer at Devizes. Entering Castle Rising were deliveries for various townsfolk, including a barrel of goods of Thomas Garret the grocer. Routes were sufficiently predictable that it was possible to hitch a lift. In August 1543, a sixteen-year-old servant known only as John asked Edmund Skaterwhight if he could join him on his oxcart on the way to London, as he did not have the money to get there. Skaterwhight had set out from Chaddesden, Derbyshire, a journey of more than 120 miles. At Kelmarsh, between Market Harborough and Northampton, John fell from the cart. In London the carrying trade was in the hands of the carmen's company. Their members featured in accidents in Southwark and St Mildred Poultry with loads including leather, vinegar and the goods of the prosperous mercer and cloth exporter, Thomas Kytson.

Big rivers carried long-distance barge trade. On the Thames a passenger barge linked London to the deep-water port at Gravesend. It served both those setting off overseas, like the three passengers who drowned on the way to board their ship in 1581, and locals heading for the capital like Thomas Pygeon, a Northfleet husbandman who fell overboard in 1568. The upriver trade from London was managed by barge owners based in the riverside ports, men such as Edward Hill of Henley-on-Thames, John Ellis of Reading, William Merye and Edward Tyler of Bisham. On the Severn operated Thomas Nicolles of Bewdley, whose boat lost its steersman at Gloucester as it set off for Tewkesbury.

Confluences linked rivers into networks. We find a boat from Beccles, on the Waveney, travelling up the Bure from Great Yarmouth to Horning. River networks were linked in turn by the coasting trade that took Yarmouth ships into the Medway, Walberswick ships into the Thames, London ships to Dartmouth, and a Buckland ship back and forth between Portsmouth and Ryde, Isle of Wight. With that trade went sailors like Zander John of Fowey in Cornwall, who met his end at Combwich in Somerset, or the many who drowned on the Tyne.

Then as now the degree of individuals' mobility depended on their occupation, age and gender. Masons and carpenters went further than most farmers. Bargemen and pedlars ventured further still. Many women just went to market or mill, though not all, as Jane Iron reminds us. Though their journeys varied, people everywhere were on the move. Crossing water was always a challenge, though bridges, fords and ferries served their turn. Roads were not good despite noticeable efforts at improvement. We still of course find ourselves queuing for bridges or tunnels and complaining about potholes and traffic jams.

These troubles did not stop economic growth and integration. That integration, though it brought with it a domination by London that may not always have been welcome elsewhere, enabled different areas to specialise in the different kinds of agriculture or industry most suited to their resources. That in turn protected England against famine better than many neighbouring countries and laid the foundations for future commercial development.

Cropping and manufacture were tied to consumption in different ways that suited different products, different landscapes and different concentrations of population. There were fairs and markets, tramping pedlars and touring dealers. For transport, different operators deployed packhorses, barges and above all carts. Like the watermill or windmill, the cart was a good solution to the challenges of its time, harnessing animal power to the movement of heavy goods. But the complexities of that solution presented a heavy price.

# 15

# Carts and Wagons

Carts and wagons accounted for nearly one in six of our accidental deaths, a rather higher proportion than road-traffic deaths now. Carts posed some of the same problems as motor vehicles, but many that were distinctive. Cart accidents were commonest in the flatter counties with their more intensive agriculture and trade. One in five accidents south and east of a line from Dorset to Lincolnshire involved a cart. In Cumberland and Westmorland, it was fewer than one in twenty. Mishaps came all year but were far more frequent in the busy summer months. They struck throughout the daylight hours, in summer from four, five or six till nine, ten or eleven, but night-time driving was rare.

Almost anything that needed carrying was put on a cart, but some loads predominated. Wood came first, making up more than a third of all recorded loads, from firewood or brushwood to beams and trees. Next came the needs of farming. In from the fields came hay, straw and grain, out to the fields went dung and marl. One cart in ten was travelling empty. The remaining one journey in five carried a vast range of things. There were food and drink, building supplies, fuels and metalware. There were wool and leather, cloth and hats, and awkward objects like ploughshares.

The reports do not make it easy to tell how varied carts were. The dozen different Latin terms used were apparently interchangeable and were often given as synonyms for each other or indeed for the commonest English words, wain and cart. Fitzherbert's *Boke of Husbandrie* suggested that a cart was lighter than a wain and made of ash wood rather than oak, but the distinction is not clear from the reports. The other main choice Fitzherbert set out was whether to have wheels with iron tyres, or plain wooden wheels, shorter-lived but cheaper and better on soft ground. Jurors noted iron-bound wheels on at least one cart in five, shod carts as they called them, or iron-bound wains. Commoner were descriptions by purpose, sometimes with a regional inflection. One cart in three given an English name was a dung-cart, dung wain, dung putt or dung crib. Others were corn wains, coal carts or beer drays.

Some vehicles were distinctive. The 'hurryicary' driven by Edmund Geton in 1568, thirty years before the pamphleteer Thomas Nashe used 'hurrie currie' for Phaeton's speedy chariot, sounds flimsy, as does the 'little curey' driven by Katherine Palmer in 1582. Each was drawn by only one horse. Tumbrils were probably designed to tip, especially useful for manure; one was a 'tumbrell or mucke carte'. Wagons were few and late, appearing only from the 1570s, but presumably large. While they were sometimes specified as having four wheels rather than the standard two, they were no juggernauts. Their standard team seems to have been four horses and as well as challenging loads such as iron or millstones they carried wheat or hay.

Sleds, presumably without wheels, were rare and apparently for unwieldy cargo: a blacksmith's trough, a barrel full of water, stone in the Yorkshire Dales. Most exotic was the 'carroche' on display in Sussex in 1578, probably a newly fashionable coach. It was drawn by two horses yoked together to make them easier to manage. When whipped they went at a 'galluppe', so fast that the driver lost control and crashed into an oak tree. Worth four or five times more than a standard cart, it seems to have belonged to the earl of Northumberland.

Most cart owners were humbler, at least two-thirds of them husbandmen or yeomen. One cart in eight belonged to the gentry and behind them came widows and a wide array of artisans and traders. Clerics, labourers and professional carriers or carmen were well behind that. The values placed on these carts by jurors rose steadily with inflation but were never large. Usual valuations ranged from 3s. to £1, with 10s. or 13s. 4d. commonest, less than the average horse. The cart body counted for little, as the complex carpentry was all in the wheels; a single wheel might easily be reckoned at 6s. 8d. or 10s. The harness too could be as valuable as the body: in 1575 six horse collars, five pairs of traces and a saddle were counted at 10s.

Carts needed to be kept in repair. Households worked together to get them ready for action and already faced dangers. Unattached wheels were unwieldy. The props used to support dismantled carts slipped or broke. Others attempted running repairs to carts heavily packed. More complex equipment presented other risks. Thomas Thaccher fell off a frame for making wain wheels and Eston Filder got out of his depth among the cartwrights in Sir William Paulet's barn at Basing House, ignoring their instructions as he tried to use a machine for lifting heavy timbers, tipping over a cart, sliding off a beam and hitting his head.

Cart teams were diverse. Seven in ten used just horses, two in ten just oxen and one in ten a mixture of the two. Oxen increased in prominence towards the west, frequent from Cornwall and Somerset through the Welsh borders to the Lake Counties, locally significant from Devon through the Midlands to Yorkshire and in the Weald. Horses might be of all sorts, stallions, mares, or geldings, and cattle more varied still, mostly castrated – oxen, bullocks or steers – but also the occasional bull or heifer.

The commonest horse teams consisted of either one animal or four, though sets of two, three or five regularly appeared. Six-horse teams were rare and seven-horse teams rarer. In general team and cart belonged to the same owner, but not always. John Elett broke his neck falling from a small cart owned by Thomas Clarke, pulled by his own black mare and William Byng's white mare. Whereas horses usually drew in a line, one in front of the other, oxen operated yoked in pairs. Jurors spoke of a yoke of oxen, a plough of oxen or a couple of steers. Teams of two, four or six were equally common. Some numbered as many as eight and Withiel, Cornwall, in 1576 saw ten.

Classic combinations for mixed teams included one horse and four cattle, two and two, and two and four, but variety was rife. For maximum power on heavy loads, teams might feature one horse and eight oxen, two horses and eight oxen or four and four. One accident shows how such mixed teams operated. John Garland and his brother Richard were taking their father's empty cart to woodland at Wrotham in Kent in May 1577 with four mares and two steers. The mares were in front, Richard leading the foremost mare by a halter, while the steers were nearest the cart, yoked to the neb or cart-pole. Richard stopped the mares, but the steers kept pulling till the cart hit a tree, overturned, and landed on John.

Few men drove their own carts and they were almost all husbandmen. It was much commoner for a servant, labourer or adolescent son to drive on the owner's behalf, making up two-thirds of identifiable drivers. Husbandmen and yeomen came next, boys after that, and then women, mostly spinsters, one driver in thirty. Less explicit reports give us half as many individuals again who may have been driving. They amplify these numbers without fundamentally altering them, adding, for example, two possible gentlemen drivers and increasing the proportion of women.

The old and the young could find driving a challenge. Nicholas Hull ran himself over in his own back yard, trying to move his dung-cart out of the heat of the May sunshine, being unable, as the jurors put it, to control the wildness of his horse because of his frailty and old age. John Ellys was described at sixty-six as old and feeble when he fell, crossing in front of his cart. Three eleven-year-olds got into scrapes. Thomas Marshall, son of a husbandman of Clowne, Derbyshire, tangled his foot in a bramble bush in Scarcliffe Park driving his father's four oxen and a horse. He fell and the cart ran over his head. Something similar happened to Henry Tybson with a briar bush on Berkhamsted Frith in Hertfordshire. John Kigges paused too long to sort out his clothes after dismounting from a draught mare as the cart rolled up behind. At fourteen, Mary Hopkys drove six oxen to bring her father's dung wain in from the fields at Sibdon Carwood, Shropshire, but could not stop them pulling it onto a bank and overturning it on top of her.

Those setting out to drive were not without advice. One good source was Leonard Mascall's thorough chapter on 'the duetie of carters'. This dealt both with the preparation of cart and team and with hazards when 'advisedly traveling on thy waie'. The great majority of accidents can be checked against Mascall's recommendations to see how well he anticipated what went wrong.

Some cart accidents were so complex that it is hard to separate out the key issues. Hugh Byrd was riding with two companions in his empty cart, none of them steering, when the yoke of the oxen nearest the cart broke. One ox ran off, chased by one of Hugh's colleagues and followed at a run by the other oxen, still pulling the cart. It hit a tree root and fell over, breaking the rope of the iron bar attaching the oxen to the cart. Four more oxen were then free to go off, leaving one ox to pull the cart a short distance to a post. There it came apart and a falling Hugh was crushed against the post. Was the fundamental problem the oxen, the yoke and rope, the collapsing cart, the tree root, the post or the initial lack of steering? At least we can say that they each played some part in the tragedy.

Driving was certainly dangerous, drivers making up around half of all victims. If we add in probable passengers, the total proportion of fatalities looks close to the 70 per cent of all current road deaths suffered by motor vehicle occupants. Today 23 per cent of victims are pedestrians. Then, 12 per cent were pedestrians clearly unconnected to the cart, to which should be added some of those recorded as walking near carts, who cannot all have been drivers or assistants. But the shocking figures are those for children. Children who were mere bystanders or playing near carts made up 5 per cent of all casualties, five times the proportion today. Mascall did warn drivers to look out for 'children and beasts'. The modern picture is completed by 7 per cent of victims on bicycles, their equivalents perhaps the 1 per cent of sixteenth-century victims who met carts while riding horses and came off worst, struck by vehicles travelling at speed or thrown by frightened mounts.

Mascall's safety advice, then, was sorely needed. Before setting off, he recommended careful checks that all the elements of the cart were 'substantiall and strong'. He gave no instructions on assembling the cart and team, but things could certainly go awry. Horses and oxen being harnessed grew restive or handlers lost control of carts as they positioned them ready for the team. Cart bodies were detachable from axle and wheels, such that when one Kent yeoman arranged to borrow a pair of wheels from another, the labourer who collected them had to lift off a heavy cart body first. As he pulled the axle out from under the propped-up body, the prop slipped, jamming his head between cart and axle.

Mascall paid no attention to loading or unloading, but he was wrong. It featured in one accident in ten. Many loaders fell off carts. The problem was often a slip or break of the cart rope with which loads were tied down. At Ilchester, Somerset, in August 1584, for example, William Hodges, senior, was working with his servant Pancras Savage in a field called 'Footes Meade'. They were loading barley, and, as the jurors put it, tying a rope around it as is the habit of the countryside. They tied a knot in one end of the rope and fixed it to the cart. Then William stood on the ground and Pancras, presumably younger and more agile, on the cart. William threw the rope up onto the cart and they each pulled it tight, but the knot slipped off the cart and Pancras fell to the ground, breaking his neck. Similar accidents added other details – loaders pulling hard with both hands, or twisting ropes tight, or losing their balance reaching for dropped ropes – that show just why securing loads was so hazardous.

Trouble with loads continued once the cart was underway. Shed loads contributed to a further one in ten accidents, striking the decisive blow in a crash, piling on top of those who fell into water or just sliding off and hitting passers-by. The risk was increased by the habit of sitting or lying on top of the cargo. Sometimes this had a clear purpose. Philip Fosset sat on two barrels of cider to stop them coming off the cart. Sometimes it must just have been comfortable. Elizabeth Smyth was lying on sacks of malt, John Elett on sheaves of barley.

Drivers were severely at risk in all the three main categories of cart accident, falls from carts, being run over and overturning. Mascall warned sternly about the commonest problem of all: 'Thou shalt keepe thy cart always upright from overthrowing.' Carts were so unstable that more than one accident in three involved overturning. Some reports describe carts rolling over twice or even three times. Overturning was so common that several victims died trying to set carts back the right way up. Richard Baker was not even righting his own cart, but helping two other men stop theirs toppling on a muddy road at Leigh-on-Sea in Essex. The wind mentioned in a score of accidents can only have made things worse.

Falls from carts – one accident in seven – were more likely for drivers who sat on the cart to drive, while being run over – one accident in five – was a risk for those who walked alongside. The two driving positions appear to have been equally common and the choice must have depended on the situation. Sitting on empty carts was frequent, perhaps on the way back from an arduous trip. Sixteen-year-old Nicholas Nasshe was tired from walking when he sat on an empty cart at eight in the evening, driving the twenty miles from Uxbridge to Wendover, only to hit a post in the road at

Amersham. The wooden frame at the front of the cart, the forecop, was a favoured place to sit, but many drivers sat on the shafts. One slip from there and one was straight under the wheels. Some stood on the cart to drive, perhaps for better visibility when manoeuvring. John Prall was driving through a field gate, and John Pett down a bank between fields and highway. Richard Butterye even drove standing on top of his load of hedge wood. Climbing on or jumping off, especially in an emergency, was another risky moment.

Walking by the cart was probably safer in difficult terrain such as woodland but slips left one in peril. Stones and bushes were the commonest trip hazards, but John Carpenter fell over a wattle hurdle, Robert Sawer a molehill, and Philip Sell a tethered pig. John Pynfold got tangled up with his whip and Robert Many with his ox-goad. A final and less common option was to ride on one of the draught animals or an accompanying horse. Fallers tended to land in front of a moving cart, and riding on a draught horse sideways, in a womanly manner as the jurors put it, must have been especially precarious. Harness could tangle around those clambering onto a cart-horse. Benjamin Hanlestons clearly found the motion of the ox he rode too comforting, as he fell asleep and came off.

Mascall warned about other dangerous situations. Hills demanded careful balance: 'when thou goest downe a hill, dragge the cart behinde, and up a hill, weigh the cart before.' Going downhill, without brakes, was indeed lethal, and one accident in twelve involved a downward slope. Juries spoke of carts going hastily downhill or explained an accident by the 'steepenesse and downfall of the said place'. Reports explain in detail how drivers and their assistants tried to retain control but ended up flattened. Edmund Gellybrand held up the left side of a cart with his shoulder all the way down Blackheath Hill until he lost his footing on ice. John Bisshope and Thomas Mylenere likewise slowed descending carts from the front end and half a dozen others tried to hold on to the shafts. Richard Smyth hung on to the back in Mascall's approved fashion, pulling hard. He got crushed between the cart and the road-bank.

Management of the team was vital. On an icy slope outside Newbury, Henry Erly and John Nashe grabbed the front horse and that between the shafts, but to no avail as their workmate John Burton was run over. Robert Colle, trying to get a cartload of beer down a hill, unhitched all the horses but one for a steadier descent, while Gervase Adams went in front of the two oxen drawing his cart downhill to direct them. Both slipped. Going uphill was much safer, but carts could roll back and flatten those behind, or horses get restive taking the hill at a run or pausing before the climb.

Mascall listed other road hazards to watch out for: 'routs, holes, and dangerous waies . . . postes, and gates'. Ruts, potholes, ditches and pits were involved in one accident in every twenty, and gates, posts, walls and hedges in a similar number, either as carts crashed or as a driver or passer-by was crushed between cart and obstacle. Hillocks, dunghills, molehills and the ridges and furrows of ploughed fields played a part in almost as many mishaps, as did trees, stumps, roots and bushes. Worse even than holes in the ground were the banks lining many roads, prime sites for overturning. Carts that got stuck needed pulling and pushing back into position. Margaret Hastings was helping get a cart off an oak tree root at Knowle in Warwickshire when the axle broke and it fell on her. Water crossings were difficult too. One accident in fifty happened at a bridge or a ford, as carts slipped or turned over, or drivers left it too late to jump onto a moving cart and ended up in the river clutching a piece of the load.

Manoeuvring in the tight spaces around homesteads was hard. Victims were jammed against walls or gates or hit by toppling carts. Richard Watridge wrongly reckoned that he could run under a cart as it came out of a barn. Jane Oker was hit in the head by the yoke of a wain as she stood at a barn door. William Levell unloaded a cart inside his master's barn, fell on his way out and was run over before he could get up. Such domestic settings also produced the heart-rending accidents in which cart owners ran over their own children. Reversing was difficult even in the open. John Smyth and his servants got his cart stuck in mud, full of marshland hay. He took four of the five horses off the front, borrowed four more from Thomas Wykes and hitched the eight-strong team to the back to pull it out, but when he unhitched, the cart rolled towards a ditch and fell on one of his crew.

In contrast to today, collisions between vehicles were vanishingly rare, though they may have been commoner on the streets of big cities for which few reports survive. Victims of multi-vehicle accidents might be pedestrians knocked over by the horse on one cart and hit by the wheel of another, or cart occupants forced off the road while passing. Most often they were squeezed between two carts. We might expect this in busy places, but Thomas Broune and Helen Olfeild, crushed in Nottinghamshire and Yorkshire villages, were presumably just unlucky.

Mascall laid great emphasis on the care and close supervision of draught animals. The carter, he wrote, must 'have alwaies patience, in moderate using' of horses and 'see well to his horse in travelling'. In different situations, different parts of the team were key. To avoid hazards ahead, one must 'have an eie to the fore horse', the horse at the front of the team. In general, one must 'look wel to the body horse', the horse in the middle. But for close control one must 'be alwaies nigh unto the thiller', the horse between the shafts, 'with thy hand nigh his head: wherby thou maiest the better rule him uppon a sodaine'. The numbers bear out his wisdom. The forehorse and the body-horse or pin-horse played key parts in a few accidents each, but the thiller and its bovine equivalents, the top oxen, wain-head oxen or nebbers, in one accident in nine.

No doubt some owners blamed the thiller to save other horses from forfeiture. But it is hard to ignore detailed accounts of drivers whipping a thiller so hard that it ran off with the cart or kicked by a thiller angry at a jerking halter as a cart accelerated downhill. Thillers that slipped, fell or stepped backwards readily caused crashes. Nebbers drew oxcarts into tight corners, stumbled in fright as drivers jumped onto carts, or bore the brunt of excessive goading. Mascall was clear that whips should be used sparingly and carefully and where possible replaced with 'fierce words'. Yet excessive or ill-timed whipping or goading caused repeated trouble.

Carelessness was as problematic as brutality. Runaway carts hit passers-by, sometimes as they tried to stop the horses: Anne Hubberd at Bacton, Norfolk, Gladys ferch Thomas in the suburbs of Hereford, Grace Atkynson at the gates of Carlton-on-Trent. Laurence Savage strolled along chatting to his neighbour John Croft as he took his master's empty cart back to their village, letting the eight oxen find their own way until he suddenly decided to run to the head of the team and fell over. At least a dozen drivers fell asleep on the job, crashing their carts or falling off the front, several late at night, but others in broad afternoon. Bad driving – negligent, hasty or aggressive – was blamed for about one accident in thirty-five. There were a few drunk-drivers, the worst Griffin Bosworth and Richard Warde, who were too inebriated to climb onto a cart without falling off or to judge whether there was space to run between a moving cart and a gatepost. Others were unlucky in the things they took with them, knives, pitchforks or walking-staffs. Nicholas Jenckes's provision for his run delivering timber on a June morning must have seemed sensible as he lodged a bottle of drink between his knees. When the cart overturned crossing the River Avon, the bottle crushed his genitals to fatal, though lingering, effect.

Care for one's animals could be counterproductive. Alan Marsh drowned when he let his horses go through a stream rather than over a bridge so they could drink. Edmund Wood lost control of his cart when he unhitched most of the horses to let them eat, and John Browne came unstuck when he paused to give his tired team some hay. Draught animals suffered an impressive range of other distractions. Mascall warned about wandering animals: running dogs and noisy pigs were indeed blamed by jurors. Thomas Everenden's oxen and mare were infuriated by the biting of gadflies or 'bremps', and Henry Nicholson's oxen ran off in fright at a bee. Other teams found their loads of rumbling barrels or clanking pewter disturbing, the sound of their own harness chains or the crunching of broken tiles in the road. In the summer months some animals were driven mad by the heat or made so sluggish that their drivers beat them into sudden movement. Simon Buckmer overturned his father's cart when the stallion drawing it saw a mare in a roadside pasture and rushed uncontrollably towards her.

Mascall's pre-trip checks included detailed attention to the cart's woodwork. Wheels and axles were of obvious importance – for smooth running he recommended greasing with crushed snails – and they played a role in many accidents, as wheels fell off, axles broke or whole carts came apart. Mascall was also concerned for the various wooden frameworks that increased the cart's carrying capacity. They should be 'whole and sound and wel furnished', made from ash wood, holly or hazel. He mentioned the rathes or raves, the rails fixed to the cart sides; the shamble staves that hung over the shafts and the thiller; and the cart-ladder, a rack extending the cart at front, back or side.

All these terms and many more came up in the reports. There were further types of load-carrying frame: cops, floats and thripples. There were the forestall or front section, the summers or beams on which the floor planks rested, the thills, sometimes called limons or blades, and the swingle-tree or crossbar to which the traces were attached. Smaller but vital were the wooden pegs, tie pins or keys that held the different parts together and the staves or spindles that supported the rathes along the sides of the cart. The jurors called some elements by regional names, notably the ear-breed, used in Yorkshire, Nottinghamshire and Lincolnshire for a crossbeam. They called some by names it is now hard to decipher: what were the 'smartstaff' and the 'bulcloshyde'?

These wooden parts of the cart body were involved in one accident in ten. Sometimes they snapped at a vital moment. More often they struck the victim as the cart overturned or crashed. Here the rathes or rathe staves were commonest, causing penetrating or crushing wounds. Metalwork contributed to fewer mishaps, but in similar ways. Carts disintegrated as staples and pins broke or bent, those holding the wheels on the axle, those holding the axle to the body and those holding together the drawing gear. Hooks, nails, pins and rings caught on clothes and ripped flesh.

Lastly, Mascall recommended that the carter keep his harness 'whole and sound'. Harness trouble featured in few accidents, but it was varied. Horses fell or drivers lost control because of breaks in the harness around the thiller, variously called the tail-rope, the ridge-rope, the ridge-with, the ridge-tie, the back band, or the crupper of the cart saddle. Drivers fell when they pulled hard on the halter and it broke, or when they tangled themselves up in straps and strings. Oxen needed metal chains – one list of forfeitures for a mixed team included two 'iron teames' for the oxen and four 'trases' for the horses – and they too could break, as could the wooden yokes.

Carts and wagons were essential for farming and trade and were simple enough that a wide range of farmers and craftsmen could own them, but they killed regularly, just as cars and lorries do now. They were versatile in how they could be drawn and driven, what they could carry and where they could carry it. Fields and woodlands presented challenges that roads did not, but even on roads, uneven surfaces, steep banks and downward slopes regularly brought disaster.

As with farming handbooks, contemporary guides gave wide-ranging but not quite comprehensive advice about how to do things right and what could go wrong. Road hazards, driver error and mechanical failure were problems common to both sixteenth-century and modern technologies, though horses and oxen were more unpredictable than engines, cart loads harder to secure than those in car boots or inside vans, and carts much more prone to overturning than modern vehicles. The resulting accidents took a particularly hard toll of child bystanders, though of course as population increased there were many children around. So much could go wrong with land transport that water carriage was an attractive alternative; but it, too, had many dangers.

# 16

## Boats and Ships

Boats and ships generated about one in twenty of our accidents. Water transport was much more prominent in the sixteenth century than it is now and fish a more important part of diet, but the reports give us a less than perfect picture of boat use. Deaths out of sight of land, in sea fishing for example, were not recorded by county or borough coroners but by the lord admiral's officers if at all. Major ports were danger spots, but the only one for which we have many inquests is Newcastle. Of the maritime counties, some like Cornwall were slack in filing reports and others like Hampshire omitted their great seafaring centres. The big difference we can detect is between inland counties with major river arteries and those without. In the Midlands, the proportion of victims dying in boats in Herefordshire, Shropshire and Nottinghamshire, along the Wye,

Severn and Trent, was five times that in Leicestershire, Staffordshire or Rutland.

Accidents happened all year, as many in the winter months as June or July, though it may be that more people were on the water in the summer but that conditions were safer. The great majority of victims drowned, either falling out of boats or when boats sank or overturned. Capsizes produced the multiple deaths far commoner on the water than elsewhere: 583 reported victims perished in just 409 accidents.

Worst was the sinking of passenger ferries. Five men and women went down on the Conquest Lode at Yaxley in 1526, seven on the Derwent at Old Malton in 1570, eight on the Tern at Allscott in 1565. Ten died on the Wye at Bredwardine in 1532 and on the Tyne at Newcastle in 1577, twelve on the Trent at Drakelow in 1506 and on the Devon at Newark in 1510. It was possible to swim or scramble to safety. Sometimes the professionals got away – Robert Sydebothom of Nottingham, boatman, Robert Welshe of York, mariner, John Fortey of Maisemore, steersman – while some of their passengers drowned. To be fair, just as many fell in while rowing ferries leaving passengers unscathed. The James Meiricke who escaped the Wilton ferry disaster of 1580 may indeed have been the same James Meyricke who drowned crossing the Wye at Wilton in a small boat in 1599.

Accidents could happen on any body of water, but three-quarters of those recorded were on rivers, the great rivers dominating the toll. Between them the Tyne, the Trent, the Severn, the Wye and the Thames in the first rank, with the Ouse, the Avon, the Parrett and the Medway following behind, accounted for more than half of all victims. Lakes, ponds, broads and marshland drainage channels saw one accident in ten, the sea, harbours and creeks rather fewer.

Some of these distinctions, of course, are rather artificial. Many who fell into rivers did so in major harbours, Newcastle, Gravesend or Combwich. Many who fell into the sea within sight of land did so within the jurisdictional boundaries of a port town or a maritime county, but those boundaries might be contested. At Watchet, Somerset, in 1582, when a ship's boat was swamped by a harbour wave, there was no debate, but in 1584, when a ship hit a rock within the low watermark, a servant of the lord admiral seized parts of the wreckage. At Wivenhoe, Essex, in March 1578, when something went wrong lifting a mast out of a grounded ketch, it was business for the county coroner, but in September that year a mishap on the way back to port after taking on ballast was found to have happened just the wrong side of the maritime boundary of Essex, in the lord admiral's jurisdiction.

Boats came in many shapes and sizes. Six in ten of those involved in accidents were just called boats. At the opposite end of the scale, one in ten was a ship. Mere boats could be valued very cheaply, especially if in poor condition: 4*d*. for a battered boat on Windermere in 1537, 12*d*. for a bad boat on the same lake in 1571. More often they were thought worth between 2*s*. and 10*s*. More valuable boats, used as ferries or for freight, might reach £1 or more.

Ships were rarely valued in inquests, but one was put at £30 and fragments of others – a mast, or a sail and some hatches – could be as valuable as a substantial boat. Ships had multiple masts and sails. Thomas Yonger was knocked overboard by a blow from the foresail sheet and John Alford hit in the forehead as a hawser tied to the foremast whipped in the wind. They had structures unnecessary in smaller craft, like the 'byttacle', the binnacle or compass-box, from which John a See fell as his ship sailed from London to Whitstable. They had smaller boats, skiffs or cockboats, to attend on them. Ships had names. Saints, though hard to tell from family names, were popular: the *Christopher of Yarmouth*, the *Katherine of Hull*, the *Margaret of Walberswick*. At Newcastle in 1527 and 1567 there were ships called the *Jesus*. Home ports were vital to distinguish the *John of Bridport* and the *John of Buckland* from the *John of London* and the *John of Wells*.

Other names came from the natural world or perhaps from heraldry: the *Primrose of Harwich*, the *Lion of Haarlem*, the *Sparrowhawk*.

For freight transport on rivers and in harbours there were large, flat-bottomed, sail-powered craft. Most generic were barges and lighters: one jury pronounced that a 'barche' might be called 'a greate lighter'. Others were locally specific. On the Severn, the Wye, the Usk and the Ebbw there were trows, used for transport but also for fishing. On the Tyne, for the coal trade, but also on the Ouse, the Wensum and the Yare, there were keels. On the Thames there were western barges. Together all these played a part in one accident in nine. A sense of their bulk comes from their value, often £5, £8 or £10, and the accidents that occurred on them. Thomas Maborne was hit by the falling mast of a western barge at Egham, Edward Merye blown off the wale of one near Windsor. Western barges even had names: the *Benjamin*, the *Thomas of Reading*, the *Samuel of Burnham*.

Similar in size and value, between ships and boats, were a range of sailing vessels for coastal and river work: ketches, hoys, barks, cobles, picards and woodbusses. Some had names, like the Medway hoys the *Swallow* and the *New John of Maidstone*. Some had smaller boats to service them. Other craft were distinguished by purpose, as ferry boats or fishing boats. On some rivers there were stock boats, probably dug out from a single log or stock. There were punts on the Thames and similar flat-bottomed carr boats on the East Yorkshire marshes. Around London there were wherries for passenger transport. On the Wye there was the occasional 'cruckle bote' or 'crocke', perhaps a Welsh coracle of wickerwork and hide.

The reports can make it hard to tell the difference between the owner of a boat before its accident and a custodian after salvage. As with carts, the owners might be more prosperous than the operators. John Gardiner, merchant of Woodbridge, owned *The Unicorn*, and William Truslowe, a yeoman of

Aylesford, Kent, owned the wood-barge worked by three of his servants on the Medway. On the other hand, many boats were owned by those who worked them: fishermen, watermen, shipwrights or bargemen. Ferry boats presumably belonged to those who leased the ferry rights from landowners. Other boats were attached to mills, used for access, maintaining dams, or servicing fish-weirs. Consortia might own bigger craft: two bargemen of Bisham, two mariners of Wivenhoe, even three owners spread around the Bristol Channel, at Watchet, Mumbles and Burton Ferry.

Those operating boats had a clearer professional identity than most of those working with carts. Sailors, watermen, bargemen, fishermen and shipwrights made up more than a quarter of all boat accident victims whose status is known. Ships' boys like Peter Jacobson of Middelburg or John Nonnyngton of Alverstoke by Portsmouth were starting a career cut short. Shipboard camaraderie can be glimpsed in the last minutes of John Awstine at Bridport Mouth, Dorset on 24 April 1582. He was a sailor from Bothenhampton, the village between Bridport and the harbour. On a small ship of twenty tons, barely afloat in six feet of water, he climbed the mast with 'a garland'. This may have been a garland of flowers to celebrate a successful voyage but was more likely a metal hoop or ring of rope designed to strengthen the mast or protect the rigging. He paused just beyond the middle of the topmast. It was not clear to his shipmates whether he was exhausted or taken by drink, but they asked him repeatedly to climb back down. Determined to reach the top, he turned around, lost his grip and fell into the sea.

Boat-handling skills were not a trade secret. Yeomen, husbandmen, labourers and clergymen wielded oars or poles, and Jane Byrde and Alice Phillippis operated a boat together on the River Thame at Cuddesdon, Oxfordshire. Ferry boats attached by a rope to posts on either bank were presumably easier to work than those that required more steering. Elizabeth Cooke, who tried to pull the Conisbrough ferry boat to her bank using a crook, or Stephen West, who swam over the stream to fetch a ferry near Sandwich, must have thought they could cope. But jurors did ascribe the deaths of some boaters to their lack of skill or carelessness.

Boat journeys had various purposes. As many as one in three were ferry crossings or longer passenger trips and one in eight for fishing. A quarter were for goods transport. Wood was commonest, as on carts, then other bulky items. One trip in six was for longer-distance trade, overseas or coasting. There was also the sheer pleasure of messing about in boats. At Cuckfield, Sussex in 1583, John Dye and Anne Umfry got into a small boat on a pond to enjoy the water, thought the jurors. In 1579, at Walthamstow in Essex, eighteen-year-old Stephen Sparke was playing in a boat on a pond by the house of Thomas Browne, esquire. He reached out a hand to Browne's son to join him in the boat, but lost his balance, fell in and drowned.

Sailing was usual at sea but also common on inland waters and larger rivers. Unfortunate sailors missed their hold when reaching for ropes or found them rotten or loose. One fell to his death as he climbed to the topcastle because the 'toppecastell rope' was so large that he could not keep a grip on it. Lowering sail was especially perilous. As his ship headed for its moorings at Harwich in September 1570, John Harryson was ordered by the master's mate to climb up and remove the main topsail from its yard. He fell to the deck clutching the sail and died at once. In the Solent in January 1572 Thomas Gimlett was blown into the sea as he tried to reef the mainsail in a storm. Masts were heavy and awkward and dangerous when they fell. Different challenges came from the speed of a well-trimmed vessel. James Wakering climbed out of his freshly ballasted ship into a boat, but drowned as the ship sailed so fast that the boat was dragged underwater.

One victim in eight was rowing, poling or steering. Rowing with one oar or two was common in smaller craft. Many lost their balance as an oar broke, caught in the water, or snagged on the bottom, as they leant hard on the oar to steer – juries called the oars in such accidents rothers or rudders, the 'sterne oare' or 'the sturringe oare' – or as they stretched to retrieve an oar dropped and floating away. Others had trouble with the oar fixings, as a tholepin fell off or a rowing-pin broke. Standing to use a single oar could be unstable, especially from the thwarts of a rowing boat or the highest part of a barge. The jolt from a broken rudder could throw even those sitting in the stern overboard. Trouble with oars could end in a sinking. Heading up the Ouse towards York in January 1580, Richard Hall's oar broke and he bent to pull it out of the river. He fell in, John Winterburne and Robert Beckwith scrambled to help, the boat turned over and all three drowned.

In shallower waters, poles were frequent, and jurors had many names for them. There were bargepoles, bumkins and quants, rowing-poles and boat-staffs. Some ended in hooks: hook-shafts, shaft-hooks, hook-poles, water-hooks. They were useful for propulsion and steering, to manoeuvre other vessels or to test the depth of the water. The classic mishap among student punters today, a pole that sticks in the muddy bottom as the boat glides onwards, was seen not only on the Thames, but also in the fens and the Kent marshes. Other poles slipped on the bank, snapped, missed the bottom, were caught by the current or were used in vain to vault from a sinking boat.

Some boats were drawn from the bank. Four men were pulling a barge at Walton-on-Thames when Clement Eller, left on board to steer, fell off. William Bilton used a rope to draw Thomas Colly in his fishing boat past the mouth of a millstream, but Thomas too slipped while steering. Horses drew barges on the Thames and the Ouse. Pulling their boat down the River Wharfe with a mare worked well for Thomas Welden and Robert Bekwit until they had to cross to the other bank at Ryther. Thomas led her onto the boat, but she knocked him out into the river and fell on top of him. More complex arrangements deployed small boats to tow larger ones.

Different stages of the journey presented their own dangers. Launching from land could be awkward. Lewis Gebon broke his leg on a lever that he and his neighbours were using to shift Tomos ap Rhys's boat into the River Rhymney. Loading or unloading, especially from one boat to another, risked overbalancing. Bystanders could be at risk. Alice Luter was washing her legs from a slipway on the Gloucester quayside when two hoopers and a sailor from Gatcombe docked their boat and set up a plank so they could roll their barrels of wine onto the quay. When she would not move out of the way, they said 'Avise ther uppon thyne own perill' and rolled the first barrel. It broke the plank and hit Alice under the right ear.

Overloading was a recurrent problem. An uneven load could be just as bad, as William and Gabriel Burton found when they piled more bundles of wood on one side of their boat than the other. Live cargo could be troublesome. Commonest were horses accompanying their riders on ferry trips – John Burton, a Kent yeoman, even stayed mounted on his bay mare for a roll-on roll-off journey – but culprits included the fifty-eight sheep who all ran to one side of the boat on their way across the Sussex Ouse, and the ox that decided to leap out of the Tamar ferry near Saltash. Sometimes the animal was not to blame. Poling his master's boat recklessly, Richard Bean hit a mare on the head. The mare fell out and the boat capsized.

Gangplanks could be slippery but alternative means of disembarking riskier yet. Thomas Deddewt jumped out of a boat holding a chain, presumably to moor it, but the current dragging on the chain pulled him in. John Gray leapt out into the water, but the boat came up behind him and pushed him under. Christopher Hudson, with the confidence of his eighteen years, jumped off a boat in a hurry to go home, but missed his hold on the bank. Simon Coven slipped on the gunwale and fell between ship and boat as he followed his shipmates into a cockboat. Boarding was as bad, as boats slipped away, or boarders fell from lowered masts onto riverside mud.

Perils continued as craft began to move. Boats wobbled when pushed off and further out wind and current played a role. Wind or storm was mentioned in one in six boat accidents, currents, whirlpools or tides in one in twelve. Winds rocked boats, drove them onto sandbanks, filled them with water, whipped up ropes. Squalls struck on rivers and lakes as well as the open sea. Currents complicated balance or steering, dragged boats off to dangerous reaches, or jammed victims in the water between boat and bank. Tides stranded ships, like the one John Grout was trying to dig out of the sand in Weymouth harbour when it fell on him.

Obstacles were another problem. Boats hit floating timber, posts in the water or waterside trees. Midwinter ice floes caused capsizes on the Wye, the Trent and the Yorkshire Ouse. Bridges and locks were worrisome too. Boats crashed into bridges at Hereford, Newport and Windsor, on the Trent at Swarkestone and the Parrett at St Michael's Borough in Lyng. John Hodgies fell in trying to fend off his boat from the western bridge over the Severn at Gloucester. Flash locks on the Thames enabled boats to pass mill-weirs or other impasses, but they were dangerous. The rush of water when Goring Lock was opened sank a boat in 1591. No wonder Richard Fruen was so afraid of taking his boat through Mapledurham Lock that he tried to jump out. To pass upstream, boats had to be dragged over the weir. Richard Webbe, a Reading bargeman, was doing just that to a western barge at 'Cotterells Locke', the lock by Shiplake Mills, on the morning of 30 October 1578. As he and his fellows strained on the rope, his feet slipped, and he fell in.

Traffic was probably more congested on rivers than on roads. Thomas Wylson was in a boat run down by a fast-sailing keel at Great Yarmouth, Richard Harryson in a punt on the Thames overrun by a barge. Sometimes we even know what warnings were shouted. When Robert Kember continued chasing ducks in a punt as a barge bore down on him, the bargemen called out 'Sway whether wyllt thow, kepe the from the barge', but Robert was oblivious.

Journey's end must have been a relief, but anchorages had their dangers. Manoeuvring in small boats to get bigger ships moored in choppy West Country harbours cost the lives of several sailors. The weight of the anchor he was dropping at Woodbridge in Suffolk pulled James Benecrofte overboard, and in a ketch at Acaster Selby on the Ouse William Hewet got the anchor rope tangled round his leg as he threw it out. Storms were a threat even in harbour. John Potter fell in at Hull fending off his ship from the horse stair when a storm blew up from the south. So was crowding. John Jacobs was crushed when another ship moored on the Tyne was forced against his by the rising tide. Safe arrival should have been a chance to consider the state of one's vessel but all too many boats were left in ill repair. One in twenty involved in an accident was described as old or damaged and at times the jurors were more eloquent: battered and full of holes, ruinous and weakened by many holes, old, decayed and full of cracks.

The needs of inland, coasting and overseas trade made plenty of work on boats. Fishing for food and ferries for travel added more. The role of the great rivers as arteries of commerce – coal down the Tyne to Newcastle, grain down the Thames to London and so on – made them prime sites for mishaps. The variety of craft developed for different needs and different waters met their purposes well, but loading, propulsion and steering could each go wrong. Rowing, poling and sailing, drawing by hand or horse all required specific skills and often put the boater in an exposed position if anything malfunctioned. Rivers and lakes – troubled by currents, winds and unstable banks and bottoms – lacked the predictability of the canal age to come, and the open sea posed many greater threats. Small boats could be dangerously unstable, especially with live cargo, and large boats and ships dangerously complex. Those who sail today are familiar with many of these issues and grateful for their lifejackets and their training courses.

Inevitably most deaths involving boats were drownings, but drownings from boats formed only around a seventh of all the drownings in our inquests. That should prompt us to think again about why certain forms of accident were so common among fatalities and why the injuries incurred in those accidents proved fatal. We should turn our eyes away from ways of living and concentrate on ways of dying.

# 17

# Ways of Dying

The main point of the coroners' inquests was to find out how people came to their deaths. We have been using their reports to find out about people's lives, but they can also tell us what was fatal under sixteenth-century conditions. Some events that killed then would likely kill now: a mauling by a bear, a bullet through the head. But there were others we are far less likely to face, or which might end with a trip to hospital or a course of antibiotics. And categories that might look familiar were in practice different.

Now around a third of accidental deaths result from falls. If we exclude drownings the figure is very similar for the sixteenth century. But we mostly fall downstairs or trip on carpets, and they fell from horses, carts and trees. Though any calculation is shaky, the rates of accidental death in our coroners' reports do not look wildly different from those recorded now. But many deaths now recorded as accidents, such as accidental poisonings or kerbside trips among the elderly, would scarcely have attracted the attention of a Tudor coroner and some of the things they counted as accidents, such as stabbings in violent confrontations, would be unlikely to count now.

Even for those comparisons we can make, the reports are not perfect evidence. Juries were meticulous in recording visible wounds, giving their dimensions down to a fraction of an inch, down to the breadth of a penny or the length of a barley grain. Some counted more than twenty separate cuts. Yet jurors viewing a corpse could have little idea of internal injuries. Different juries, moreover, recorded what may have been similar events in very varied terms. How much difference was there really between being killed by a fall, being killed by the dizziness that caused the fall, being killed by having a battered body sustained in the fall, and being killed by the broken left arm, or three broken ribs, or badly bruised buttocks that were the most visible result?

Sometimes juries were more specific but still, to our minds, mysterious, because their explanations are hard to translate into our terms. One fall killed a man instantly because it knocked all the breath out of his body, while another victim died three days afterwards because the fall caused his blood to coagulate. One man worked so hard and sweatily that, when exposed to cold immediately afterwards, his intestines and internal organs were affected by exhaustion and illness, so that he died eleven days later.

There are special issues with the time of death. For accidents where the event causing the fatal injury and the resulting death were clearly separable, reporting could be precise: one could die immediately upon falling and hitting one's head, or fall and hit one's head and die two hours, or two days, later. Other kinds of fatality were different. Few deaths by drowning were said to be instant because one either drowned or one did not. The same went for suffocation. Some injuries were so obviously catastrophic – bodies crushed, suffocated and burnt, or multiply wounded with the skull broken in various places – that it seemed needless to explain that they caused immediate death. Death by exposure was not often assigned a specific time, as it was not clear at what point of a cold night or a bitter storm the victim had succumbed. The result is that an approximate time of death is known for the great majority of straightforward injuries, but far fewer for categories like these.

It is hard to map the inquests' causes of death onto modern classifications such as the International Classification of Diseases (ICD-10) with its hundreds of finely distinguished forms of injury. Did William Pigge, struck in the neck and killed instantly by a piece of timber falling from an overturning cart, succumb to one of ICD-10's S11.0–S11.9, different varieties of open neck wound, or S12.0–S12.9, a neck broken at different points, or perhaps S17.0, a crushing injury of the larynx and trachea; or maybe even to I46.1, a sudden cardiac arrest? And in any case, should we count as the underlying cause of his death, as many modern mortality statistics would, not the injury, but the accident in which it was incurred, perhaps under code V80.0, as an occupant injured by a fall from an animal-drawn vehicle in a non-collision accident?

Despite these reservations, we can learn much from the ways of dying described in the reports. Drownings made up by far the largest category, at a proportion more than twenty times what it is today in England, though some African and Asian countries have drowning rates five or ten times ours and in some ways closer to the Tudor experience. Drowning was a characteristically female death: 60 per cent of women's accidental deaths came by drowning and only 38 per cent of men's. Travel, work and recreation took men and women to the open water in the landscape, but domestic tasks took women especially often to ponds, wells or streams. If they fell in, their long skirts and shifts of rapidly waterlogged wool and linen must have been terribly hampering.

Jurors understood the mechanics of drowning. They explained how water went into the mouth and nostrils and stopped the victim's breath. Sometimes they recounted how a victim was knocked unconscious by a blow on the head or struggled to get out but was too weak. A few juries added what they called relaxation of mind, perhaps a recognition of the shock of falling into cold water. Jurors also explained drowning's social dynamics, that people drowned for lack of help: no one there or, occasionally, no one bold enough to try. And they had an idea of how long it took to drown, saying that a victim was in the water for a quarter of an hour or half an hour before they were found dead.

Head injuries, still prominent among fatalities today, produced the next largest category after drowning, one death in six. Contemporaries recognised the importance of the brain, seen as the seat of the soul, the animal spirits and the five wits or faculties. Juries mentioned the brain often, especially to account for instant death. They talked of how cartwheels struck a man's head such that his brain fell out of his skull, of how machinery crushed a woman's head so that her brains were scattered all over the mill, of brains penetrated by sharp impacts or forced out through noses or ears. They explained how a blow to the forehead deprived one victim's body of its spirit and how a head-first fall from a mare left another with 'her animall spyryttes or facultys' stupefied.

More likely to kill instantly than head wounds were broken necks, mostly incurred in falls. Almost as fast, but rarer, were broken backs and the multiple injuries caused by being dragged over rough ground. Neck and throat wounds could be dangerous even where the jurors did not report a broken neck, given the risks to arteries and windpipe. Another large category bringing a comparatively quick end, one death in nine, comprised the crushing and bruising injuries caused by collapsing trees and buildings, trampling animals and runaway carts.

Presumably many such deaths were caused by internal injuries, but damage to internal organs was rarely identified. The spleen, the bladder and the lungs were each mentioned once, while the one broken 'bludbuk' might have been the liver or the spleen. The kidneys came up sometimes and the entrails or intestines more often still, crushed or ruptured, wounded such that excrement flowed out through the hole, or falling out of the bellies of those gored by animals. Most prominent was the heart, penetrated by deep wounds or hit by blows to the chest. Medical books treated it as the 'seat of life' where the 'spirit of life' was generated. Jurors knew its importance.

Jurors also emphasised blood, just as medical works, for which blood was one of the four humours governing the body's operation, stressed the role of blood loss in death. In head wounds and broken necks, they noted blood coming from the ears, mouth and nose. Blood was also important in explaining how peripheral wounds could kill. Arm and hand wounds, for example, caused few deaths, as they still do today. They also caused them slowly. Two-thirds of victims took two or more days to die, even after a major trauma, like John Pilgreme who lasted twenty-four days after his left arm was pulled off in a watermill. Recalling blood loss when a wound was fresh helped make sense of what happened when death came later.

Leg, hip and foot injuries caused many more deaths than those to arms, as they do now, and more of them were instant. The speed was due in part to the large arteries that might be severed in the thigh, where at least one in five fatal leg wounds fell. Juries sometimes identified wounds to a principal blood vessel, one of them flowing unstoppably from ten in the morning till five in the afternoon. Some victims bled so freely that death was instant. Others lasted an hour or two but expired by great effusion of blood.

Common injuries that are hard to classify in modern terms were generic falls and blows, cases of multiple injury where especially vulnerable parts were not mentioned, and a range of injuries to the chest, back or abdomen. Jurors reached for familiar terms in describing some of them, for spirits stunned, a battered body, blood accumulating in the belly after a kick in the back from a horse. Most victims died fast, but some suffered long before they succumbed, William Burre lasting nearly eleven months with his crushed back. Slower to kill even than arm wounds were wounds to the genital area. A few women were gored by bulls or fell awkwardly onto stakes, but six times as many victims were men. Some lingered for two weeks, three or even four.

Burns and scalds were horribly slow-acting. Only a quarter of victims died at once, one in five later the same day, another quarter the next day and the remainder later still. At least one in three victims was under the age of seven, and small children are still very vulnerable to fire and hot liquids. Occasional juries felt the need to spell out the effects of immersion in boiling water, great sores all over the body or skin peeling off, or to add that fire victims were burnt to ashes. Poisoning, though rarer, acted more slowly but likewise dispatched some sufferers at each stage. Jurors made intermittent mention of swollen bodies or copious vomiting.

Though fatal infection after injury was not much understood, jurors perhaps gave indications of it. Several delayed deaths from leg injuries were attributed jointly to the leg wound and to a fever and some victims were described as gravely ill between accident and death. After Nicholas Dyckenson caught his left hand in a mill, it swelled up so that his heart was affected and he died eleven days later. Thomas Hatche died from illness, shock and pain in his leg fourteen days after he broke it. John Palmer was thrown by a young gelding on 20 March, crushing his chest and upper back; he languished until 15 June, recovered partly and then languished again until 10 July, when he died.

Jurors knew the signs of impending death from normal deathbeds. One was speechlessness. Two men with head injuries could not speak between accident and death, while a woman struck to the ground by a tree branch died without speaking a word. A man crushed in a windmill lasted three days, first without vital breath and later without use of his tongue. An alternative state of moribundity was paralysis. One man was paralysed for five days with a wound an inch deep between upper lip and left eye. Accounts of exposure sometimes enumerated its physical symptoms, a numbing of all parts, a weakness in the heart, an inability to get up after lying down.

What happened in the aftermath of an accident depended on the state of the victim and who else was there. Children were more likely to be the target of search parties, whereas most adults were found by those who had no identifiable connection to them, though they may have been workmates or neighbours. Complete lack of connection was most likely in river drownings, where bodies could be washed downstream and found days or weeks after death. Corpses needed to be recovered for the inquest process, if needs be with a grapnel from the bottom of a well or with the help of neighbours from an ice-covered pond, but those still alive might be rescued or cured.

Fellow-bathers or bystanders regularly tried to help those in trouble in the water. Sometimes they lost their own lives in the process: William Chivall going after his daughter, Laurence Aborne after his sister, Margaret Earle trying to stop her mother from drowning herself. Sometimes the rescuer survived, but the rescue failed. Thomas Chadwycke and his servants arrived too late to get Richard Christian out of a well. Lord Bergavenny's well-fed under-cook Ambrose Johannes proved too heavy to manhandle out of the water.

Some rescues seemed for a time to have been successful. Richard Gatys, a seventy-year-old shepherd, fell asleep by a well, slid in and was dragged out spluttering. Thomas Stalybrasse's wife and servant managed, together with John Kynges who had heard their cries for help, to haul him out of a pond. Quick-thinking Alice Doo used an iron hook to fish out Helen Munder, and others were pulled to the bank after being swept down river. But each of these expired after some hours.

Scalded children were rescued in vain as they screamed, and so was little Richard Geslyng after an hour in a tanning pit. The most stomach-turning of such fates befell Anthony Layfelld, a labourer from Huby in Yorkshire. On 27 May 1586, at four in the afternoon, he was unloading firewood from a cart in the yard by the house of Thomas Clarke, husbandman, at Sutton-on-the-Forest. As he finished, he jumped down to the bank of a pond full of mud and 'stinkinge watter', presumably a slurry pit, only to collapse and fall in. Thomas ran over, pulled him out and put him to bed. All that night he was vomiting up putrid water and mud. Next day he got up and went home, but there too he continued to retch until he died at 7 a.m. on 1 June.

Many victims of falls and crushes were taken away in the hope of recovery. Extracting them from their situation could be difficult. It took three men to get John Longe out from under a cartload of timber and carry him off to his master's house. Time was of the essence. One set of rescuers used a cart, another a sled, but details are often sketchy. Roughly equal numbers went back to their home parish or stayed on to expire near the accident site. Fewer head-injury patients were moved than others, though the differences are small.

We can be more specific in some five dozen cases. The great majority died either in their own home, in that of their parents, or in that of their master or mistress. In some instances that was the accident site, in others the obvious place for recovery. John Holyns, a Yorkshire yeoman, fell out of his armchair with a palsy and hit his head on a stone. His servants carried him to his bed and he died there three hours later. John Barett, a Suffolk clergyman, was gored by a bull in a pasture and carried by his neighbours to his rectory, where he died after four days.

Sometimes parents could not get children home but did reach them before they died. Henry Butcher lay for two hours in the field where he had been thrown by a horse and kicked in the head, but at least his mother was there, having arrived shortly after his fall. Thomas Knight's father found him alive when he fell out of a cart at Bracebridge just south of Lincoln and broke his neck. He took him not back to their home in Doddington, but to Thomas Burgh's house nearby, where he died three hours later.

Good masters and mistresses made provision for injured servants. John Pemble junior, servant of a Kent yeoman, was kicked in the head by a horse in his master's stables and died a fortnight later in his master's house. Robert Beckett, servant of a Kent tailor, fell off a horse on the road and died at his master's house six days later. Temporary employers sometimes felt the same duty. Hugh Sandwich died in the house of Ralph Fynche, esquire, after he was injured ploughing Fynche's fields. Morris ap John died at Edstaston Hall, Shropshire, the home of George Maynwaringe, gentleman, the day after he fell off a ladder daubing the walls there. Other worthies took in those for whose accidents they might feel some responsibility. Joan Manvell was attacked at Launceston in Cornwall by a cow belonging to Thomas Hicke, gentleman. She languished at Hicke's house for four days before she died.

There are some signs of a wider expectation that the gentry and clergy take a lead. William Dawtrey, esquire, of More House at Petworth, Sussex, and William Nycholson, rector of Barming in Kent, hosted local victims. Others who took in the injured may have been good neighbours or may have offered hospitality or nursing on a commercial basis. We know too little of William Rutkyn of Morcott, Rutland, husbandman, of Thomas Crannefeilde of Shefford, Bedfordshire, or of Thomas Barton alias Pyp, butcher of Shrewsbury, to be sure.

Wherever victims were, they seem to have been faithfully watched. Their times of death are often given to the nearest hour, or as falling between two times, between ten and eleven in the morning, for instance, between five and six in the evening, or even between midnight and 1 a.m., as though they were being attended. The hours or days of languishing gave time to reflect on life, to receive the last rites or to make a will. That brought them closer to the deathbed experience of the far larger number of their contemporaries who died in less dramatic ways, from plague and influenza, from dysentery and respiratory disease, from old age and the many afflictions of childhood. Many of that group would have suffered accidents but survived – as the pole-vaulting Henry VIII did – while a few no doubt breezed through sixteenth-century life without mishap.

Like those around their deathbeds, we too have been watching the victims. Their enormous variety, in age, rank, residence and occupation, and the variety of their passage from daily life to sudden death, make their stories a marvellous source of insight into Tudor life. To us, their England looks familiar in some ways and strange in others. Its landscapes are recognisable but the centrality of agriculture in the economy and the predominance of rural over urban population made variations in terrain a bigger determinant of daily life than they are for us. We can spot streets and buildings we know among its townscapes, but we might not last long there without an eye for excitable livestock and open tannery pits.

Their bodies were subject to a comparable range of disabilities, diseases and injuries to ours, and they took steps to maintain their health, but they lacked some of our most vital remedies and their strategies for keeping well, notably bathing in open water when unable to swim, entailed risks we would generally avoid. Our sports test skill, speed, strength and stamina in rather safer ways, and the end of legal animal baiting has saved human as well as animal lives.

Their two-generation households in family homes make sense to us, but the proliferation of servants seems odd. The practicalities of timber-framed and thatched householding, the constant fetching of water, riverside laundry and home brewing would challenge us, but then so do our own domestic arrangements, which kill more of us than road accidents. We have not, for example, improved much on their experience with ladders, which still account for a few dozen of us each year. Their young and their old were vulnerable as ours are, sometimes in the same ways – the toddler by the pond, the old person on the stairs – but sometimes differently.

The basics of agriculture have not changed – fertilising, ploughing and planting, harvest and storage, feeding livestock, milking cows, shearing sheep – but the technology or patterns of work to complete them are for the most part profoundly different. Most of us have far less to do with trees than they did and while inland fishing and horse-riding have changed less than most of our interactions with the animal world, they are now more about leisure than livelihood. We still have to calculate how a cow and a calf will react to a dog, but usually in the context of a weekend ramble rather than everyday work. The dangers of extractive industries and powerful machinery still demand respect, but few of us now dig anything more alarming than garden soil, and the peculiar perils of mills powered by wind and water with wooden gearing are behind us.

They had to be careful with travel and transport as we do, but their technologies were heavily dependent on the horse and the ox. Some features of their vehicles would alarm us, if, for example, we had to take a cart downhill with no brakes. So would some of their traffic situations, watching more carefully for small children asleep by the roadway or for collapsing maypoles than for collisions with other vehicles. Sailing and rowing have changed rather less, though fifty-eight sheep on a ferry boat might be problem enough for the most expert boater.

Their England was changing over the Tudor century and those changes affected how people died. Some changes had a direct impact. There were more mishaps with guns, more forge-hammers and blast-furnaces, more labourers in areas where big farming advanced and more accidents in enclosed fields, more paupers on the roads. Other developments showed up more tangentially. Economic integration diversified farming regimes and their associated repertoire of accidents, put more barges on rivers and more carts and packhorses on the roads. Urban growth filled towns with scaffolding and building supplies and overcrowded the bulging suburbs.

The Reformation changed what happened at church on Sundays, brought in clerical wives and children, modified the built environment with the Dissolution of the Monasteries, and accelerated changes in literacy and education. A growth in governance was evident in the regulation of vagrancy, the organisation of road-mending and the parliamentary provision for Wilton bridge. It blended with a longer-term but ongoing consolidation of the legal system and of popular participation in it, seen both in the inquest process and in arrests and imprisonments.

Are we fooling ourselves if we think we have got to know some of the unchronicled people of the Tudor past? It partly depends how we weigh up the strengths and weaknesses of the inquest reports. They were formal documents, undoubtedly shaped by legal and social dynamics, yet their accounts had to be plausible to sceptical contemporaries. The victims and their neighbours are only a dozen generations away from us, though on the far side of an industrial revolution, the rise and fall of empires, two world wars and a cold war, the coming of mass democracy and welfare states. Yet the little touches of human detail in the reports seem to draw them near: Christopher Conyers and his reading glasses, Barbara Reder reaching out for her husband's arm, Thomas Beettes heading home as he began to feel tipsy, even the teenage spat between Alice Bennett and John Onley. We feel we have met people quite like Richard Browne the officious watchman or William Hall the comedy ram-rider. Accidents at places we can still visit give us another kind of connection to them, to the prisoners in the dungeon of Colchester Castle, to Thomas Newlandes keeping watch on the walls at Carlisle, to Robert Michell peering up at the Sherborne Abbey vault.

The reports also show that sixteenth-century people met the challenges of their world resourcefully. They looked for ways to do things safely. Sometimes their thinking makes obvious sense: reaping in a staggered line, steering a falling tree with a rope, replacing a muddy pond with a draw-well or a well with a pump. Sometimes we have to trust that it made sense to them. At present carrying heavy or awkward loads on the head is more widely seen in other parts of the world than in England, but it clearly worked in Tudor times, especially for women. Playing football with a knife at one's belt looks alarming to us, but with ill-defined pitches and teams, where was one supposed to leave one's knife safely, and if one went back to a pile of similar knives, how was one to be quite sure which was one's own and which someone else's? And might picking up the wrong one start a quarrel? Tying a horse or cow halter round one's arm or chest goes against all current advice, but as a child servant left in charge of a strong, wilful and valuable animal, what else was one to do?

It is also tempting to see things through the eyes of the jurors, to share their pity for babies in unsafe homes and for friends who drowned trying to save one another, if not their disapproval of young servants who ran away from overbearing masters. We can relate, perhaps with some surprise, to their search for practical explanations, their apparent disinclination, for example, to blame misfortune on witchcraft, and we can appreciate their attempts to use the science of their day, whether humoral theory or astrology or the animal spirits of the brain. Then again, the jurors were middle-aged men, husbands and fathers, somewhere in the middle of the social pyramid of their day, so some of us might imagine ourselves more naturally than others on the jury alongside them.

Probably all but the most patient of us can share those jurors' exasperation with grown men and women who should have known better. Surely John Dowe was unwise to try to pass water without dismounting from his horse. Couldn't Joan Hammon have been more careful not to drop her shears on her son? How on earth could Thomas Pert shoot himself in the head with a longbow? What was John Cheeseman thinking of, dancing drunkenly in that heaving crowd with his grievous hernia?

Yet most of us have taken short-cuts of some sort, like Edward Hall jumping on the millrace floodgate, or Robert Bakar polevaulting across the parson's pond, or all those who scraped away just a little more sand or marl in an overhanging pit. We know the urge to be helpful even when it may not be prudent, like those who tried to catch runaway cart-horses or fiddled with a neighbour's malfunctioning gun or jumped in after swimmers in trouble. We can often recall split-second miscalculations or failures to spot risk. For one of us it led to falling off a chair balanced on a chancel step while trying to photograph a Tudor tomb, for the other to flying off the front of a bike going fast downhill through a gate that was narrower than the handlebars. Maybe looking at our predecessors tells us more about ourselves than we expect.

Let us turn back to our victims and their accidents one last time. Once it was evident that they were dead, the coroner was called in. He arrived and the jurors assembled. Together coroner and jury began to open that window through which we have been peering so intently at them, their neighbours and their world. Now it is time to leave them to bury their dead in peace.

# *Acknowledgements*

We must begin by thanking the Economic and Social Research Council and the taxpayers whose money it spends for funding the main four years of research on this project. In a different way we are indebted to those inspiring historians who have worked on coroners' inquests in the past, whose work we describe in the bibliography. Additional research funding was provided by Merton College, Oxford, and the development of an interactive map of accidents was supported by the Digital Scholarship at Oxford scheme. We are grateful to Merton and to Wolfson Colleges and our colleagues and students there and in the History Faculty for providing a supportive environment for research and teaching.

Such a wide topic cannot be tackled without the help of many colleagues. We have benefited from the wise comments of Paul Cavill, Martin Ingram, Samuel Johnson, Stephen Mileson, Margaret Pelling and Phil Withington, who read sections of the book in draft, and in particular from the heroic assistance of Ian Archer and Jacquie Gunn, who read the whole book, sometimes in multiple versions. For other advice and references we are grateful to Brianne Dolce, Alex Gajda, Dorian Gerhold, Steve Hindle, Jenni Hyde, Angela McShane, Shannon McSheffrey, Robert Peberdy, Simon Stevenson and Lucy Wooding.

Since we began work on this subject we have presented our findings at dozens of Historical Association, local history and history festival groups and research seminars. The participants' questions and comments have shaped our thinking again and again. For encouraging and facilitating the public dissemination of our research we owe special thanks to Victoria McGuinness and others at TORCH, the Oxford Research Centre for the Humanities. At John Murray, Joe Zigmond and Siam Hatzaw have been supportive and insightful editors. Lastly and above all we should thank our families for all their sustaining love and encouragement.

*Illustration Sources*

Chapter 1: Michael Coignet, *Abraham Ortelius his epitome of the Theater of the worlde* (London, 1603) / Alamy Stock Photo.
Chapter 2: Anon., *The cryes of London*, late 16th century (detail).
Chapter 3: John Fitzherbert, *The boke of surueyeng and of improume(n)tes* (London, 1523) / Alamy Stock Photo.
Chapter 4: Stephen Batman, *A christall glasse of christian reformation* (London, 1569) / British Library Archive / Bridgeman Images.
Chapter 5: Anon., *Tenor of the whole psalmes in foure partes* (London, 1563) / Alamy Stock Photo.
Chapter 6: Antoine de La Sale, *The fyftene joyes of maryage* (London, 1509) / Alamy Stock Photo.
Chapter 7: Ranulf Higden et al., *Chronicles of England* (London 1510) (detail) / Alamy Stock Photo.
Chapter 8: Edmund Spenser, *The Shepheardes Calender* (London, 1579) / Alamy Stock Photo.
Chapter 9: Anon., *The ordenarye for all faythfull Chrystia(n)s to leade a virtuous and Godly lyfe herein this vale of miserie* (London, 1548).
Chapter 10: George Gascoigne, *The noble arte of venerie or hunting* (London, 1575) / Alamy Stock Photo.
Chapter 11: William Gilbert, *De Magnete* (London, 1600) / Alamy Stock Photo.
Chapter 12: William Kempe, *Kemps nine daies wonder, performed in a daunce from London to Norwich* (London, 1600) / Alamy Stock Photo.
Chapter 13: Anon., *A students lamentation* (London, 1595).

Chapter 14: Georg Braun and Franz Hogenberg, *Civitates Orbis Terrarum*, 6 vols (Cologne, 1593-1618), v (detail) / Alamy Stock Photo.

Chapter 15: Thomas Harman, *A Caueat or Warening for Commen Cvrsetors* (London, 1567) / Alamy Stock Photo.

Chapter 16: *Civitas Londinum* (detail), also known as the 'Agas' map of London, early 1560s / Alamy Stock Photo.

Chapter 17: Geffrey Whitney, *A Choice Of Emblemes, and Other Devises* (Leiden, 1586).

# Bibliography

## General

The inquest reports we have used, found in The National Archives (TNA) classes KB8 and KB9, contain rich detail about many individual accidents that we could not include here. We aim to deposit all this data in a simple but robust format so that it can be useful both to local and family historians and to those who want to use it to ask new questions about Tudor life in general. It should in due course be available under the title 'Sixteenth-century English accident inquests' both from the UK Data Service (https://ukdataservice.ac.uk/) and the Oxford University Research Archive (https://ora.ox.ac.uk/). County inquest reports expertly edited by R. F. Hunnisett include *Calendar of Nottinghamshire Coroners' Inquests 1485–1558*, Thoroton Society Record Series 25 (Nottingham, 1969), *Sussex Coroners' Inquests 1485–1558*, Sussex Record Society 79 (Lewes, 1985) and *Sussex Coroners' Inquests, 1559–1603* (London, 1996).

Reference works, read both online and in hard copy, have been invaluable in making sense of the reports. Our fundamental dictionaries have been the *Dictionary of Medieval Latin from British Sources*, the *Oxford English Dictionary*, the *English Dialect Dictionary* and the *Middle English Compendium*. For dates, we have used C. R. Cheney, *Handbook of Dates for Students of English History* (multiple editions, London, 1945–2000). To identify well-known individuals, we have used the *Oxford Dictionary of National Biography*, *History of Parliament: The House of Commons 1509–1558*, ed. S. T.

Bindoff, 3 vols (London, 1982), *The House of Commons 1558–1603*, ed. P. W. Hasler, 3 vols (London, 1981) and, for lawyers, J. H. Baker, *The Men of Court 1440 to 1550: A Prosopography of the Inns of Court and Chancery and the Courts of Law*, 2 vols, Selden Society supplementary series 18 (London, 2012). Acts of Parliament are cited from *Statutes of the Realm*, ed. A. Luders et al., 12 vols (London, 1810–18). To identify places, we have been dependent on Frederic A. Youngs, *Guide to the Local Administrative Units of England. Vol. I, Southern England; Vol. II, Northern England* (London, 1979–91) and the publications of the English Place-Name Society. For local context, the many volumes of the Victoria County History have been endlessly enlightening. The practicalities of everyday life are set in their material context in *The Oxford Handbook of Later Medieval Archaeology in Britain*, ed. Christopher Gerrard and Alejandra Gutierrez (Oxford, 2018), the outlines of society and culture well presented in *A Social History of England, 1500–1750*, ed. Keith Wrightson (Cambridge, 2017), long-term economic trends quantified in S. N. Broadberry, B. M. S. Campbell, Alexander Klein, Mark Overton and Bas van Leeuwen, *British Economic Growth, 1270–1870* (Cambridge, 2015) and the law brilliantly analysed in J. H. Baker, *The Oxford History of the Laws of England. Vol. VI, 1483–1558* (Oxford, 2003). What follows is not an exhaustive bibliography, but a list of works we have found particularly useful or from which we have drawn points of comparison or analysis. Many are of course relevant to several overlapping chapters but appear only once.

Inquest reports have been used by previous scholars and we are much indebted to their example. Barbara Hanawalt notably used them to explore the lives of medieval peasants in *The Ties That Bound: Peasant Families in Medieval England* (New York and Oxford, 1986). The Towners deployed them for comparative studies in public health: E. Towner and J. Towner, 'Developing the History of Unintentional Injury: The Use of Coroners' Records in Early Modern England', *Injury Prevention*, 6 (2000), 102–5; eidem, 'The Hazards of Daily Life: An Historical Perspective on Adult

Unintentional Injuries', *Journal of Epidemiology and Community Health*, 62 (2008), 952–6. Several scholars have investigated suicide through them, Michael MacDonald and Terence Murphy on a broad through canvas (*Sleepless Souls: Suicide in Early Modern England* (Oxford, 1990)), and Simon Stevenson in detailed local context ('Social and Economic Contributions to the Pattern of "Suicide" in South-East England, 1530–1590', *Continuity and Change*, 2 (1987), 225–62). Others again have used them to look at murder: K. J. Kesselring, *Making Murder Public: Homicide in Early Modern England, 1480–1680* (Oxford, 2019) and J. A. Sharpe and J. R. Dickinson, 'Revisiting the "Violence We Have Lost": Homicide in Seventeenth-Century Cheshire', *English Historical Review*, 131 (2016), 293–323. For an investigation of accidents and the light they shed on economy and society using a different source, the London bills of mortality, see Craig Spence, *Accidents and Violent Death in Early Modern London 1650–1750* (Woodbridge, 2016).

## Chapter 1: Another Tudor England

T. R. Forbes, 'London Coroner's Inquests for 1590', *Journal of the History of Medicine and Allied Sciences*, 28 (1973), 376–86; E. A. Wrigley, 'Rickman Revisited: The Population Growth Rates of English Counties in the Early Modern Period', *Economic History Review*, n.s. 62 (2009), 711–35; E. E. Rich, 'The Population of Elizabethan England', *Economic History Review*, n.s. 2 (1950), 247–65. Cheshire inquest reports can be found in TNA, CHES24/71–106 and contain material similar to that for other counties, as do the Welsh coroners' reports preserved in series such as *Montgomeryshire Court of Great Sessions: Calendar of Criminal Proceedings 1541–1570*, ed. Murray Chapman (Aberystwyth, 2004), while Admiralty inquests in TNA, HCA1/78–81 appear on preliminary examination to be unsurprisingly dominated by drownings.

## Chapter 2: All Sorts of People

E. A. Wrigley and Roger Schofield, *The Population History of England, 1541–1871: A Reconstruction* (London, 1981); Alexandra Shepard, *Accounting for Oneself: Worth, Status, and the Social Order in Early Modern England* (Oxford, 2015); Cordelia Beattie, *Medieval Single Women: The Politics of Social Classification in Late Medieval England* (Oxford, 2007); Amy M. Froide, *Never Married: Singlewomen in Early Modern England* (Oxford, 2005); Julian Cornwall, 'The Early Tudor Gentry', *Economic History Review*, n.s. 17 (1965), 456–71; A. J. Tawney and R. H. Tawney, 'An Occupational Census of the Seventeenth Century', *Economic History Review*, 5 (1934), 25–64; E. P. Taylor, 'The Representations of Millers, Tailors, and Weavers in Popular Print, c. 1500 to c. 1700', Exeter University PhD thesis, 2016; Leigh Shaw-Taylor, 'The Rise of Agrarian Capitalism and the Decline of Family Farming in England', *Economic History Review*, n.s. 65 (2012), 26–60; Paul Glennie and Nigel Thrift, *Shaping the Day: A History of Timekeeping in England and Wales 1300–1800* (Oxford, 2009); W. Mark Ormrod, Bart Lambert and Jonathan Mackman, *Immigrant England, 1300–1550* (Manchester, 2018); Marcel F. Backhouse, 'The Strangers at Work in Sandwich: Native Envy of an Industrious Minority 1561–1603', *Immigrants & Minorities: Historical Studies in Ethnicity, Migration and Diaspora*, 10 (1991), 70–99; Miranda Kaufmann, *Black Tudors: The Untold Story* (London, 2017); Scott Smith-Bannister, *Names and Naming Patterns in England, 1538–1700* (Oxford, 1997). For Cambridge student drownings, see http://venn.lib.cam.ac.uk/Documents/acad/2018/search-2018.html, searched 24/4/2020; for Thomas Egglesfeld's and William Bryswood's pardons, *Letters and Papers, Foreign and Domestic, of the Reign of Henry VIII*, ed. J. S. Brewer et al., 23 vols in 38 (London, 1862–1932), I, i. 1083 (49), XIII, i. 190 (36); for John Lyes's pardon, *Calendar of Patent Rolls 39 Elizabeth I (1596–1597): C66/1458–1476*, ed. Simon R. Neal and Christine Leighton, 2 vols, List and Index Society 322–3 (2008), i.

859; for James Poke's and William Ridge's wills, West Sussex Record Office, Chichester, Archdeaconry of Lewes wills, Book A7, fos. 101v–102r and Book A8, fo. 323v; for Robert Elwood and William Staveley's wills, Borthwick Institute, York, Probate Register 16, fos. 73v–74r and Probate Register 27, fos. 232r–3r; for John Glanvile, Edward Foss, *The Judges of England*, 9 vols (London 1848–64), v. 494–6.

## Chapter 3: At the Coroner's Court

R. F. Hunnisett, *The Medieval Coroner* (Cambridge, 1961); Matthew Lockwood, *The Conquest of Death: Violence and the Birth of the Modern English State* (New Haven and London, 2017); S. J. Stevenson, 'The Rise of Suicide Verdicts in South-East England, 1530–1590: the Legal Process', *Continuity and Change*, 2 (1987), 37–75; Sara M. Butler, 'Degrees of Culpability: Suicide Verdicts, Mercy, and the Jury in Medieval England', *Journal of Medieval and Early Modern Studies*, 36 (2006), 263–90; J. A. Sharpe and J. R. Dickinson, 'Coroners' Inquests in an English County, 1600–1800: A Preliminary Survey', *Northern History*, 48 (2011), 253–69; Carrie Smith, 'Medieval Coroners' Rolls: Legal Fiction or Historical Fact', in *Courts, Counties and the Capital in the Later Middle Ages*, ed. D. E. S. Dunn (Stroud, 1996), 93–115; Steve Hindle, '"Bleedinge Afreshe"? The Affray and Murder at Nantwich, 19 December 1572', in *The Extraordinary and the Everyday in Early Modern England; Essays in Celebration of the Work of Bernard Capp*, ed. A. McShane and G. Walker (Basingstoke, 2010), 224–45; James McComish, 'Defining Boundaries: Law, Justice, and Community in Sixteenth-Century England', in *Legalism: Community and Justice*, ed. Fernanda Pirie and Judith Scheele (Oxford, 2014), 125–50; R. A. Houston, *Punishing the Dead? Suicide, Lordship, and Community in Britain, 1500–1830* (Oxford, 2010); idem, 'What did the Royal Almoner do in Britain and Ireland, c.1450–1700?', *English Historical Review*, 125 (2010), 279–313; Carol Loar, '"Under Felt Hats and Worsted

Stockings": The Uses of Conscience in Early Modern English Coroners' Inquests', *The Sixteenth Century Journal*, 41 (2010), 393–414; eadem, 'Conflict and the Courts: Common Law, Star Chamber, Coroners' Inquests, and the King's Almoner in Early Modern England', *Proceedings of the South Carolina Historical Association* (2005), 49–60; eadem, 'Medical Knowledge and the Early Modern English Coroner's Inquest', *Social History of Medicine*, 23 (2010), 475–91; Anthony Fitzherbert, *In this booke is contayned the offices of sheryffes, bailliffes of liberties, escheatours constables and coroners & sheweth what euery one of them maye do by vertue of theyr offices, drawen out of bokes of the comon lawe & of the statutes* (London, 1538); Thomas Smith, *De republica Anglorum* (London, 1583); Alan Hassell Smith, *County and Court: Government and Politics in Norfolk, 1558–1603* (Oxford, 1974); Diarmaid MacCulloch, *Suffolk and the Tudors: Politics and Religion in an English County, 1500–1600* (Oxford, 1986); R. Somerville, *A History of the Duchy of Lancaster, I, 1265–1603* (London, 1953); Steven Gunn and Tomasz Gromelski, 'Coroners' Inquest Juries in Sixteenth-Century England', *Continuity and Change*, 37 (2022), 365–88; Anna Pervukhin, 'Deodands: A Study in the Creation of Common Law Rules', *American Journal of Legal History*, 47 (2005), 237–56; Teresa Sutton, 'The Nature of the Early Law of Deodand', *Cambrian Law Review*, 30 (1999), 9–20; Mark Overton, 'Prices from Probate Inventories', in *When Death Do Us Part: Understanding and Interpreting the Probate Records of Early Modern England*, ed. Tom Arkell, Nesta Evans and Nigel Goose (Oxford, 2000), 120–41; Michael Witmore, *Culture of Accidents: Unexpected Knowledges in Early Modern England* (Stanford, CA, 2001); Barbara Spackman, 'Machiavelli and Gender', in *The Cambridge Companion to Machiavelli*, ed. John M. Najemy (Cambridge, 2010), 223–38; Alexandra Walsham, *Providence in Early Modern England* (Oxford, 2001); *The workes of Geffray Chaucer newly printed* (London, 1532); William Lyndwood, *Constitutions prouincialles, and of Otho, and Octhobone, translated in to Englyshe* (London, 1534); Eamon Duffy, *The Stripping of the Altars: Traditional Religion in England, 1400–1580*, 2nd edn (New Haven CT, 2005); *The Great Chronicle of London*, ed.

A. H. Thomas and I. D. Thornley (London, 1938); *The Customs of London, otherwise called Arnold's Chronicle*, ed. F. Douce (London, 1811); *The Diary of Henry Machyn, Citizen and Merchant-taylor of London, from A.D. 1550 to A.D. 1563*, ed. J. G. Nichols, Camden Society o.s. 42 (London, 1848); *Three Fifteenth-Century Chronicles: with Historical Memoranda by John Stowe, the Antiquary, and Contemporary Notes of Occurrences written by him in the reign of Queen Elizabeth*, ed. James Gairdner, Camden Society n.s. 28 (London, 1880); John Rastell, *Exposiciones terminorum legum anglorum* (London, 1523); K. J. Kesselring, *Mercy and Authority in the Tudor State* (Cambridge, 2003); Laura Gowing, 'Secret Births and Infanticide in Seventeenth-Century England', *Past and Present*, 156 (1997), 87–115; K. J. Kesselring, 'Bodies of Evidence: Sex and Murder (or Gender and Homicide) in Early Modern England, c.1500–1680', *Gender and History*, 27 (2015), 245–62; *Proceedings in the Parliaments of Elizabeth I*, ed. T. E. Hartley, 3 vols (Leicester, 1981-95); Simonds d'Ewes, *The Journals of All the Parliaments During the Reign of Queen Elizabeth* (London, 1682); C. S. Knighton, 'The Reformed Chapter, 1540–1660 ', in *Faith and Fabric: A History of Rochester Cathedral 604–1994*, ed. Nigel Yates (Woodbridge, 1996), 57–76; John Field, *A godly exhortation, by occasion of the late iudgement of God, shewed at Parris-garden* (London, 1583). Witness depositions from an investigation into a jury are in TNA, KB9/694/18 and evidence from Exeter civic records of cash redemption of a deodand is at Devon History Centre, EAB1/2, fo. 52r. Inquests used here which do not appear in our dataset because not found to be accidents include TNA, KB9/617b/121, 641a/172, 644a/271, 644a/323, 644a/324, 652b/326, 656a/149, 657a/114, 657a/158, 665a/134, 665a/135, 665b/225, 670a/143, 675a/148, 675a/156, 673a/80, 1021/1/43, 1036a/81, 1063b/198.

## Chapter 4: In Sickness and in Health

*Health, Medicine and Mortality in the Sixteenth Century*, ed. Charles Webster (Cambridge, 1979); Mary J. Dobson, *Contours of Death and Disease in Early Modern England* (Cambridge, 1997); Elis Gruffudd, 'The "Enterprises" of Paris and Boulogne, 1544', ed. M. B. Davies, *Fouad I University Bulletin of Faculty of Arts*, 11 (1949), 37–95; Alanna Skuse, *Constructions of Cancer in Early Modern England: Ravenous Natures* (Basingstoke, 2015); Louise Hill-Curth, *English Almanacs, Astrology and Popular Medicine, 1550–1700* (Manchester, 2007); Thomas Moulton, *This is the myrour or glasse of helth necessary and nedefull for euery person to loke in, that wyll kepe theyr body from the syckenes of the pestylence: and it sheweth howe the planettes raygne, in euery hour of the daye and the nyght: with the natures and exposicions of the .xii. sygnes, deuided by the .xii. monthes of the yere. And sheweth the remedyes for manye diuers infyrmytes and diseases, that hurteth the body of man* (London, 1531); Wendy J. Turner, *Care and Custody of the Mentally Ill, Incompetent and Disabled in Medieval England* (Turnhout, 2013); Linda Pollock, *With Faith and Physic: The Life of a Tudor Gentlewoman, Lady Grace Mildmay 1552–1620* (London, 1993); Margaret McGlynn, 'Idiots, Lunatics and the Royal Prerogative in Early Tudor England', *Journal of Legal History*, 26 (2005), 1–24; Margaret Pelling, *The Common Lot: Sickness, Medical Occupations and the Urban Poor in Early Modern England* (Harlow, 1998); Isla Fay, *Health and the City: Disease, Environment and Government in Norwich, 1200–1575* (Woodbridge, 2015); Andrew Wear, *Knowledge and Practice in English Medicine, 1550–1680* (Cambridge, 2000); Andrew Boorde, *The breuiarie of health vvherin doth folow, remedies, for all maner of sicknesses & diseases, the which may be in man or woman* (London, 1587 edn); Georges Vigarello, *Concepts of Cleanliness: Changing Attitudes in France since the Middle Ages* (Cambridge, 1998); Nicholas Orme, *Early British Swimming, 55 BC–AD 1719. With the First Swimming Treatise in English 1595* (Exeter, 1983); William Langham, *The garden of health conteyning the sundry rare and hidden vertues and properties of all kindes of simples and plants, together with the maner how they are to be vsed and applyed in medicine for the health of mans body, against diuers diseases and infirmities most common amongst men* (London, 1597). For French Weir, Taunton, see http://www.thisisthewestcountry.co.uk/news/14602317.Fond_farewell__Gazette_readers_share_their_memories_of_learning_to_swim_at_St_James_Pool/, consulted 20/7/2022.

## Chapter 5: Families and Households

Jane Whittle and Mark Hailwood, 'The Gender Division of Labour in Early Modern England', *Economic History Review*, n.s. 73 (2020), 3–32; Charmian Mansell, 'The Variety of Women's Experiences as Servants in England (1548–1649): Evidence from Church Court Depositions', *Continuity and Change*, 33 (2018), 315–38; *The booke of common prayer, and administracion of the sacramentes, and other rites and ceremonies in the Churche of England* (London, 1559). Alice Sherwood's inquest is at TNA, KB9/657a/114.

## Chapter 6: Houses and Homes

Matthew Johnson, *English Houses 1300–1800: Vernacular Architecture, Social Life* (Harlow, 2010); Malcolm Airs, *The Tudor and Jacobean Country House: A Building History* (Stroud, 1995); Chris Skidmore, *Death and the Virgin: Elizabeth, Dudley and the Mysterious Fate of Amy Robsart* (London, 2010); Tara Hamling and Catherine Richardson, *A Day at Home in Early Modern England: Material Culture and Domestic Life, 1500–1700* (New Haven CT and London, 2017); Craig Muldrew, *Food, Energy and the Creation of Industriousness: Work and Material Culture in Agrarian England, 1550–1780* (Cambridge, 2011).

## Chapter 7: Townscapes

*The Cambridge Urban History of Britain, Vol. I: 600–1540*, ed. D. M. Palliser (Cambridge, 2000); *The Cambridge Urban History of Britain, Vol. II: 1540–1840*, ed. Peter Clark (Cambridge, 2000); *The English Urban Landscape*, ed. Philip Waller (Oxford, 2000); Martha Carlin, *Medieval Southwark* (London, 1996); Jeremy Boulton, *Neighbourhood and Society: A London Suburb in the Seventeenth Century* (Cambridge, 1987); M. A. Katritzky, '"A Plague o' These Pickle Herring": From London Drinkers to European Stage Clown', in *Renaissance Shakespeare / Shakespeare Renaissances: Proceedings of the Ninth World Shakespeare Congress*, ed. Martin Procházka, Andreas Höfele, Hanna Scolnicov and Michael Dobson (Newark DE, 2013), 149–51; C. P. Graves and D. H. Heslop, *Newcastle upon Tyne, the Eye of the North: An Archaeological Assessment* (Oxford, 2013); *Newcastle and Gateshead before 1700*, ed. Diana Newton and A. J. Pollard (Chichester, 2009); Richard Welford, *History of Newcastle and Gateshead*, 3 vols (London, 1885); C. M. Fraser, 'The Early Hostmen of Newcastle upon Tyne', *Archaeologia Aeliana*, 5th series, 12 (1984), 169–79; Gwendolynn Heley, *The Material Culture of the Tradesmen of Newcastle upon Tyne 1545–1642: The Durham Probate Record Evidence*, British Archaeological Reports British Series 497 (Oxford, 2009); J. R. H. Moorman, *The Grey Friars in Cambridge* (Cambridge, 1952); Mark S. R. Jenner, 'From Conduit Community to Commercial Network? Water in London, 1500–1725', in *Londinopolis: Essays in the Cultural and Social History of Early Modern London*, ed. P. Griffiths and M. S. R. Jenner (Manchester and New York, 2000), 250–72; Thomas Almeroth-Williams, *City of Beasts: How Animals Shaped Georgian London* (Manchester, 2019); Emily Cockayne, *Hubbub: Filth, Noise, and Stench in England, 1600–1770* (New Haven CT and London, 2007); John Rhodes, 'The Severn Flood-Plain at Gloucester in the Medieval and Early Modern Periods', *Transactions of the Bristol and Gloucestershire Archaeological Society*, 124 (2006), 9–36; J. F. Merritt, *The Social World of Early*

*Modern Westminster: Abbey, Court and Community, 1525–1640* (Manchester, 2005).

## Chapter 8: Landscapes

*Rural England: An Illustrated History of the Landscape* ed. Joan Thirsk (Oxford, 2000); Oliver Rackham, *The History of the Countryside* (London, 1986); Francis Pryor, *The Making of the British Landscape: How We Have Transformed the Land, from Prehistory to Today* (London, 2010); *The Agrarian History of England and Wales, Volume IV, 1500–1640*, ed. Joan Thirsk (Cambridge, 1967); Angus Winchester, *The Harvest of the Hills: Rural Life in Northern England and the Scottish Borders, 1400–1700* (Edinburgh, 2000); Joan Thirsk, *English Peasant Farming: The Agrarian History of Lincolnshire from Tudor to Recent Times* (London, 1957); John Leland, *The Itinerary of John Leland in or about the Years 1535–1543*, ed. L. T. Smith, 5 vols (London, 1906–10); John Hare, *A Prospering Society: Wiltshire in the Later Middle Ages* (Hatfield, 2011); David Hall, *The Open Fields of England* (Oxford, 2014); Mark Overton, *Agricultural Revolution in England: The Transformation of the Agrarian Economy 1500–1850* (Cambridge, 1996); S. A. Mileson, *Parks in Medieval England* (Oxford, 2009); Briony McDonagh, 'Disobedient Objects: Material Readings of Enclosure Protest in Sixteenth-Century England', *Journal of Medieval History* 45 (2019), 254–75; Nicola Whyte, *Inhabiting the Landscape: Place, Custom and Memory, 1500–1800* (Bollington, 2009); Paul Cavill, *A New Dictionary of English Field-Names* (Nottingham, 2018); Ronald Hutton, *The Stations of the Sun: A History of the Ritual Year in Britain* (Oxford, 1997); Alexandra Walsham, *The Reformation of the Landscape: Religion, Identity, and Memory in Early Modern Britain and Ireland* (Oxford, 2011). For Kent beacons see William Lambarde, *A Perambulation of Kent, increased and altered* (London, 1596), map facing 6.

## Chapter 9: Seedtime and Harvest

Anthony Fitzherbert, *The Book of Husbandry*, ed. Walter Skeat (London, 1882); Thomas Tusser, *Five Hundred Points of Good Husbandry*, ed. Geoffrey Grigson (Oxford, 1984); *Food in Medieval England: Diet and Nutrition*, ed. C. M. Woolgar, D. Serjeantson and T. Waldron (Oxford, 2006).

## Chapter 10: Wild and Tame

John Edwards, *Horse and Man in Early Modern England* (London, 2007); Alison Locker, *Freshwater Fish in England: A Social and Cultural History of Coarse Fish from Prehistory to the Present Day* (Oxford, 2018); Roger Lovegrove, *Silent Fields: The Long Decline of a Nation's Wildlife* (Oxford, 2007); Leonard Mascall, *The First Booke of Cattell* (London, 1587). For the Mantuan ambassador, see *Calendar of State Papers Relating to English Affairs in the Archives of Venice, Volume 6: 1555–1558*, ed. R. Brown (London, 1877), 1672.

## Chapter 11: Places of Work

*English Medieval Industries: Craftsmen, Techniques, Products*, ed. John Blair and Nigel Ramsay (London and Rio Grande OH, 1991); John Hatcher, *The History of the British Coal Industry: Volume 1: Before 1700: Towards the Age of Coal* (Oxford, 1993); M. B. Donald, *Elizabethan Copper: The History of the Company of Mines Royal 1568–1605* (London, 1955); John Langdon, *Mills in the Medieval Economy: England, 1300–1540* (Oxford, 2004); John Oldland, 'The Economic Impact of Clothmaking on Rural Society, 1300–1550', in *Medieval Merchants and Money: Essays in Honour of James L. Bolton*, ed. Martin Allen and Matthew Davies (London, 2016), 229–52; Michael Zell, *Industry in the Countryside: Wealden Society in the Sixteenth Century* (Cambridge, 1994); Margaret Yates, *Town and Countryside in Western*

*Berkshire c.1327–c.1600: Social and Economic Change* (Woodbridge, 2007); the English Heritage county by county *Building Stone Atlas* series is useful to identify likely quarry types. For Horner Wood, see https://www.exmoorher.co.uk/Monument/MSO7424 consulted 23/1/2024.

## Chapter 12: Faith and Festivity

Peter Marshall, *Heretics and Believers: A History of the English Reformation* (New Haven CT and London, 2017); Ronald Hutton, *The Rise and Fall of Merry England: The Ritual Year 1400–1700* (Oxford, 1994); Christopher Marsh, '"At it ding dong": Recreation and Religion in the English Belfry, 1580–1640', in *Worship and the Parish Church in Early Modern Britain*, ed. Alec Ryrie and Natalie Mears (Farnham, 2013), 151–72; Steven Gunn and Tomasz Gromelski, 'Sport and Recreation in Sixteenth-Century England: The Evidence of Accidental Deaths', in *Sports and Physical Exercise in Early Modern Culture*, ed. Angela Schattner and Rebekka von Mallinckrodt (Abingdon, 2016), 49–63; C. L. Kingsford, 'Paris Garden and the Bearbaiting', *Archaeologia*, 70 (1920), 161–6; *Records of Early English Drama: Newcastle Upon Tyne*, ed. J. J. Anderson (Toronto, 1982). Details of the careers of parish clergy can be found in the Clergy of the Church of England Database, https://theclergydatabase.org.uk/ consulted 29/1/2024.

## Chapter 13: Crime and Control

C. V. Phythian-Adams, 'Rituals of Personal Confrontation in Late Medieval England', *Bulletin of the John Rylands Library*, 73 (1991), 65–90; Steven Gunn, 'Archery Practice in Early Tudor England', *Past and Present*, 209 (2010), 53–81; Steven Gunn and Tomasz Gromelski, 'Firearms Accidents in Sixteenth-Century England', *Arms and Armour*, 20:2 (2023), 149–59.

## Chapter 14: Trade and Travel

John Chartres, *Internal Trade in England, 1500–1700* (London, 1977); Dorian Gerhold, *Carriers and Coachmasters: Trade and Travel before the Turnpikes* (Chichester, 2005); Mark Brayshay, *Land Travel and Communications in Tudor and Stuart England: Achieving a Joined-Up Realm* (Liverpool, 2014); Ian Cooper, 'The Speed and Efficiency of the Tudor South-West's Royal Post-Stage Service', *History*, 99 (2014), 754–74; David Harrison, *The Bridges of Medieval England: Transport and Society, 400–1800* (Oxford, 2004); Keith Challis, 'Drowned in "a Whyrlepytte": the River Trent in the Nottinghamshire Coroners' Inquests of 1485–1558', *Transactions of the Thoroton Society of Nottinghamshire*, 108 (2005), 115–23. For Henry VIII and the ditch, see Edward Hall, *Hall's Chronicle* (London, 1809), 697.

## Chapter 15: Carts and Wagons

James Arnold, *Farm Waggons and Carts* (Newton Abbot, 1977); J. Geraint Jenkins, *The English Farm Wagon: Origins and Structure* (3rd edn, Newton Abbot, 1981); John Langdon, *Horses, Oxen and Technological Innovation: The Use of Draught Animals in English Farming from 1066 to 1500* (Cambridge, 1986). Modern road accident statistics can be found at https://www.gov.uk/government/statistics/reported-road-casualties-great-britain-annual-report-2021 consulted 23/01/2024.

## Chapter 16: Boats and Ships

T. S. Willan, *River Navigation in England, 1600–1750* (London, 1936).

BIBLIOGRAPHY

## Chapter 17: Ways of Dying

Danae Tankard, 'Defining Death in Early Tudor England', *Cultural and Social History*, 3:1 (2006), 1–20. Modern death registration statistics for England using ICD-10 can be found at https://www.nomisweb.co.uk/datasets/mortsa, international comparisons can be made using World Health Organization data at https://platform.who.int/mortality and a useful presentation of the UK figures for 2005 grouping injuries to different parts of the body is available at https://www.realfirstaid.co.uk/injury-statistics (all consulted 4/4/2023). Current statistics on many health-related phenomena can be found at https://www.ons.gov.uk/peoplepopulationandcommunity/ and the website of The Royal Society for the Prevention of Accidents at https://www.rospa.com is a useful source of information of all sorts on accidents today.

# Index

For reasons of space, individual people and places are not included in this index. They can be traced using the 'Sixteenth-century English accident inquests' data deposit (see bibliography).

abortion 39
accident, idea of 34–46
acorns 158
admiral, lord 5, 28, 249, 251
Africa, Africans 20, 263
agrarian capitalism 15–16, 124, 271
alabaster 174
ale 54, 55, 66, 91, 202
alehouses 64, 202, 208
All Souls' Day 214
*Alltagsgeschichte* 2
almanacs 35, 50
almoner, royal 30
alms 16–17, 191
almshouses *see* hospitals
almsmen 12
angling *see* fishing
Anglo-Saxons 22, 115
ants 151, 209
apothecaries 55
apples 51, 92, 131, 139, 140–1, 230
apprentices 55, 74, 184, 186–7
aprons 63, 93
archaeology 2–3, 183
archery 3, 23, 39, 41, 70, 97, 111, 113, 137, 152, 192, 194, 201, 209, 213–15, 219, 273
Arches, Court of 209

Armada, Spanish 2, 8
artisans *see* craftsmen
Ash Wednesday 190
ashes 51, 91, 94, 266
assizes 3, 5
astrology 34–5, 50, 273
autopsies 33
axes, hatchets 30, 85, 143–4, 147, 148, 153, 154

bachelors, singlemen 13
bacon 83, 158
bags 65, 141, 165, 196
bailiffs 27, 211,
bakehouses 88, 92
bakers 31, 57, 96
ballads 35, 63
baptism 21, 191
bargemen 222, 233, 253, 257
barley 30, 75, 120, 122, 125, 131, 134, 137–9, 166, 229, 231, 240, 241, 262
barns 12, 17–18, 64, 75, 76, 77, 81, 82, 84, 86, 88, 97, 112, 135, 136, 138–9, 154, 157, 160, 192, 196, 237, 243
barrels 8, 66, 88, 90, 93, 103, 183, 231–3, 236, 241, 246, 256
barrows (landscape) 38–9, 127–8

# INDEX

baskets 64, 91, 142, 146, 172, 210, 229, 231
batfowling 153
bathing, swimming 1, 20, 25, 29, 34, 43, 44, 49, 50, 56–9, 71, 88, 95, 104, 109, 111, 114, 130, 138, 140, 141, 168, 177, 186, 192, 227, 250, 254, 256, 267, 270, 273
beacons 4, 127
beans 120, 134, 136, 137
bears 39, 45–6, 114, 151, 200–1, 261
beating, whipping 16, 37, 38, 55–6, 76–7, 204, 210
beds 4, 7, 29, 35, 48, 50, 54, 55, 65, 72, 81, 84, 96–7, 103, 122, 129, 145, 191, 193, 200, 268
beef 83, 159, 200
beer 54, 103, 114, 202, 229–30, 243
bees 154, 246
beggars, begging 17–19, 153, 172
bells 16, 108–9, 154, 193–4, 204, 222
bell towers 8, 108, 193
belts 63, 73, 93, 157, 194, 224, 272
benches 65, 66, 87, 158, 183, 193–4, 197, 217
Bible 21–2, 127
bills, billhooks, reaping hooks, wood-hooks 72, 138, 141, 143, 146, 147, 204, 208–10, 215, 267
birds 42, 73, 118, 119, 131, 136–7, 153–4, 156, 217; bird-catchers 153; nests 42, 114, 153–4, 159, 168; *see also* individual species or genus
bishops, archbishops 2, 7, 20, 87, 109, 125, 163, 191, 193, 209
bladders 58–9, 95, 264
bladesmiths, cutlers, furbishers 92, 182–3, 187
blankets 102, 212
blindfolds 70–1, 94
blindness 51–2, 82, 110, 163
blood 55, 59, 73, 262, 265
boats 8, 15, 19, 24, 41, 44, 67, 68, 96, 104, 107, 111–12, 114, 118–19, 142, 147–8, 177, 192, 204, 216, 221, 228, 230, 249–59; construction and repair 104, 105, 144, 258; barges and lighters 43, 104, 109, 112, 113, 148, 231, 233–4, 252–3, 255, 257, 271; cargo boats 75, 87, 122, 135–6, 145, 148, 172, 176, 229, 231, 251, 252, 254; coracles 252; fishing boats 128, 154–6, 210, 252, 254, 255; keel-boats 31, 105, 252, 257; ketches and hoys 111, 251, 252, 258; punts 68, 252, 255, 257; skiffs 210, 251; trows 252; wherries 114, 252; *see also* ferries
bookbinders 216
books 3, 71, 109, 127, 190, 191; *see also* Common Prayer, Books of; handbooks; pamphlets
boots 44, 94,
bottles 93, 245
bowls (game) 130, 197, 204
bowls, basins 65, 70, 88, 89, 92, 93
bracken 141
brains 127, 139, 219, 264, 273
brambles 123, 147, 239
brasiers 111, 183
brass 25, 91, 93, 154, 187, 231
bread 92–3, 157, 176, 186, 191, 203
breast-cloths 93
breeches 48, 93, 95, 102–3, 179
brewers 15, 19, 31, 103, 114, 186, 195, 202
brewhouses 67, 88, 102, 112, 183
brewing 66, 78, 88, 91, 92, 98, 106, 131, 140, 176, 179, 183, 197, 205, 270
bricklayers 86
brickmakers 114, 175, 223, 225
bricks 83, 85, 87, 226
bridewells 17,
bridges 20, 43, 50, 52, 67, 94, 97, 104–6, 112–15, 129, 148, 154, 181, 197, 203, 223, 226–7, 230, 232, 234, 243, 245, 257, 271; drawbridges 73, 120

# INDEX

bronchitis 49
broom 125, 141
brooms, sweeping 83, 181
buckets, pails 1, 66, 69, 70, 85, 89–90, 91, 93, 94, 157, 158, 159, 197, 230
bucklers 38–9, 213
building 14, 77, 81, 82, 84–7, 98, 105, 108, 147, 171, 174–5, 223, 236, 271; *see also* demolition
burial 3, 22, 33, 189, 274
burns and scalds 9, 35, 40, 51, 52, 65, 66, 72, 78, 82, 91–3, 106, 136, 146, 183, 196, 219, 262, 266, 267
butchers 23, 55, 107, 114, 157, 160, 162, 190, 194, 202, 222, 223, 269
butter 159, 230, 232

cakes 67, 190
canals 128, 258
cancer 49
candles 81, 93, 107, 130, 131, 181, 218; rushlights 142, 231
candlesticks 55, 87, 193
canvas 52, 93, 178, 231
cappers 103, 111
carpenters 75, 86, 108, 143, 144, 212, 222–3, 233
carriers 232–3, 237
carters 35, 75, 232
cart-houses 52, 86
carts 9, 20, 41, 52, 97, 103, 113, 114, 121, 122, 124, 125, 128, 138–9, 142, 147–8, 152, 156, 161, 176, 182, 185, 186, 196, 199, 224–7, 229–33, 235–47, 263, 264, 268, 271; beer carts, drays 23, 103, 236; coal carts 114, 130, 146, 172, 201, 236; dung-carts 72, 113, 115, 135, 236, 239; collapses 107, 192, 246; collisions 16, 32, 35, 53, 62, 67, 87, 106, 107, 108, 114, 126, 138, 241, 244, 245; driving 8, 40, 54, 69–70, 74, 75, 140, 176, 238–47; falls from 32, 41, 49, 54, 55, 106, 118, 138, 139, 184, 232–3, 241, 261, 268; forfeiture 6, 30, 33–4, 42, 237, 247; loading 62, 136, 137, 138, 141, 145, 175, 240–1, 243, 267; repair 65, 75, 77, 237; *see also* cattle; horses
castles 8, 28, 70, 94, 105, 109, 110, 120, 154, 212, 216, 272
cathedrals 45, 101, 110, 202
cats 127, 157
cattle 62, 66, 70, 81, 120–1, 122, 124, 128, 129, 140, 151, 156, 159–61, 168–9, 199, 228; bullocks 134, 160; bulls 41, 52, 105, 118, 151, 159–60, 166, 200, 201, 265, 268; calves 114, 159–60, 232, 270; cows x, 6, 24, 68, 70, 78, 111, 112, 118, 122, 123, 126, 159–60, 166, 232, 269, 270, 272, *see also* milking; heifers 75, 107, 159, 237; oxen 51, 52, 68, 123, 126, 159–60, 184, 256; traction 33, 69, 70, 114, 121, 122, 130, 134, 159, 168, 233, 237–47, 271
cauldrons 76, 89, 91, 103, 184, 197, 203
causeways 129, 191, 211, 227, 232
cellars 83, 107
censuses 4
chains 90, 104, 107, 134, 156, 173, 200, 201, 212, 246, 247, 256
chairs 32, 65, 73, 87, 193, 268, 273
chalk 23, 75, 120–2, 125, 136, 149, 174–5, 187
chamber pots 96
chambers 7, 40, 48, 52, 83–4, 87, 212, 217, 218
charcoal 92, 146, 182, 187
cheese 91, 92, 93, 122, 131, 159, 186, 230
cherries 140
chests 65, 87
chickens, cocks 158, 200
childbirth, pregnancy 13, 64, 161, 191
children 12–13, 17–18, 20, 23, 29, 32, 34, 40, 42, 48, 52, 54, 55, 61–79, 82, 87, 88, 91, 93–6, 98, 103, 106, 107, 108, 111, 113, 126–30, 135, 138, 154,

297

children (*cont.*)
156, 158, 176, 178, 181, 184, 190, 192, 198, 201, 214, 217, 240, 243, 247, 266–71; babies 4, 9, 21–2, 35, 39–40, 65, 76, 83, 96, 122, 129, 158; play 4, 57, 65–8, 70–1, 84, 108, 109, 113, 114, 122, 157, 158, 195–7, 199, 202, 240, 273; travel 41, 119, 164, 165, 189, 226, 232; work 62, 68–70, 78, 88–90, 92, 117, 158, 159–60, 166, 168, 179–80, 239, 253, 273
chimneys 8, 73, 83, 193, 204
chisels 95
Christmas 19, 141–2, 158, 190, 196, 197, 199, 205, 212, 219, 226, 228
chronicles 35–6, 44
churches 2, 16, 20, 28, 51, 105, 108–9, 113, 119, 154, 189–94, 195, 204, 208, 210, 213, 214, 222–3, 228, 271
churchwardens 2, 31, 190
churchyards 2, 41, 110, 123, 195–6, 202
cider 62, 181, 241
clay 23, 82, 108, 114, 121–2, 125, 127, 134, 175–6, 177, 187
clergy 23, 25, 35, 45–6, 54, 57, 74, 83, 84, 88, 95, 153, 157, 160, 162, 164–5, 174, 189–93, 204, 212, 228, 237, 253, 268, 269, 217; *see also* bishops, archbishops; friars; monks; nuns
cliffs 17, 42, 118, 141, 153, 174, 191
cloaks 95, 98
clocks 16, 87
cloth, clothworking 12, 15, 20, 56, 75, 94, 117, 118, 176, 180–1, 184–7, 229, 231, 236
clothiers 94, 185–6, 232
clothing 3, 7, 25, 39, 50, 57, 93–5, 98, 128, 179, 187, 239, 247, 263; *see also* laundry; individual garments
coaches 237
coal 31, 105, 146, 252; mining 7, 118, 121, 125, 171–3, 187
coats 179, 196

coinage, money 7, 24, 30, 52, 92, 210, 211, 230
colliers 146, 201
Common Pleas, court of 25, 67
Common Prayer, Books of 7, 21, 35, 64, 204
commons 1, 89, 118, 126, 131, 176, 195, 197, 226
compost, manure 121, 125, 135–6, 148–9, 184, 236; *see also* carts; dunghills
confession 35, 191
confirmation 191
constables 16, 27, 31, 33, 37, 78, 190, 209, 211
cooking 77, 82–3, 91–2, 198
cooks 35, 83, 267
coopers 103, 143
coots 153
copper 91, 183; mining 20, 118, 173
coroners 3, 5, 27–30, 32, 33, 41, 42, 44–6, 122, 189, 251, 261–2, 274
Corpus Christi 201
Council in the North 25
court, royal 1, 28, 36, 113, 204
cradles 9, 35, 55, 65, 158
craftsmen 14, 19, 31, 74, 83, 143, 164, 182, 184, 186, 195–6, 214, 216, 222, 225, 228, 237, 247
cramp 50
cranes 67, 186
crayfish 155
crossbows 23, 54, 153
crosses, wayside and churchyard 3, 105, 109, 128, 201, 202, 224, 230
crows 66, 136–7, 153, 218
crutches 52
cupboards 87
curriers 184

daggers 38–9, 179, 196, 197, 198, 201, 208–9, 213
dancing 53, 127, 198–9, 205, 273
darkness 52, 54, 64, 90, 95, 97, 103,

# INDEX

105, 107, 115, 120, 130, 131, 153, 181, 226
deer 121, 124, 141, 147, 152, 156, 168, 184
demolition 8, 75, 84–7, 98
deodands 6, 30, 33–4, 39, 41, 42, 159, 162, 244, 247, 251
dialects 20–1, 118, 236, 246
dinner 88, 91–2, 154, 198
dishes 66, 89, 93
ditches 19, 49, 52, 62, 67, 89, 92, 94, 96, 102, 109, 110, 114, 124, 127, 129, 146, 155, 192, 202, 203, 228, 230, 243, 244; see also drains, sewers
dizziness 49, 262
dogs 30, 82, 104, 113, 134, 151, 156–7, 158, 159, 166, 168, 186, 208, 209, 210, 218, 245, 271; bloodhounds 156; greyhounds 24, 50, 66, 152, 156; mastiffs 50, 92, 103, 156, 200; spaniels 156
domestic violence 37, 64, 76–7
doors 18, 75, 84, 85, 97, 139, 186, 212, 243; doorframes, doorposts 19, 82; trapdoors 83
doublets 95
doves, pigeons 123, 154, 158, 218, 230
drains, sewers 72, 83; drainage ditches 42, 118, 119, 173, 250
drapers 95, 192
drowning 6, 8, 19, 24, 32, 34, 36, 39, 40, 42, 45, 48, 56, 62, 66–8, 77, 91, 93, 94, 96, 107, 109, 112, 114, 119, 122, 128, 142, 145, 146, 155, 158, 159, 162, 165, 173, 174, 184, 186, 191, 199, 202, 203, 222, 223, 230, 258–9, 262–4, 267; see also bathing; ferries; laundry; millponds; moats; ponds; rivers; streams; water collection; wells
drums 201
drunkenness 4, 20, 22, 37, 53, 54, 64, 95, 96, 97, 98, 102, 105, 110, 114, 158, 165, 192, 198, 202–5, 208, 211, 229, 245, 253, 273

ducks 68, 151, 153, 156, 158, 191, 257
duels 39
dunghills 113, 135, 243
dyeing, dyers 106, 184, 187, 199; dye-houses 65, 112, 196
dysentery 48

epilepsy 39, 51, 60, 178
estate mapping 136
evening prayer 35, 108, 190
executors 24
exposure 17, 18, 39, 50, 64, 77, 97, 128, 203, 224, 263, 266

fairs 172, 183, 230, 234
famine 16, 35, 105, 234
fences 42, 87, 103, 123, 124
fenland 42, 49, 118–19, 120, 130, 131, 142, 152, 176, 227, 230, 231, 255
ferrets 152
ferries 42, 43, 223, 227, 228–9, 250–4, 256, 258, 271
fevers 17, 24, 37, 48–9, 75, 118, 155, 266
field forms 51, 87–8, 97, 120–6, 140, 185, 192, 195, 196, 214, 271
fires, fireplaces 4, 7, 35, 49, 51, 52, 63, 65, 73, 77, 83, 85–7, 89, 91, 97, 136, 147, 157, 175, 176, 186, 198, 203, 209, 212, 218, 219, 266; see also houses, house fires
firewood 69, 77, 91, 109, 113, 115, 120, 123, 126, 142, 146, 146–9, 212, 229, 235, 267; storage 66, 82, 87, 108, 202, 209
fireworks 8, 36
first finders 16, 19, 31, 62, 64, 67, 68, 69, 72, 75, 78, 88, 103, 154, 161, 186, 189, 221, 224, 267
fish 75, 91, 203, 231, 249; eels 155, 227; herring 93, 103, 231; lamprey 155; mackerel 230; pike 155, 230; sand-eels 154; turbot 210
fishermen 24, 118, 155, 226, 253

299

## INDEX

fishing 14, 51, 57, 63–4, 70, 77, 93, 111, 119, 128, 154–6, 210, 249, 252, 254, 255, 258, 270
fishing nets 24, 119, 155
fishmongers 210, 230
fish-traps 75, 155–6, 168, 253
flails 77, 140
flint 175, 217
floods 52, 82, 83, 96, 110, 119, 126, 128, 129, 131, 173, 189, 226, 230, 232
flour 157, 209
flowers 66, 131, 147, 177, 199, 205, 252
football 37, 53, 113, 194–5, 205, 272
fords 20, 42, 58, 95, 161, 165, 227, 234, 243
forges 20, 182, 183, 218, 271
Fortuna 34
founders 183
foxes 151, 152
France, French 20, 104, 207, 216
friars 8, 109, 191, 204
friendship 44, 55, 58–9, 71, 195, 273
fruit 57, 69, 108, 127, 140–1, 149, 210; *see also* individual varieties
fuller's earth 176
fullers 42, 180, 195, 225
fulling-mills 66, 112, 118, 176, 180–1, 184, 186
furnaces 65, 182, 183, 271

gadflies 245–6
gallbladder 33
gallows 127
gambling 196
gardens, yards, courtyards 36, 51, 66, 72, 81, 84, 87–8, 91, 96, 108, 109, 119, 122, 123, 135, 138–40, 148, 156, 166, 176, 192, 193, 214, 229, 238, 267, 271
gates, gateposts 17, 32, 87, 124, 154, 225–6, 243, 245, 273; field gates 97, 232, 242; town gates 18, 105, 107, 109, 110, 113, 245

geese 66, 75, 158
gentry 7, 13, 22, 23–4, 39, 50, 51, 52, 55, 67, 73–4, 78, 114, 162–4, 167, 185, 193, 208, 217, 221–2, 224, 225, 228, 231, 237; as administrators 7, 17, 25, 28, 31, 43, 84, 173, 208; as landlords 15, 121, 141, 159, 191, 209, 223; homes 82–4, 86–7, 92, 108, 120, 156, 237, 269; manual work 86, 88, 138, 143, 238; recreation 44, 57, 153, 163, 191, 192, 214–16, 218, 254
Germany, Germans 2, 19, 20
glass 142
glasses (drinking) 93
glasses (spectacles) 191, 272
glaziers 187
glovers 15, 121, 160
goads 76, 134, 242, 244–5
goldsmiths 57, 103, 183
Good Friday 202
gorse 119, 136, 141
gout 47, 49
gowns 73, 179
grapes 140
gravel 19, 67, 70, 107, 108, 125, 130, 175, 177, 187, 225
greens 67, 109, 113, 126, 185, 195, 199, 214, 230
grinding mills 92, 176, 182, 187
grocers 233
guildhalls 28
gunpowder 8, 9, 109, 144, 201–2, 215–19
guns 9, 23, 30, 40, 42, 95, 96, 102, 110, 113, 137, 153, 182, 187, 193, 199, 201, 215–19, 271, 273
gypsum 176

haberdashers 103, 108
hair 128, 179, 208
halberds 210
halls 64, 82–3, 91, 97, 192, 196, 198, 200, 217

halters 67, 159, 160, 167–8, 238, 244, 247, 272
hammers 68, 180, 182, 271; throwing 41, 198, 205
handbooks: animal care 157–63, 239–47; farming 35, 133–42, 148–9, 158, 236; government 27–9, 33; medical 50, 56–7, 59, 265; swimming 57–8
hanging 40, 127, 156
hares 24, 152, 156
harness 134, 165–6, 188, 237, 240, 242, 246, 247
harrows, harrowing 112, 125, 135, 148–9
harvest 17, 48, 63, 65, 74, 84, 112, 115, 122, 126, 135–40, 142, 149, 209, 214, 270
hats, caps 67, 71, 94, 98, 128, 187, 196, 215, 229, 231, 236
hawks 153, 228, 252
hay 24, 41, 51, 62, 63, 66, 106, 112, 114, 118, 122, 125, 126, 137–9, 142, 166, 232, 236, 244, 245
hay-crooks 139
haystacks 12, 63, 92, 121, 138, 144, 149, 196
hearts 49, 139, 219, 265, 266
hedges 2, 23, 66, 77, 120, 122, 123–4, 126, 129, 131, 136, 144, 152, 153, 203, 213, 242, 243
hemp 131, 140, 196
henhouses 82
herbs 69, 140
herdsmen 121, 126, 160
heresy 51
hermits 192
hernias 47, 53, 273
herons 154
highway repairs 42, 225, 234, 271
hoes 175
holly 141–2, 246
Holy Rood Day 190
homicide 3, 16, 36–40, 219; accidental 23, 37; murder 6, 35, 41, 208, 219; self-defence 37, 38, 63, 207
hoopers 256
hops 131, 140, 230, 232
hornets 9
horse-mills 15, 17, 67, 69, 112, 163, 176, 179–80
horses 7, 16, 29, 30, 39, 41, 43, 44, 66, 108, 109, 110, 112, 114, 118, 130, 136, 151, 156, 162–8, 177, 191, 192, 193, 196, 199, 208, 265, 268, 272; colts 70, 163–4, 166; fillies 163; geldings 24, 52, 105, 112, 162–3, 165, 229; mares 6, 7, 24, 162–7, 246, 256; packhorses 68, 118, 155, 165, 176, 183, 185, 186, 229, 230, 232, 271; horse care 24, 34, 69, 74, 92, 183, 196; dead 152, 166–7, 198; fighting 92, 103, 166; racing 199–200; riding 8, 9, 22, 23–4, 25, 36, 42, 49, 68, 69, 73, 105–6, 110, 111, 114, 129, 130, 138, 143, 162, 166, 184, 191, 200, 203, 204, 221, 222, 224–7, 230, 232, 240, 256, 261, 266, 268–9, 270, 273; traction 30, 33–4, 65, 67, 69–70, 107, 121, 122, 134–5, 144, 145, 149, 162, 201, 204, 236–45, 247, 255, 258, 264, 271, 273
horseshoes 76, 166, 187
hospitality 50, 77, 82, 157, 269
hospitals, almshouses 9, 18, 109, 110, 261
house martins 154
houses 2, 4, 7, 23, 24, 29, 44, 48, 54–6, 65–9, 71–9, 81–99, 104–8, 113, 114, 120, 122–3, 126, 135, 143, 145, 153, 156, 157, 159, 176, 181, 185, 191, 192, 198, 200, 201, 204, 209, 211–13, 215, 217, 219, 223, 254, 267–9; house collapses 82, 96, 108, 119, 129; house fires 52, 81–2, 96, 105, 193
humours 55, 265, 273
hurdles 90, 159, 161, 174, 242

# INDEX

husbandmen 15–16, 31, 48, 50, 52, 57, 62, 74, 83, 86, 87, 135–9, 143, 147, 160, 162, 164, 195–6, 199, 214, 222, 223, 225, 228, 231, 233, 237–9, 253, 267, 269

ice 111, 129–31, 145, 147, 152, 226, 243, 257, 267
idiocy 52–3
infanticide 39–40
inflation ix, 16, 17, 148, 237
influenza 48, 269
innkeepers 162
inns 22, 28, 53, 83, 95, 102, 107, 108, 111, 166, 202–3, 208, 218
inquests 3, 27–46, 74, 78, 261, 267, 271, 274, 279; reports, accuracy of 4–7, 11–12, 16, 23, 27–34, 47–8, 57, 122–3, 137, 152, 236, 249, 252, 262–3, 272
insanity 50
insults 38–9, 77, 186, 204, 208
intestines 30, 53, 262, 264–5
invasions 4, 8, 127, 207
Ireland, Irish 19
iron 4, 8, 69, 87, 103, 108, 124, 135, 146, 147, 156, 173, 181, 198, 200, 212, 213, 231, 236, 239, 247, 267; mining 173; processing 20, 146, 172, 182–3
ironmongers 114, 231
Israel 21
Italy, Italians 20, 103, 164, 213
ivy 141–2, 199

javelins 9
jerkins 93, 179
joiners 76, 179, 199, 223
jugs 89
juries, jurors x, 6, 17–19, 27–33, 42, 45, 46, 51, 57, 67, 78, 85, 90, 94, 103, 109, 111, 122, 164, 178, 189, 195, 209, 232, 236, 237, 240, 245, 274; difficult verdicts 16, 36–40, 54–6, 84, 207–8, 262; social views 12, 35, 40, 41, 48, 50, 53, 58, 59, 62, 64, 65, 70, 72, 76–7, 95, 97, 134, 144, 157, 159, 162, 167, 168, 175, 182, 194, 203, 213, 217, 219, 225, 254, 273; vocabulary ix, 9, 20–1, 29, 36, 44, 58, 82, 86, 89, 93, 96, 102, 110, 112, 118, 123, 125–8, 134, 136, 139, 141–7, 152, 155, 156, 158, 163, 173, 175, 190, 195, 200, 201, 215, 217, 223–4, 226, 228, 238, 242, 246, 252, 255, 258, 263–6
justices of the peace 17, 28, 43, 198, 212

keelmen 31, 201
kettles 65, 66, 72, 89, 91, 93, 231
kidneys 49, 264
kilns 97; *see also* lime; malt
King's Bench, court of 3, 30, 36, 208
kissing 62, 63
kitchens 48, 61, 66, 73, 77, 82–3, 86, 91, 97, 154, 158, 192, 196, 198, 217, 218, 219
kites 158, 163
knives 48, 50, 63, 71, 73, 91, 95–6, 122, 124, 153, 154, 157, 158, 166, 190, 194, 196, 197, 202, 224, 245, 272; in confrontations 24, 38, 77, 98, 204, 208–9; and eating 92–3, 186, 191; manufacture 183, 187

labourers 15–16, 18, 22, 65, 69, 74–5, 83, 88, 97, 146, 160, 163, 164, 190, 193, 216, 222, 228, 230, 237, 253, 271; recreation 57, 195–6, 197, 199, 200, 202, 214; work 8, 42, 84, 86, 91, 122, 127, 136–9, 143, 144, 147, 162, 223, 238, 240, 267
ladders 31, 40, 83, 84–5, 91, 106, 108, 121, 136, 138–9, 141, 143, 154, 157, 173, 195, 204, 269, 270
lakes 68, 118, 119, 176, 250, 251, 254, 257, 258
last rites 35, 191, 269
lattices 86; lattice-makers 14

# INDEX

laundry 12, 48, 51, 67, 75, 93–4, 98, 111, 115, 130, 177, 183, 203, 270
law, lawyers, litigation 2, 18, 25, 28, 33, 36, 39, 52, 113, 209, 211, 271
lead 91, 110, 183, 193, 217; mining 118, 173
leather 89, 93, 137, 159, 165, 187–8, 196, 233, 236; leatherwork 14–15, 103, 121, 184
leeks 140
lentils 166
leprosy 49
levers 62, 144–5, 177, 186, 256
lice 54
lightning 35, 36, 39, 128–9, 131
lime 87, 108, 174, 184; lime kilns 24, 105, 174–5
linen 12, 57, 66, 67, 75, 93–5, 123, 218, 231, 263
lions 201, 252
litany 35
liver 33, 264
locks (rivers) 97, 257
locksmiths 57, 182
lofts 29, 82, 83, 139, 158, 192
lunacy 50
lungs 33, 264

madder 184
Maid Marian 127
malaria 49
malt 64, 70, 91, 183, 229, 241; malt kilns 7, 52, 61, 91; malt mills 17, 69, 176, 179, 232; malthouses 88, 112
manorial courts 31, 43, 125
maps 2, 127, 136
markets, marketplaces 105, 107, 118, 160, 165, 185, 200, 201, 203, 221, 222, 224, 229–30, 234
marl 23, 75, 112, 125, 127, 136, 148–9, 208, 236, 273
marriage 13, 23, 62–4, 72, 74, 96, 138, 157, 181, 204, 267, 271
marshes 24, 49, 63, 97, 112, 114, 118–19, 126, 142, 152, 217, 227, 243, 250, 252, 255
masons 51, 75, 86, 87, 108, 173–4, 175, 195, 223, 233
mass 35, 51, 190
mattocks 112, 136, 139, 175, 225
May Day 8, 107, 213
maypoles 109, 113, 198–9, 205, 271
meadows 52, 53, 70, 112, 113, 122, 126, 131, 136, 137, 141, 189, 195, 197, 198, 223, 227, 240
mercers 157, 192, 200, 233
merchants 31, 82, 105, 201, 232, 252
metalwork 14, 15, 182–3, 216
mice 139
Michaelmas 214
midwives 13
migraine 49
militia 4, 14–15, 216
milk, milking 55, 56, 74, 93, 119, 120–2, 156, 157, 159, 168, 270
millers 15, 57, 130, 155, 177–81, 198
millponds 8, 42, 123, 177, 181, 199, 211
millraces, millstreams 65, 71, 96, 177, 255
millstones 178, 180, 236
miners, mining 14, 20, 91, 118, 171–3
minstrels 49, 201, 223
mistletoe 141–2
moats 42, 58, 65, 73, 89, 91, 92, 94, 95, 120, 128, 140, 192
moles 152, 195, 242, 243
monastic and religious houses 8, 105, 108–9, 112, 154, 191, 193, 199, 212, 272; dissolution 1, 8, 108, 128, 271
monks 8, 154, 191, 204
moorhens 153
moorland 17, 119, 126, 129, 142, 166, 176, 183
morning prayer 35, 190, 208
mortar 105, 174; mortar boards 85
mosquitoes 49
mud 51, 56, 58, 62, 67, 70, 93, 102, 135, 164, 224, 227, 228, 241, 244, 255, 256, 267–8, 272

303

## INDEX

mufflers 95
murder *see* homicide
music 2, 113, 202
musters 4, 9, 216

nails 76, 85, 86, 166, 182, 247
naming practices 18–19, 20–22
National Archives 6
neckerchiefs 93
negligence, recklessness 37, 40–2, 62, 65, 67, 71, 84, 92, 95, 144, 168, 175, 186, 198, 215, 218, 219, 226, 245, 254, 256
neighbours 17, 23, 30, 32, 51, 57, 64, 65, 72, 76, 77–8, 86, 103, 107, 145, 160, 190, 192, 194, 195, 203, 207–11, 214, 216–17, 221, 224, 232, 245, 256, 267–9
Netherlands, Netherlanders 19–20, 103, 104–5, 216, 252, 253
nobility 2, 4, 7, 8, 20, 25, 87, 114, 124–5, 162, 164, 166, 181, 200, 237, 267
nuns 191
nuts 69, 71, 140–1, 157; hazelnuts 140; walnuts 140

oats 61, 64, 120
old age 4, 12–13, 17–19, 51, 52, 74, 82, 83, 87, 95, 98, 110, 118, 142, 163, 192, 203, 228, 238–9, 262, 267, 269, 270
onions 91, 140
orchards 88, 92, 140, 141, 158, 210
otters 152
ovens 105
oysters 92, 119, 155

painters 194
Palm Sunday 190
palsy 49–50, 268
pamphlets 35, 44, 45–6, 236
paralysis 49, 266
pardons 5, 23, 37–8
parish registers 2, 12, 22–3

parks 9, 106, 121, 124–5, 127, 142, 147, 152–3, 193, 214, 239
parliament, statutes 3, 16, 17, 43, 98, 124, 158, 213, 217, 225; MPs 24–5, 43, 87, 121
parlours 83
partisans 213
Passion Sunday 190–1
pastures 24, 51, 52, 78, 118, 120–6, 163, 196, 197, 226, 246, 268
paving 106, 193, 211
pears 92, 131, 140–1
peas 63, 114, 120, 125, 128, 134, 137–9, 192, 232
peat 69, 111, 118, 176
pedlars 222, 229, 233, 234
pegs 30, 86, 180, 197, 246
petticoats 93, 179
pewter 231, 246
pewterers 232
physicians 54
pickaxes 136, 174
pigs 9, 35, 40, 70, 112, 122, 126, 151, 156, 157–8, 166, 168, 181, 242, 245
pigswill 158
pikes, pikestaffs 9, 198, 208
pillows 96
pinners 103
pitchforks 6, 41, 69, 86, 135, 138, 139, 167, 192, 196, 209, 211, 245
plague 33, 35, 48, 269
plaster, plasterers 85–6, 176, 223
plays 1–2, 34, 127, 141, 199, 201–2
ploughs, ploughing 69, 70, 75, 76, 112, 121–6, 129, 133–5, 148–9, 164, 165, 167, 198, 209, 236, 238, 243, 269, 270
plough-staffs 81, 134
ploughwrights 143
plums 140–1
poaching 152–3, 155, 168
poisoning 39, 55, 59, 262, 266; *see also* ratsbane
pole-vaulting 152, 227–8, 255, 269, 273
poling 255, 256, 258

304

ponds 16, 21, 36, 49, 78, 93–4, 96, 98, 109, 119–20, 123, 127, 128, 130, 141, 143, 157–9, 173, 183, 189, 192, 203, 210, 228, 250, 254, 263, 267, 273; and animals 41, 118, 127, 152, 153, 158, 160, 165, 167, 224; and children 62, 65, 66, 69, 71, 77, 182, 196, 270; fishponds 119, 155; *see also* bathing; millponds; water collection
population increase 5, 11, 12, 16, 98, 102, 148, 247
porters 104
posnets 89
potash 176
pots, pottery 54, 69, 77, 89, 93, 107, 126, 183–4, 209
poulterers 211, 230
pounds 110, 167
poverty 4, 16–18, 88; *see also* vagrancy
prison base 197
prisons 102, 103, 109, 211–13, 219, 271, 272
probate valuation 30
Protestantism 20, 21, 44, 45, 190
providence, divine 34–5, 44–6
prunes 231
pumps 90–1, 110, 173, 272
purgatory 35
purses 52, 93, 230

quarries 173–4
quays, wharves, landing-stages 24, 58, 94, 104, 105, 111, 113–14, 115, 210, 218, 228, 231, 256, 258
quoits 198

rabbits 123, 127, 152–3, 166
rabies 156
rakes 141
raspberries 140
rats 139, 157
ratsbane 35, 39, 54, 59, 157, 168, 187
reading, literacy 3, 28, 31, 35, 71, 191, 271, 272

rectories, vicarages 28, 71, 157, 192–3, 196, 202, 228, 268
reeds 63, 142, 202
Reformation 21, 51, 128, 190–2, 271
Renaissance 21–2, 58
revolts, riots 2, 28, 110, 124, 209
rivers 8, 17, 20, 22, 48, 52, 75, 91, 93–7, 105, 110–11, 118–20, 122, 126, 128–30, 137, 142, 147, 181, 183, 186, 192, 197, 202, 214, 221, 253–7, 267; and animals 111, 153, 155–6, 160, 161, 165; and children 40, 62, 67, 70–1, 73, 103, 157, 202; crossings 43, 50, 109, 112, 121, 203, 210, 211, 226–9, 232, 243, 245, 250; as transport routes 14, 31, 41, 87, 104, 111–12, 114, 135–6, 146, 148, 172, 182, 228, 231, 233, 249–50, 252, 255, 257–8, 271; *see also* bathing; laundry; water collection
roads 5, 6, 14, 16, 32, 42, 64, 65, 126, 128, 129, 135, 148, 156, 190, 196, 198, 199, 201, 208, 211, 221, 223–6, 231, 232, 235, 241, 243, 244, 247, 269, 271; road-banks 34, 106, 122, 140, 197, 224–5, 239, 242, 243, 247; Roman roads 115, 223–4; *see also* highway repairs
roasting spits 73, 198
robins 23
rollers 86, 104, 144–5; field rollers 67, 122, 135
roofs 49, 76, 82, 84–5, 86, 98, 108, 154, 157, 190, 193, 204; *see also* slate; thatch, thatching; tiles, tiling
rooks 153–4, 168
ropes 19, 40, 59, 67, 85, 90, 111, 119, 140, 143–5, 155, 157, 172–4, 178, 180, 193–4, 200, 201, 211, 212, 239, 240–1, 247, 253–8
rowing 67, 104, 114, 153, 210, 250, 254–5, 258, 271
rye 104, 120

sabbath 45–6
saddles 113, 141, 165, 230, 237, 247
sailing 19, 114, 210, 251–2, 254, 257, 258, 271
sailors 19, 20, 31, 33, 57, 104, 200, 216, 222, 233, 250, 253–8
St Bartholomew's Day 197
St George's Day 197, 213
salt 83, 91, 176, 231
salters 232
saltpetre 9
samphire 141
sanctuary 39
sand 23, 69, 108, 125, 127, 175, 187, 225, 257, 273
sarsen stones 127
saws, sawing, sawyers 75, 76, 105, 144–5, 147, 223
scaffolding 45, 51, 85, 86, 105, 108, 139, 201, 271
scall 54
schools 71, 109, 196
scoops 90
Scotland, Scots 7, 19, 110, 207
scythes 62, 68, 124, 137–8, 182, 187, 223
sea 5, 28, 112, 119, 176, 249–58
seamstresses 13, 55
seasonality of accidents 56–7, 84–5, 88, 94, 98, 130, 134–47, 152–4, 160–2, 190, 194, 198, 199, 202, 214, 229, 235, 246, 250
seaweed 136
sedges 41, 118, 119, 142
servants 13, 20, 28, 31, 35, 48, 64, 68–9, 74–9, 82, 83, 96, 97, 103, 155, 158, 164–7, 182, 192, 193, 210, 217, 221, 228, 233, 251, 270, 273; and children 9, 42, 55, 65, 67, 72–4, 83, 84, 92; and masters 24, 35, 37–8, 45, 48, 51, 52, 62, 74–7, 86, 138, 139, 191, 228, 240, 267, 268–9; and mistresses 37, 61, 75; recreation 57, 59, 130, 195–201, 214; work 1, 63, 70, 88, 91–3, 107, 111, 114, 118, 122, 136, 138, 154, 159, 162, 176, 181, 225, 238, 243, 253
sewing 4, 73, 84, 95
sex ratios 13, 57, 67, 164, 197, 202, 214, 216, 217, 221, 228, 263, 265–6; in work 69, 88, 93–4, 134–6, 138, 141–3, 147, 154, 158–9, 161, 174–5, 225, 229, 238
sexual assault 37–8, 63
shearmen 185
shears, scissors 87, 95, 140, 161, 166, 273
sheds, hovels 84, 86, 128, 139
sheep 68, 70, 117, 119, 121–2, 125, 142, 156, 161–2, 168, 210, 256, 270, 271, 272
sheepskins 165, 184
sheets 65, 93, 94, 96
shelves 87, 187
shepherds 57, 68, 125, 267
shifts 63, 263
ships 15, 20, 31, 104–5, 114, 145, 210, 216, 217, 233, 251–8
shipwrecks 2
shipwrights 104, 253
shirts 48, 52, 57, 58, 93–4, 179
shoemakers 1, 15, 19, 31, 57, 107, 111, 186, 199, 216, 229
shoes 28, 52, 57, 70, 73, 93, 94, 95, 195, 202, 230
siblings 57, 65–9, 72, 74–5, 77, 96, 129, 141, 155, 161, 195, 219, 221, 238, 267
sickles 63
sieves 61
skillets 93
skirts 141, 263
slagheaps 2,
slate 84, 174, 187
slaters 84
sleds 236, 268
sleep 4, 18, 41, 55, 65, 69, 71, 77, 83, 87, 96–8, 102, 126, 129, 138, 139, 146, 165, 184, 191, 195, 203, 231, 242, 245, 267, 271

# INDEX

slings 136–7
smiths, blacksmiths 19, 68, 76, 105, 112, 114, 172, 183, 216, 218, 223, 236
snails 66, 246
snakes 65
snow 49, 77, 82, 119, 129, 131, 143, 145
soap 94
soldiers 36, 48, 57, 107, 216
sowing 134–7
spades, shovels 62, 77, 92, 136, 144, 145, 175, 225
Spain, Spaniards 2, 8–9, 20, 207
spices 55
spinning 184–6
spinsters, singlewomen 9, 13, 39, 57, 62, 221; recreation 199, 202; work 88, 93, 225, 238
spleen 33, 49, 264
spurs 94, 167, 225
squirrels 127, 152
stables 4, 7, 68, 84, 92, 97, 108, 160, 166, 224, 268
staffs 52, 64, 72, 89, 104, 118, 152, 153, 180, 204, 208, 210, 213, 245, 255
stairs, steps 4, 8, 22, 29, 48, 52, 65, 72, 83–4, 89, 92, 94–6, 98, 107, 192, 226, 261, 270, 273
Star Chamber, court of 30, 32
starlings 154
stepping stones 118, 131
stiles 121, 124, 130, 137, 203, 229
stillbirth 4, 39, 64–5
stinging nettles 167
stitch 50
stockings, hose 57, 70, 93, 95
stocks 37, 190
stone 25, 66, 110, 125, 127, 136, 137, 143, 154, 156, 173, 176, 195, 198, 204, 208, 227, 242, 251; as building material 8, 43, 48, 82–7, 89, 106, 109, 123, 173–5, 190, 193, 202, 209, 212, 225, 226, 228, 237, 268; *see also* millstones; stepping stones
stools 71, 73, 77, 86, 87, 103, 107, 203
storms 35, 44, 64, 107, 117, 122, 128–9, 134, 146, 161, 178, 254, 257–8, 253
straw 52, 56, 65, 69, 81, 84, 85, 91, 131, 139–40, 158, 161, 236; *see also* hats, caps
strawberries 140
streams 17, 21, 57, 62–4, 69, 70, 75, 78, 93–4, 118, 119, 130, 155, 162, 165, 192, 203, 211, 222, 226, 228, 245, 254, 263; *see also* bathing; millraces, millstreams; water collection
string 30, 215, 247
suffocation, smothering 18, 35, 55, 85, 103, 136, 138, 146, 158, 182, 212, 231, 262
suicide 5, 6, 30, 36–40, 45, 84, 208
surgeons 33, 49, 53–4, 56, 194, 223
swans 153
sweating 55, 59, 138, 262
swimming *see* bathing
swords 38–9, 50, 152, 187, 198, 204, 208, 209, 213

tables 28, 87, 92, 95, 199, 217, 218
tailors 14, 15, 29, 52, 57, 59, 76, 95, 195, 211, 225, 268
tallow 179
tankards 89, 93
tanners 37, 50, 52, 121, 157, 184, 195
tanning, tanyards 67, 112, 122, 146, 184, 210, 267, 270
tar 232
taxation 2, 43, 275
tea 9
tennis 197, 204
thatch, thatching 84–5, 118, 139, 142, 270
thatchers 4, 12, 84, 223
theft 140, 209–10, 217
threshing 75, 140
tides 42, 97, 111, 119, 154, 257, 258
tilemakers 160, 175–6
tilers 84, 108, 223

307

# INDEX

tiles, tiling 84, 87, 108, 246
timber-framing 81–6, 108, 129, 180, 191, 270
time of death 16, 23, 25, 37–9, 50, 53, 54, 62, 66, 104, 124, 146, 190, 208, 210, 219, 262–9
tin mining 173, 211
tinkers 103, 223
tip-cat 197
toilet facilities 29, 48, 95–6, 98, 102, 108, 110, 165, 273
tongs 160
towels 57, 93, 165
towns 2, 4, 5, 17, 83, 84, 94, 101–15, 183–6, 201–2, 214–16, 223; and countryside 14, 53, 69, 112–13, 115, 148, 221–2, 229–33; governance 24, 27, 28–9, 31, 41, 43, 46, 102, 211, 212, 249; growth 98, 102, 104, 108, 148, 271; streets 103, 105–7, 214, 244, 270; suburbs 102–4, 113–15, 245; walls 105, 110, 113; water supply 104, 110–11; *see also* gates; markets
trade 14, 43, 104–5, 111–12, 229–34, 235, 254, 258, 271
treadwheels 91
trees 3, 20, 89, 92, 97, 108, 120, 129, 152, 153–4, 159, 168, 190, 195, 199, 215, 219, 235, 238, 239, 243, 257, 261, 264, 266, 270; coppicing 146; felling 9, 69, 70, 75, 117, 121, 128, 143–4, 147, 222, 272; lopping 71, 121, 142–3, 147; alder 69, 120; apple 51, 92, 127, 140–1; ash 9, 25, 32, 120, 123, 143–4, 199, 236, 246; aspen 120; beech 62, 120, 144, 146; birch 120, 143, 199; blackthorn 120; damson 127; elm 6, 8, 71, 78, 120, 144, 145, 147, 200; hawthorn 120; hazel 37, 55, 209, 246; holm oak 120; hornbeam 120; lime 120; maple 120, 144; oak 105, 120, 124, 142–4, 147, 158, 184, 236, 237, 243;

pear 77, 123, 140–1; plum 127, 140, 141; poplar 120; service 120; walnut 127, 141; willow 17, 59, 62, 120, 123, 124, 131, 145–6; wych elm 120; yew 39
Trinity Sunday 214
tripe 91
troughs 67, 236
tuberculosis 49
tubs, vats 66, 67, 78, 91, 93–4, 105, 122, 154, 158, 183, 187
typhus 48

ulcers 53
universities, colleges 22, 58, 87, 113, 155, 190, 255

vagrancy 4, 16–19, 50, 57, 97, 161, 223, 271
vaulting horse 4
veins 53, 160
vestments 45
vetches 140
vinegar 233
visitation, divine 36–7, 39, 46, 56

wafer-sellers 14,
Wales, Welsh 18–19, 43, 48, 252
washing-beetles 94, 130
watchmen 37, 211, 272
water collection 1, 68–71, 75, 82, 87–90, 98, 104, 110–11, 130, 177, 270; *see also* wells
watermen 57, 63, 75, 104, 114, 253
watermills 15, 42, 65, 69, 74, 96, 109, 112, 130, 155, 176–82, 222, 234, 253, 257, 265, 271
waterweeds 58, 227
waterwheels 20, 41, 177, 179, 182, 222
weavers 14, 88, 95, 103, 184–5, 187, 195, 202, 203
weeds 125, 135
wells 56, 59, 67, 69, 72, 75, 83, 87–91,

93, 96, 97, 98, 106, 108, 109, 110–11, 115, 119, 158, 160, 187, 192, 212, 263, 267; draw-wells 69, 70, 90–1, 103, 157, 272; well-digging 42, 75, 85, 98
wet-nursing 62, 65
wheat 18, 75, 120, 121, 125, 131, 136, 138, 178, 209, 229, 230, 236
wheelbarrows 135, 180
wheelwrights 143
whey 78, 91–2, 106, 122
whips 16, 70, 134, 135, 164, 167, 237, 242, 244–5
whirlpools 58, 161, 165, 257
Whit Sunday 53, 190, 193, 214
whittawers 184
whooping cough 47, 49
widows 4, 9, 13, 18, 33, 71, 72, 74, 77, 88, 91, 93, 95, 138, 142, 159, 164, 200, 203, 217, 221, 237
wills 23–4, 269
wimbles 76
winches 69, 90, 103
wind 43, 68, 77, 82, 85, 94, 107, 109, 113, 124, 126, 130, 136, 143–4, 189, 192, 199, 214, 215, 226, 241, 251, 257, 271; *see also* storms; windmills
windlasses 90, 145, 212
windmills 4, 15, 32, 40, 68, 112, 119, 125, 176–9, 181, 266, 271

windows 82, 84, 86, 96, 107, 139, 153, 185, 193, 200, 209, 212, 218
wine 202, 231, 256
wire-drawers 103
witnesses 7, 32, 46, 53, 104, 189
woad 184, 187
wood, timber 6, 15, 18, 49, 53, 55, 62, 75, 105, 106, 108, 120, 124, 141, 144–6, 155, 235, 242, 253, 254, 256; wooden objects 4, 30, 52, 66, 67, 70, 83, 84, 89, 90, 91, 93, 96, 106, 112, 139, 158, 173, 179, 180, 185, 193, 197, 202, 212, 213, 222, 226, 236, 241, 246, 247, 271; *see also* firewood; timber-framing; trees
woodcock 154
woodland 25, 75, 77, 92, 120–2, 126, 131, 136, 143–4, 147, 148, 151, 152, 183, 217, 221, 238, 242, 247
wool ix, 121, 180, 184–7, 229, 236
workhouses 185, 186; *see also* bridewells
worms 54
wrestling 36, 186, 194–6, 205, 208

yeomen 7, 15–16, 31, 37, 39, 58, 62, 72, 74, 83, 86, 88, 90–1, 94, 114, 138, 143, 153, 157, 160, 162–4, 192, 194–5, 199, 201, 203, 207, 214, 216–17, 223, 228, 232, 237, 238, 240, 252, 253, 256, 268